WHERE ARE WE GOING?

HUMAN NATURE AND THE STRUGGLE FOR OUR DEMOCRACY

BRUCE BRODIE

CONTENTS

INTRODUCTION

These are troubled times. It seems that not too long ago, our country was filled with hope for a better future. The fall of the Berlin Wall in 1989 symbolized the end of the Cold War, and democracy was on the rise. The United States led a coalition of democracies in the advancement of globalization, market economies, the rule of law, and the protection of human rights and political freedoms (Ikenberry, 2018). Progress was in the air.

But the dream has faded. In the United States, the hope that international trade and capitalism would bring economic progress and security has not been fulfilled. Working- and middle-class Americans have largely been left behind by globalization, automation, and corporate greed. Incomes and opportunities for middle-class and blue-collar workers have stagnated, while the wealth of those at the top has soared. Globalization and capitalism seem more like tools for the connected and elite than a system to promote the economic security and well-being of all Americans. As the income gap has grown, the American Dream of rising from the depths of poverty to social and economic success through hard work and perseverance has become an illusion. The United States, despite its failings, once had a national identity based on shared values of equality, liberty, and justice for all that transcended religious, ethnic, and socioeconomic groups, but America has regressed into divisiveness and tribalism. We now identify with membership in tribes, largely defined by identity politics: African Americans, Hispanics, LGBTQ people, and liberal elites mostly on the left, and Evangelical Christians, working-class European Americans, and plutocrats mostly on the right. Our collective American identity, which had united the country's many subgroups, has lost its way.

The alienation and resentment felt by the White working class who were left behind fueled a populist movement that looked for new leadership.

Donald Trump seized the opportunity, captured the presidency, and moved our country closer to autocracy. Our fragile democracy barely survived the transfer of power after Trump's defeat in the 2020 election and his attempts to overturn the election. Our democracy remains in great peril.

We are now engaged in a great struggle between autocracy and democracy, both at home and abroad. Throughout human history, autocratic regimes have dominated over democracies, and many experts believe this is because evolution has given humans a genetic predisposition for hierarchically structured social and political systems that favor autocracy.

Many people are surprised to learn that our opinions and social perspectives have a strong genetic component. We all have inherited a mix of hierarchical and authoritarian traits and egalitarian traits. Those with predominantly hierarchical and authoritarian traits have a genetic predisposition to believe that some groups are superior to other groups and should dominate other groups. People with these genetic predispositions have an intrinsic bias toward authoritarian rule and a mindset to follow authoritarian leaders. In contrast, those with predominantly egalitarian traits have a predisposition to believe that all humans are morally equal and should have the same rights and opportunities. People with these innate predispositions have a bias favoring democracy over autocracy. We all have a mix of authoritarian and egalitarian traits, but most of us have predispositions favoring one or the other. Those with mostly authoritarian traits present a challenge to the preservation of our democracy.

Natural selection has given us selfish traits that help us in our struggle for resources, status, prestige, mates, and survival. While selfish traits, such as greed and deception, may promote individual success, they are counterproductive in social groups because they inhibit cooperation. Natural selection has also given us tribal instincts that promote cooperation and loyalty toward members of our own tribe but foster hostile and xenophobic behavior toward outsiders. Tribal instincts make it difficult for us to cooperate with those who are different than we are—those of another race, religion, socioeconomic group, or political party—and this damages democracies.

Despite these obstacles, much of our human nature supports a cooperative society. This is evidenced by the transition of our societies from small hunter-gatherer tribes to large nation-states with diverse populations. Cooperation has become the driving force of evolution. We humans are social animals and experience love, empathy, altruism, and kindness toward one another. Our need to connect with something larger than ourselves has given us a sense of grand purpose and has promoted self-sacrifice for the betterment of the group. Many of us have a genetic predisposition to egalitarian traits, believe in the equality of all human beings, and strongly support a democratic society.

Human nature provides a template that guides our behavior, but our behavior is greatly shaped by our material and cultural environment. Psychologist Steven Pinker has shown, for example, that the establishment of nation-states and the rule of law, maintained by the legitimate use of force, has reduced human violence to the lowest level in human history. The rise in domestic and international commerce and the exchange of ideas through new technologies facilitating communication and travel have promoted better understanding and cooperation between diverse groups.

In contrast, two major inequities in our current cultural environment have unleashed the darker side of our human nature. Structural racism and socioeconomic inequities have bred anger and resentment and have led to great divisions and polarity in our society. They have unleashed our tribal instincts and have led to a right-wing populist movement that threatens our democracy.

Our challenge is to create a cultural environment that will heal the great divisions in our society and bring out the better side of our human nature. Will we be able to address and improve the racial and socioeconomic inequities that divide our nation and threaten our democracy? Can we create a more egalitarian society that will bring out the better angels of our nature so we can achieve a national identity and solidarity that will allow us to preserve and strengthen our democracy? Can we meet these challenges?

We begin *Where Are We Going?* with Part I, which outlines the origins and evolution of our hybrid human nature. We discuss in Part II the dual racial and socioeconomic inequities of our society that bring out the worst in our human nature. In Part III we describe the ongoing conflict between democracy and autocracy in America and abroad, and in Part IV we discuss how human nature and our cultural environment shape our behavior and impact the struggle between democracy and autocracy. Let's begin the story.

PART I
EVOLUTION OF HUMAN NATURE

CHAPTER 1

HUMAN NATURE: THE NATURE-NURTURE DEBATE

Every human brain is born not as a blank tablet (a tabula rasa) waiting to be filled in by experience but as "an exposed negative waiting to be slipped into developer fluid."

—E. O. Wilson, *Sociobiology: The New Synthesis*

English philosopher John Locke in his 1690 *An Essay Concerning Human Understanding* advocated the concept that the human mind is born with a "blank slate" (tabula rasa) upon which our culture and environment etch our personality and behavior (Loehlin, 2009). The term "tabula rasa" implies we start life from scratch, without innate ideas or character, and that our experiences and perceptions of the outside world define our identity and behavior. We now have a different perspective. Evolutionary psychologists and biologists now believe that much of our behavior is shaped by behavioral traits that we have inherited through the long journey of evolution. Let's explore the debate.

The Nature Versus Nurture Debate

Charles Darwin in his 1859 publication of *On the Origin of Species* argued that much of animal and human behavior is innate and that behavioral traits, like physical traits, evolved by natural selection. Behavioral traits that promoted survival and reproductive success were selected and passed to subsequent generations (Darwin, 1859). Darwin characterized these innate behavioral traits, which he called instincts, as automatic, unconscious behaviors that require no judgment and are shared by members of an individual species. He distinguished instincts from habits, which are behaviors learned during a lifetime through repetition. Instinctive behavior is not learned and can be performed by animals that have been raised in isolation. Birds, for example, have an innate ability to build nests for their offspring with no tutelage from their parents (Image 1.1). Darwin did not discuss human instincts in *Origin*, but he did make it clear there were analogies between instinctive behavior in animals and similar behavior in humans (MacNeill, 2009).

Image 1.1 Brown Boobies Building a Nest. This behavior is not learned—
it is embedded in the birds' genes

In one of his last books, *The Expression of the Emotions in Man and Animals,* Darwin advocated that emotions evolved by natural selection and are an innate behavioral trait in animals and humans (Darwin, 1872; Image 1.2). He concluded "that the chief expressive actions exhibited by man and by the lower animals are now innate or inherited—that is, have not been learnt by the individual—is admitted by everyone." Darwin's beliefs set the stage for the new field of evolutionary psychology, but his ideas were not immediately accepted (MacNeill, 2009).

Image 1.2 Charles Darwin (1809–1882)

English sociologist and anthropologist Sir Francis Galton (1822–1911), perhaps best known as the founder of the controversial pseudoscience of eugenics, was greatly influenced by his half cousin Darwin's *On the Origin of Species.* Galton was a pioneer in the study of inheritance of behavioral traits and introduced the term "nature and nurture." He introduced twin studies to estimate the relative importance of inheritance and environment in shaping human behavior and intelligence, and he concluded that hereditary factors play a dominant role in human behavior (*Origins*, 2020). Darwin and Galton were on the nature side of the nature-nurture debate, but they did not have much company. Their ideas about the inheritance of behavioral traits fell into disfavor and did not come back into the mainstream until the late twentieth-century.

The Evolution of Social Behavior

In 1975, eminent Harvard biologist E. O. Wilson rekindled the debate on the origins of human nature with the publication of his classic book *Sociobiology: The New Synthesis* (Wilson, 1975). *Sociobiology* looked at social behavior through the lens of Darwinian evolution. Wilson provided a synthesis of what was known about the evolution of social behavior. He drew from theories and models of previous investigators, beautifully described social behavior in animals, and provided insights into the origins of social behavior in humans. Wilson advocated that much of human social behavior, like animal social behavior, was innate and instinctual—a product of evolution and natural selection. He, like Darwin, believed that behavioral traits evolved through natural selection because they provided survival and reproductive advantages. He provided many examples: empathy provides survival and reproductive advantages for the individual and the group because it helps us connect and cooperate with other members of our society. Maternal love provides support for the survival of offspring so that shared genes will survive and be passed to subsequent generations. Disgust provides protection against pathogens and infectious diseases by helping us avoid spoiled foods, sick or unhygienic animals, and bodily wastes. Darwin and Wilson believed that human nature consists of psychological traits and behavioral traits common to all human beings and that these traits evolved because they provide adaptive advantages.

Early reviews of *Sociobiology* were very positive, and the book achieved widespread acclaim. There followed a groundswell of new ideas and publications that viewed human social behavior as a product of Darwinian evolution. These concepts became more mainstream in the 1980s as sociobiology morphed into the field of evolutionary psychology.

Eminent Harvard psychologist Steven Pinker was one of the strongest and most vocal supporters of Wilson's views. In 2002, Pinker published the best-selling book *The Blank Slate: The Modern Denial of Human Nature*, in which he argued against tabula rasa (clean slate) models and argued that much of human behavior is shaped by innate behavioral traits, which are a product of natural selection. This stimulated a revival of the nature versus nurture debate, pitting the empiricists (strong advocates of the nurture school) against the nativists (strong advocates of the nature school). Pinker's belief that we have an inherited innate human nature is based to a great extent on the commonality of hundreds of behavioral traits across all human cultures, ranging from the ability to learn language, the desire to be socially accepted, and the capacity for empathy and other human emotions.

What Can Twin Studies Tell Us?

Studies of identical and fraternal twins have provided the most powerful data to untangle the competing influences of genes and environment on behavioral traits (Image 1.3). Identical (monozygotic) twins are formed when a single sperm fertilizes a single egg, forming a zygote that then divides and produces two embryos that develop into identical twins with identical genes. Fraternal (dizygotic) twins are formed when two separate sperm fertilize two separate eggs, forming two zygotes that produce two embryos and fraternal twins who share approximately 50% of their genes. Most twin studies compare the concordance of a trait in identical twin pairs with the concordance of the same trait in fraternal twin pairs assuming the identical twin pairs are raised in a similar environment and the fraternal twin pairs are raised in a similar environment. Concordance is defined as the probability that if one of the twin pairs has a trait, the other twin pair will also have that trait. If the concordance for reading skills in identical twins is 60%, for example, and in fraternal twins is 30%, we can conclude there is a genetic component to reading skills.

Image 1.3 Identical Twins. Separated at birth, the Seifert twins meet accidentally after 30 years in the patent attorney's office with identical inventions

The role of genetic and environmental influences in determining intelligence has been one of the most controversial topics in psychology. Twin and sibling studies have provided valuable information in sorting this out. The correlation of IQ scores between identical twins reared at home is greater than the correlation of IQ scores between fraternal twins reared at home (Plomin & Spinath, 2004). Similarly, the correlation of IQ scores between siblings reared together in the same home is greater than the correlation between two adopted children reared together in the same home (McGue et al., 1993). Since identical twins share all their genes, while fraternal twins share only half their genes, and since siblings share half their genes while adopted children share far less, these data support the strong influence of genes on intelligence. These and numerous other studies have emphasized the strong influence of heredity on measures of intelligence.

Studies on genetic influences on sexual orientation have received great attention. One study found that if one identical twin is gay, the probability that the other identical twin is gay is 66%, while if one fraternal twin is gay, the probability that the other twin is gay is just 30% (Whitam et al., 1993). These data suggest that sexual orientation has a strong genetic component.

The Emergence of Evolutionary Psychology and Behavioral Genetics

Evolutionary psychology endeavors to explain behavioral and psychological traits as adaptations that evolved through the process of natural selection to promote survival and reproductive success. Behavioral genetics is a related field of scientific research that studies genetic and environmental influences on behavior. As we discussed earlier, Sir Francis Galton's late nineteenth-century twin studies launched the field of behavioral genetics, but it fell into disfavor because of its association with the eugenics movement. Behavioral genetics regained prominence in the late twentieth and early twenty-first centuries and has now become mainstream. Evolutionary psychology and behavioral genetics are now complementary fields, committed to learning about the roles of evolution, natural selection, genetics, and environment in shaping behavior.

There is now a consensus that our behavior has a strong genetic component and is shaped by our cultural and material environment. The question is no longer whether behavior is a product of nature or nurture but rather what are the strengths of the genetic and cultural influences, and how do these two interact. In the latter chapters of this book, we will examine how our cultural environment can act on our innate behavioral traits—our basic human nature—to shape our behavior. Our goal is to create a cultural environment that will bring out the better part of our human nature.

CHAPTER 2

EMPATHY: EVOLUTION'S PRECIOUS GIFT

Empathy is seeing with the eyes of another, listening with the ears of another and feeling with the heart of another.

—Alfred Adler

With the American Civil War approaching, esteemed American poet and humanist Walt Whitman captured the essence of empathy in his epic poem "Song of Myself," published in *Leaves of Grass* (1855): "I do not ask the wounded person how he feels, I myself become the wounded person." Empathy is the ability to *understand* and *share* feelings and emotions of another individual. It is not enough to just recognize and understand another's emotions: empathy requires sharing those emotions. It is an emotional mirroring.

The success and dominance of *Homo sapiens* rest on our capability for bonding and cooperating with one another, and this, in turn, is greatly dependent on our capacity for empathy—our ability to feel what others feel. We have inherited this precious trait through the long process of evolution, and it is hardwired in our genes. Empathy is possessed by many mammals and some birds, but it has reached its highest level in us humans.

Origins of Empathy

German psychologist Theodor Lipps (1851–1914) described his feeling of suspense while watching a high-wire artist navigate across a great abyss. He vicariously entered the performer's body and shared his experience—he was on the wire with him. He used the German term *Einfühlung* (feeling into) to describe the experience but later proposed the Greek equivalent *empatheia* (experiencing strong affection or passion), which was embraced by British and American psychologists as "empathy" (de Waal, 2009). Lipps was one of the first to call empathy an "instinct"—an innate behavioral trait—a product of evolution. Evolutionary psychologists now believe empathy goes far back in evolutionary history to before the origin of our species.

Esteemed Dutch American biologist Frans de Waal in *The Age of Empathy* describes how empathy may have started in mammals with the bond between mother and offspring (de Waal, 2009; Image 2.1). For a mother to tend to her offspring's needs, she needs to understand and be sensitive to signals of hunger, pain, and distress and respond appropriately. Sharing emotional experiences with her offspring would greatly facilitate this process, and empathy likely evolved for this purpose.

Image 2.1 Chimpanzee and Infant. Empathy may have had its origins in facilitating the bond between mothers and infants in early mammals

Oxytocin, a peptide hormone produced in the hypothalamus and released from the pituitary gland (a pea-sized structure at the base of the brain), plays a key role during pregnancy and maternal infant bonding (Pappas, 2015). The hormone promotes uterine contractions during labor and helps shrink the uterus after delivery. When the infant suckles the mother's breast, oxytocin is released and triggers the breast to "let down" milk for the infant. Higher oxytocin levels during pregnancy have been correlated with closer bonding behavior between mother and infant (Feldman et al., 2007).

Perhaps not coincidentally, oxytocin also plays a major role in fostering empathy. Oxytocin is released during the active experience of empathizing with another person, and higher levels of oxytocin are associated with greater empathetic connection (Barraza & Zak, 2009). Normal male volunteers given intranasal oxytocin score higher than controls on the Multifaceted Empathy Test and achieve scores comparable to untreated women (Hurlemann et al., 2010). Low levels of oxytocin are associated with poor performance on empathy tests and have been linked to autism and poor social functioning (Daughters et al., 2017). Amazingly, the hormone also seems to facilitate gaze-mediated bonding between dogs and their owners (Nagasawa et al., 2015). Mutual gazing between dogs and their owners increases oxytocin levels in both, and nasally administered oxytocin increases gazing behavior in dogs toward their owners.

All this evidence—the relationship between oxytocin and empathy and the role of oxytocin during pregnancy and maternal-infant bonding—supports de Waal's hypothesis that empathy may have had its beginnings in early mammalian species with bonding between mother and infant.

Empathy in Animals

Most of us think of empathy as a uniquely human trait, but empathy has been widely documented in primates and other mammalian species. In his role as director of the National Primate Research Center at Emory University, Frans de Waal (2005) has studied and detailed empathetic traits in chimpanzees and monkeys. Chimps are very consoling. If a chimp is a victim of aggression by another chimp and is sitting alone, pouting, licking an injury, and feeling dejected, a friend or relative will often provide consolation. The friend gives a hug, checks the injury, and grooms the victim. The encounter appears quite emotional. Chimps seem to empathize with the plight of victimized chimps and seem to want to relieve their suffering.

In another example, de Waal describes an episode at the Arnhem Zoo, where bonobos (pygmy chimpanzees) live on an island surrounded by a moat (2009, pp 91–92). The moat is full of ducks and ducklings. One day juvenile bonobos picked up a little duckling and were swinging it around a bit too roughly. When they tried to grab another duckling, an adult bonobo ran over and intimidated the juvenile bonobos, causing them to scatter. The bonobo then directed the young duckling into the water where it was safe. The bonobo appeared to share the young duckling's distress.

Investigators at Northwestern University trained rhesus monkeys to pull a chain that delivered food to themselves (Masserman et al., 1964). After they became accustomed to this, the investigators rigged the chain so that it would also deliver a shock to a companion monkey in an adjoining cage in plain sight. After witnessing their companion receiving a shock, most monkeys stopped pulling the chain. One monkey stopped pulling the chain for 12 days. The monkeys were literally starving themselves to avoid seeing their companions in distress.

There are many examples of empathy in primates, but the evidence for empathy in other mammals has only been demonstrated recently. Investigators at the University of Chicago devised an experiment to evaluate empathy in rats (Bartal et al., 2011). They arranged for two rats to share a cage for two weeks so they would get to know one another. The investigators then placed one of the rats in a restraining device with severely cramped space. The other rat was free to roam outside the device, while observing the plight of its pal. The free rat became agitated after observing the distress of its companion—indicating there was sharing of emotions. The free rat bit and clawed at the restraining cage until it figured out how to open the door and free its companion. The investigators gave the free rat the choice of opening another cage with a reward of chocolate inside or freeing its pal. The free rat almost invariably released its pal. If it did open the cage with chocolate, it would share the chocolate with its pal. This experiment was one of the earliest to show that mammals other than primates are able to exhibit empathy (Image 2.2).

Image 2.2 Empathy in Rats. Perhaps surprisingly, rats have shown empathy in experiments in which they helped free fellow rats that were trapped in cages and were in distress (Bartal et al., 2011). These experiments were among the first to demonstrate that mammals other than primates experience empathy.

Mammals also appear able to show empathy toward other species. Marine ecologists aboard a research vessel off the coast of the West Antarctic Peninsula encountered an unusual and marvelous event involving humpback whales, orcas, and a Weddell seal (Brethel-Haurwitz, 2016). Eleven orcas were attacking a Weddell seal that had sought refuge on an ice floc. As the orcas closed in, two massive humpback whales intervened, surging into the middle of the action. The seal swam toward the humpbacks, and one of the humpbacks rolled over and helped the seal to safety onto its belly with a nudge of its flipper. The seal then swam off to shelter. The humpbacks seemed to empathize with the Weddell seal in distress. The interference of these humpback whales appeared to be an altruistic act initiated through shared emotions. There are numerous other examples of humpbacks intervening to protect unrelated species from attacks by orcas. There are also many stories of dolphins rescuing humans and dogs from shark attacks, and of apes helping injured animals who fall into their zoo enclosures (Brethel-Haurwitz, 2016). These episodes are uncommon but not rare.

How can we explain such apparent altruistic acts? What possible evolutionary advantage could this type of selfless behavior have for these helpers? The acts cannot be explained by kin selection—helping kin so that shared genes will be passed to the next generation. They also cannot be explained by the other theory of altruism in humans—reciprocal altruism—because there is no possibility of payback in the future. Could these actions result from genuine psychological altruism—selfless concern for the well-being of others? It doesn't seem possible. Animals do not have the cognitive complexity and ability for abstract thought needed for psychological altruism. This suggests that these episodes do not necessarily arise from high-level concerns about justice and morality but rather from lower-level emotional processes. If an observer animal empathizes with another animal in distress, it will share in that distress. This may create a desire to relieve the other animal's distress, which, in turn, will relieve the observer animal's own shared distress. Emotional empathy may provide an explanation for this type of altruistic behavior in some human situations as well (Brethel-Haurwitz, 2016; de Waal, 2008).

Why Empathy?

Behavioral traits, like physical traits, must provide adaptive advantages if they are to be preserved through natural selection. Empathy is no exception. Empathy likely evolved because it facilitates pair-bonding and cooperation in humans and other social animals. It can be seen as a tool that has evolved to facilitate cooperative interactions (Image 2.3).

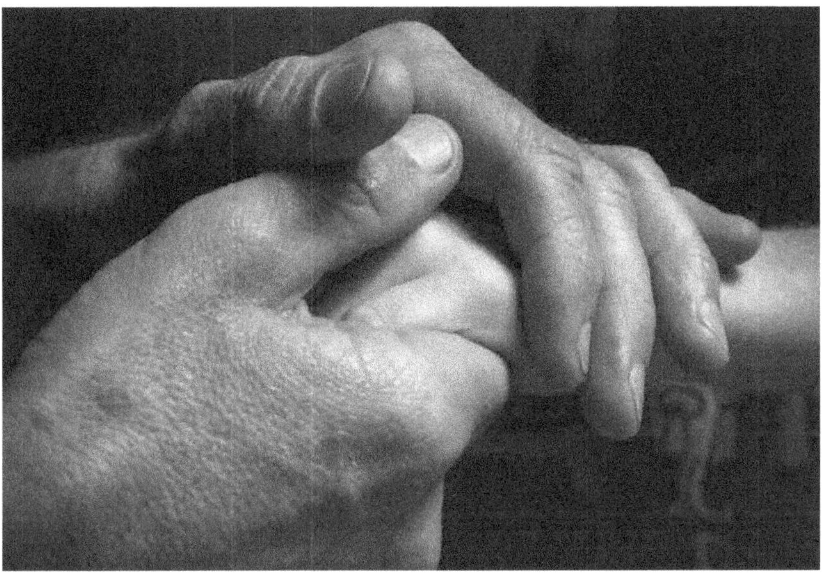

Image 2.3 Empathy. Empathy can be seen as a tool that has evolved to facilitate communication, bonding, and cooperation in social animals

Pair-bonding is essential for several types of human love (Allott, 2019). We have already seen that empathy is a critical component and facilitator of mother-infant bonding and motherly love. Empathy also facilitates erotic love. Lovers can share and feel each other's emotions and become one with one another. The hormone oxytocin is released during the early stages of erotic love and during sexual activity and orgasm (Schneiderman et al., 2012). Empathy is also a major part of romantic love—the long-term pair-bonding between mates or parents that evolved to support child-rearing. (Fletcher et al., 2014). The human brain is not fully developed at birth, and children are helpless and dependent on adults for more than a decade after birth. Pair-bonding between parents enduring over decades is required for cooperative child-rearing, which is so important for the survival and success of the next generation. Empathy facilitates all these types of pair-bonding. Without empathy, human love would not be possible.

Empathy appears to be important for all types of human cooperation, but its significance has perhaps been best studied in indirect reciprocity: we humans often help and cooperate with strangers without expecting them to pay us back, but we do expect strangers to help and cooperate with us when we need it. Investigators at the University of Pennsylvania sought to determine whether cooperation through indirect reciprocity can work without empathy (Radzvilavicius, 2019). They created computer models of a society in which there was not general agreement on good and bad reputations and there was little empathy. The results were very disappointing. Over time the society became less altruistic, and cooperation almost vanished. The investigators knew that humans have a remarkable capacity for empathy—adopting another person's point of view. When humans interact with strangers and empathize with them, they are much more likely to judge the strangers in a favorable light and be willing to cooperate with them. When the investigators incorporated empathy into their models, cooperation skyrocketed, and altruism triumphed over selfish behavior.

While empathy's greatest adaptive advantages appear to be related to its facilitation of bonding and cooperation, it has other benefits. Empathy can help group communication through shared emotions, and such exchanges can provide important survival advantages. Evolution designed and fine-tuned emotions to prepare us for action. One of the clearest examples of a shared emotion that facilitates survival is fear (Schulz, 2019). Suppose a lion is stalking a herd of wildebeests. The first wildebeest to see the lion reacts with fear—characterized by panting and trembling—triggering the flight response and causing it to flee. A second wildebeest that doesn't see the lion right away and doesn't flee is at risk of being caught and killed. But if the second wildebeest and others in the herd see the first wildebeest's fear, they can mirror the fear reaction through empathy, flee much sooner, and survive. The emotion fear, shared with the herd through empathy, has provided a survival advantage.

How Does Empathy Work?

How often have you watched a horror movie in which the heroine is in great fear for her life, and you are engulfed with the same fear? How do we react at such a gut level to someone else's emotions? How do we understand so instinctively another's thoughts and feelings? How does empathy work? Neuroscientists believe they may have some answers with the discovery of mirror neurons. These are brain cells that respond similarly when either we perform an action or when we witness someone else performing the same action.

In the 1980s, Italian neuroscientist Giacomo Rizzolatti and colleagues implanted electrodes in the premotor cortex of the brains of macaques and identified specific neurons that fired when the monkeys picked up a peanut. Then they noticed something very surprising. When the investigators themselves picked up a peanut to give to the monkeys, they noticed that the same neurons fired in the monkeys' brains as when they themselves grasped the peanut. The investigators published their results and called their discovery **mirror neurons** (di Pellegrino et al., 1992; Gallese et al., 1996; Winerman, 2005).

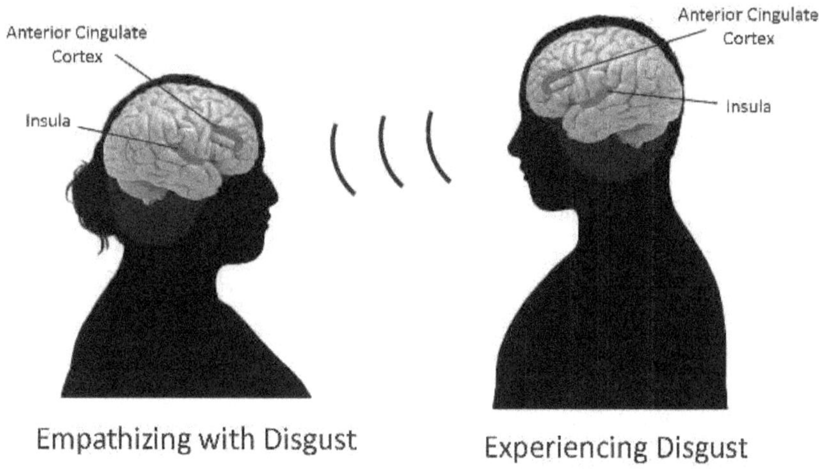

Image 2.4 Mirror Neurons. A man experiencing a strong emotion such as disgust (right) will activate brain activity in the insula and anterior cingulate cortex, as assessed by fMRI. A woman empathizing with the man (left) will activate the same sites in her brain. The activated areas of shared emotions in the woman's brain are called mirror neurons (Wicker et al., 2003)

Once researchers identified mirror neurons in monkeys, the obvious next step was to look for mirror neurons in humans (Image 2.4). French and Italian investigators took up the task (Wicker et al., 2003). They asked volunteers to inhale foul odorants, producing a strong feeling of disgust, and they measured their brain activity with functional magnetic resonance imaging (fMRI). The investigators then asked the same volunteers to observe video clips showing emotional facial expressions of disgust in other volunteers and repeated the fMRI studies. When the volunteers observed disgust in others, they activated the same sites in the brain (anterior insula and the anterior cingulate cortex) as when they experienced the foul-smelling oder and disgust themselves. Some experts believe the discovery of mirror neurons has provided a biological basis for empathy (Wicker et al., 2003).

The process of mirroring the emotional state of another in our own brain is automatic. We don't have to think about it or learn how to do it. We have inherited this trait through our evolutionary past, and the process occurs subconsciously. We *Homo sapiens* are fortunate to have this trait hardwired in our genes. It ties us all together.

Emotional Empathy Versus Cognitive Empathy

Empathy in its simplest form consists of sharing emotions at the subconscious level. This basic level of empathy—emotional empathy—is what we have seen in most of the animal examples described earlier. As our hominin and human ancestors formed larger societies with more complex social environments and personal interactions, a higher level of interpersonal communication and understanding was required. Cognitive empathy evolved to meet this need (Smith, 2006). Cognitive empathy is emotional empathy plus the additional capacity to recognize and understand the contents and perspective of another person's mind. This requires high levels of cognitive ability and is probably experienced only by humans.

Cognitive empathy is closely related to **theory of mind (ToM)**, which is the ability to understand the mental and emotional states of other individuals and to then use that information to predict the behavior of those individuals (Smith, 2006). The major difference between the two traits is that ToM, in contrast to cognitive empathy, does not require sharing or mirroring the emotional state of others (Smith, 2006). ToM and cognitive empathy are crucial for everyday human social interactions and are used when analyzing, judging, and predicting the behavior of others. These traits enable us to understand whom we can trust and cooperate with, who is trying to cheat us, and, yes, how we can manipulate or deceive others to our own advantage. Cognitive empathy and ToM are greatly responsible for the cooperation that has led to the dominance of *Homo sapiens*.

ToM and cognitive empathy are inherited traits, but both require social experience over many years for their full development. People develop various skill levels for ToM; those with autism have a deficit in ToM.

Neuroscientists have studied regions of the brain, such as mirror neurons, that are active in individuals during emotional and cognitive empathy (Dvash & Shamay-Tsoory, 2014). Emotional empathy, not unexpectedly, activates regions of the brain that mediate emotional experiences (the insula, amygdala, and anterior cingulate cortex), while cognitive empathy activates regions in the neocortex dealing primarily with cognitive functions (the medial prefrontal cortex, superior temporal sulcus, and temporal poles) (Dvash & Shamay-Tsoory, 2014; Uribe et al., 2019). Although emotional and cognitive components of empathy may work autonomously, in natural social situations, almost every empathic response activates both emotional and cognitive regions of the brain to some extent (Dvash & Shamay-Tsoory, 2014).

There has been much confusion about the meanings and definitions of sympathy, empathy, and compassion. Sympathy is the experience of understanding and caring for another person who is suffering or unhappy. In contrast with empathy, sympathy does not include feeling or sharing the emotions of another person. For example, if someone's father has passed away, you may not be able to viscerally feel that person's pain. However, you can employ your cognitive skills and emotional experience to understand that your friend is sad and feel sympathy for her. Compassion takes empathy and sympathy a step further. When you are compassionate, you feel the pain of another (empathy) or you recognize that the person is in pain (sympathy), and then you do your best to alleviate that person's suffering. Compassion—real compassion—is empathy or sympathy put into action.

A word of caution. Without empathy, sympathy and compassion may lead to resentment. Individuals who are targets of sympathy and compassion have heightened sensitivity to actions that do not include empathy. They may feel that acts of charity are degrading forms of pity.

Are Women Really More Empathetic?

We know the stereotype—women are better than men at understanding other people's perspectives, feeling their pain, and demonstrating compassion. Evolutionary psychologists often link this to the belief that empathy evolved in mammals millions of years ago as a tool for bonding mother and infant. There is now ample evidence to support the view that women are indeed more empathetic than men.

Numerous studies using standard empathy questionnaires have revealed that women show a greater empathetic response than men (Rueckert et al., 2011). Women have also shown greater mirror neuron activity than men (Derntl et al., 2010). In one study, investigators asked volunteers to lie down in an MRI scanner and view a video clip of a human hand being mutilated with a sharp needle. Female participants showed higher activation in areas of the brain associated with pain than their male counterparts—they had greater mirror neuron activity (Olmos, 2019).

Oxytocin plays an important role in facilitating empathy. Women have higher baseline plasma oxytocin levels than men, and oxytocin levels increase more in women than men in response to active empathy (Marazziti et al., 2019; Miller et al., 2015). These and other studies document that oxytocin is responsible for some of the greater empathy seen in women compared with men, but the role of oxytocin is complicated, and there are many unanswered questions (Moore, 2016).

We will discuss in later chapters how the empowerment of women has a pacifying influence in today's societies. Both domestic violence and international violence are less frequent in societies with greater empowerment of women. Gender differences in human nature, including differences in empathy, may be responsible.

The Tribal Nature of Empathy

Our ancient hunter-gatherer ancestors exhibited prosocial, altruistic, and cooperative behavioral traits toward members of their own tribes, but projected hostile, xenophobic behavior toward outsiders, who were seen as enemies. This combination of traits represents our tribal instincts. Empathy is tribal. We empathize with those who are like us—those within our tribe—and we , and we have more difficulty empathizing with those who are different from us—those outside our tribe. Unfortunately, this constitutes a major limitation in promoting cooperation in today's diverse societies. We are innately more empathetic toward people who look, act, speak, and think like we do. The inadequate federal and local response to the devastation of Hurricane Katrina in New Orleans in 2005 may provide an illustrative example (Doherty, 2013). Katrina roared ashore on the Gulf Coast and left images of poor, mostly Black New Orleans residents stranded on rooftops or crowded into the Louisiana Superdome amid putrid conditions. More than 1,000 died. Many have attributed the poor federal response to a lack of empathy for the predominantly Black victims from predominantly White bureaucrats in Washington, DC.

Can we overcome the tribal nature of our empathy? Surprisingly, rats may give us some insight. As we saw earlier, researchers at the University of Chicago found that rats seemed to empathize with fellow rats who were trapped in a restraining device, and they went to great lengths to free their companions (Bartal et al., 2011). But the investigators found that the rats' empathy was not indiscriminate (Bartal et al., 2014). There are several strains of rats, with coats in a variety of colors—white, brown, black, and spotted. Rats exhibit empathy for rats of their own strain but not for rats of different strains. However, if rats are raised with rats of other strains, they will empathize with them. These experiments demonstrate that rats' empathy, like ours, is selective, but they also suggest we may have opportunities to expand our empathy. One thing we can do is expose ourselves and our children to a variety of people, places, and cultures. This will reduce the tendency to see any group as different and should broaden the scope of empathy to more diverse groups.

We have another challenge. Empathy appears to be declining. Investigators from the University of Michigan reviewed 72 self-evaluating studies assessing empathy over the past 30 years that asked college students to affirm or deny such statements as "I often have tender, concerned feelings for people less fortunate than me." (Konrath et al., 2011). Based on these questionnaires, they found current students showed 40% less empathy than students in the 1980s and 1990s. The authors speculated that the reasons for the decline may be that students are communicating through smartphones and social media—and are having fewer face to face interactions. Can we reverse this trend? Possibly. Most psychologists believe we can improve our empathy with practice (Loehr, 2016). Practice being a good listener, be fully present in your interactions with others, smile (it's contagious), give genuine recognition, try to empathize with people whose beliefs you don't share, and challenge yourself to have deeper conversations with colleagues—go beyond the weather. Practice can make a difference.

Evolution has given us a precious gift. It is a universal trait with the potential to bring us all together in common purpose. But empathy is tribal. Tribal boundaries expanded throughout human history from small hunter-gatherer tribes to large, complex societies and nation-states, but we still have tribes within those nation-states. The challenge of our time is to expand our circle of empathy to include those outside our tribes—those of different races, religions, and politics. With progress, the next great step will be to expand our circle of empathy beyond our national borders to a global scale so that we can feel empathy for all of humanity.

CHAPTER 3

EMOTIONS: THE ESSENCE OF HUMANITY

The best and most beautiful things in the world cannot be seen or even touched. They must be felt with the heart.

—Helen Keller, *The Story of My Life*

Imagine what life would be like without emotions. How could we be happy? How could we be sad? Where could we find love? Or joy? Or a sense of pride and accomplishment? Sure, emotions can bring a rollercoaster ride of agony and ecstasy, but without emotions we would be robotic, filled with boredom.

Emotions sharpen our focus and fuel the energy to direct our lives. They give value and meaning to our existence, our relationships, our dreams, and our aspirations (Fisher, 2019). They make us human. Our emotions are the essence of who we are.

Origins of Emotions

As we have seen, Darwin's treatise *The Expression of the Emotions in Man and Animals* postulated how emotions, a special type of behavioral trait, evolved by natural selection (1872). Darwin observed that people around the world, including in very isolated areas, expressed emotions in much the same way. This made him believe that emotions were not learned behavior or culturally transmitted but rather had evolved by natural selection and were an innate part of human nature.

Current research provides compelling evidence that animals experience a wide range of emotions ranging from fear, anger, and disgust to excitement, pleasure, and pain (Bekoff, 2000). Emotions are obvious in many mammals. Can you deny your dog's excitement when you pull out his leash to take him for a walk? He seems to come out of his skin, wagging his tail, wiggling his behind, jumping up and down, and panting, ready to run out the door. Or can you deny his shame when he lowers his head, tucks his tail between his legs, and has drooping eyes after being scolded for an accident on the living room rug?

Darwin argued that the spectrum of emotions in animals provides evidence that there are transitional stages in the evolution of emotions from their origins in our ancient ancestors (Bekoff, 2000). Once emotions emerged, he thought they evolved incrementally through natural selection. Most experts believe reptiles demonstrate basic emotions, including anxiety, fear, excitement, pleasure, and pain (Lambert et al., 2019; Texas A&M University Veterinary Medicine & Biomedical Sciences, 2011). Iguanas may show pleasure by closing their eyes and holding still when being stroked by a human. In one study, gentle handling of iguanas resulted in a small rise in body temperature and heart rate, well known responses to emotional states in humans and other mammals (Cabanac, 1999). The author concluded these responses represented an emotional response by these reptiles to gentle handling.

Basic emotions, such as fear and disgust, are believed to have evolved among our ancient reptilian ancestors; bonding emotions, such as a mother's love for her offspring, probably evolved among early mammals; and social emotions, such as guilt and pride, are believed to have evolved as primates came together in social groups (Kisak, 2016).

Adaptive Advantages of Emotions

Emotions are strong feelings in response to internal and external events and are generally associated with physiological changes (such as arousal), an expressive reaction (such as a distinctive facial expression), and a behavioral response. Emotions must have provided adaptive advantages for survival and reproductive success for them to have persisted through natural selection. Emotions motivate animals and people to focus attention and respond quickly to events in their environment—actions which may help to improve the chances of survival (Tyng et al., 2017). Although our rational minds help make decisions to guide behavior, rational thinking is often too slow to react to an immediate threat, such as an attacking predator. We need to react more quickly, and emotions, like fear and surprise, help us do that. They are nature's way of facilitating behavioral responses.

Anthropologist John Tooby and psychologist Leda Cosmides (2008), a husband-and-wife team that have been pioneers in evolutionary psychology, believe a major function of emotions is to control which behavioral responses are active and which responses are suppressed in response to external stimuli. When a deer sees a predator in the brush, it reacts with fear, and this helps it to react quickly and flee from the predator. Fear activates the flight response, but to be effective, it must suppress most other responses. The brain can be thought of as containing many algorithms that dictate behavioral responses to various environmental and internal inputs: foraging for food in response to hunger, courting a mate in response to libido, sleep in response to fatigue, and flight in response to the sight of a predator. The appropriate and optimal response to the threat of a predator depends on activating the flight response and suppressing the other responses.

Neural Correlates of Emotions

Investigators have long sought to understand the relationships between brain activity and human emotions. Surgical removal of the temporal lobe in monkeys, including the amygdala and hippocampus, has resulted in what is known as Klüver-Bucy syndrome, which is characterized by compulsive eating, hypersexuality, and blunting of emotional expression (Roxo et al., 2011). Patients with tumors and other lesions in the hippocampus and cingulate gyrus have shown ongoing emotional disorders. American physician and neuroscientist Paul MacLean used these findings and others to promote the concept of the limbic system, a complex neural network fundamental in controlling basic emotions (Roxo et al., 2011). He included in his proposed limbic system the thalamus, hypothalamus, hippocampus, cingulate cortex, amygdala, and prefrontal cortex (Image 3.1). MacLean proposed an evolutionary theory that the vertebrate brain evolved in three phases: the oldest phase is the "reptilian brain," which is responsible for instinctual behaviors. The second phase is the limbic system, responsible for emotions (which evolved in early mammals). The third phase is the neocortex, responsible for cognitive function (which evolved in mammals and reached its pinnacle in primates and *Homo sapiens*).

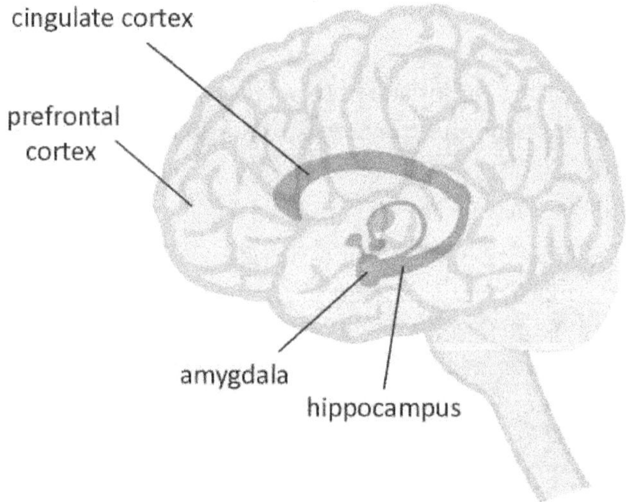

Image 3.1 Limbic system. Initially promoted by neuroscientist Paul MacLean, the limbic system is an ancient evolutionary neural network fundamental to controlling basic emotions. Today, it is widely accepted that the majority of emotional processes occur in the amygdala, anterior cingulate cortex, hippocampus, and insula (not shown), with cognitive components taking place in the prefrontal cortex

New imaging technologies have provided a wealth of new data correlating brain activity with emotional states. MacLean's concept of a subcortical limbic system that is responsible for emotions is probably oversimplified and is now used mostly as a historical perspective. Today, it is widely accepted that most emotional processes are correlated with activity in the amygdala, anterior cingulate cortex, hippocampus, and insula, with cognitive components and conscious awareness in the prefrontal cortex (LeDoux & Brown, 2017; Roxo et al., 2011).

Basic Emotions

Our hottest, most animalistic, and usually most self-serving emotions have been characterized as our "basic" or "primary" emotions. American psychologist Paul Ekman famously described these basic emotions and their characteristic facial expressions in isolated tribesmen in Papua New Guinea (Ekman, 1992). The characteristic facial expressions associated with the basic emotions in these isolated tribesmen are nearly identical to the expressions associated with these emotions in other cultures that have had no exposure to the tribesmen. This provides evidence that the basic emotions are innate and not a product of culture. The classification of basic emotions has been based on this historical perspective and today is somewhat controversial, but Ekman's classification has persisted. Ekman's basic emotions include fear, disgust, anger, joy, sadness, and surprise. We'll consider several of these.

A deer hears rustling in adjacent grass that may be a predator and reacts with **fear** (Image 3.2). This triggers a cascade of events (Cosmides & Tooby, 2008). The deer focuses its attention. It listens intently and watches for signs of movement. Priorities of behavior change: safety becomes the highest priority. Hunger is suppressed, and the search for food is postponed. Libido and the search for a mate are subdued as well. Sleep is delayed. If the deer determines the rustling and movement are indeed a predator, but the predator does not see the deer, the deer may hide. If the predator sees the deer and an ambush occurs, the deer responds with the flight response—an adrenaline rush, a rapid heart rate, and signals to the muscles to run.

Image 3.2 Fear. The universal facial expression of fear includes wide eyes, raised eyebrows, flared nostrils, and a mouth pulled back toward the ears

Fear and other emotions can also act as great communicators. If the deer experiences fear in response to detection of a nearby predator, other deer may sense the emotion, allowing them to escape through early detection. Fear provides an adaptive advantage to the group.

Fear was an important emotion for the survival of our ancient hominin ancestors on the savannas, but it is less helpful and even sometimes harmful in today's modern, civilized life. Threats on the savannas from predators were immediate, but modern-day threats are usually in the future and are less physical. These include loss of a job, financial crises, failing in school, and more. Without an immediate threat to address, our fear frequently turns to anxiety, which can often be counterproductive.

Disgust, another basic emotion, evolved because it provided adaptive advantages in protecting animals against infection (Curtis et al., 2011). Objects and entities eliciting disgust include bodily wastes, spoiled foods, and sick, dead, or unhygienic people or animals—substances or beings that contain pathogens that pose risks of infection. The behavioral response associated with disgust includes a characteristic facial expression—wrinkled nose, lowered brows, narrowed eyes, and a protruded tongue—and withdrawal from and avoidance of the disgusting object (Image 3.3). These reactions can provide communications to human companions about the risks of contaminated objects and help to protect the group. The universality of disgust in humans and its presence in animals that predate the evolution of humans provide strong evidence that disgust is an evolved trait.

Image 3.3 Disgust. The characteristic facial expression of disgust includes trembling and a wrinkled nose, lowered brows, narrowed eyes, and, often, a protruded tongue

Anger has long been regarded as a negative and destructive emotion worthy of suppression. If we feel mistreated or cheated, we often become angry, and our anger galvanizes us into action. The small, almond-shaped amygdala in the limbic system of the brain becomes active, the adrenal glands release adrenaline, and, in men, the testes release testosterone, preparing us for physical aggression and attack (Devlin, 2019). The behavior can sometimes be constructive but is often very destructive.

If anger has survived through the long journey of natural selection, it must have its advantages. A growing number of evolutionary biologists and evolutionary psychologists have provided new perspectives on this ancient emotion (Rodgers, 2017). Sometimes, we suppress our immediate aggressive reaction to anger, allowing for a more measured response. Our prefrontal cortex, which is responsible for reasoning and decision-making, can often put our anger into context and help us address our problem in socially acceptable ways (Devlin, 2019). Anger is now recognized as a powerful motivator of behavior that has fueled ambitions great and small (Rodgers, 2017). In contrast to fear and disgust, which cause individuals to withdraw and avoid challenges, anger propels the enraged to initiate actions they would otherwise shun. Many of our greatest accomplishments are triggered by anger. If you are a long sufferer of domestic abuse, your anger can reach a boiling point where you muster the energy and courage to leave the relationship. If you are angered by injustices to African Americans in our society, your anger may give you the strength, motivation, and perseverance to protest.

Anger plays a major role in addressing conflicts with other individuals. It is a bargaining tactic used to resolve disputes in favor of the angry individual. When others insult or exploit us to benefit themselves, natural selection has wired us to get angry. Our anger causes those who are hurting us to re-evaluate the cost of damaging our relationship. For example, if a co-worker treats me with disrespect by leaving their work undone for me to do, I may get angry. And if that person values our relationship, my anger may make them recalibrate our relationship and be much less likely to treat me with disrespect in the future. This recalibration theory of anger, put forth by Sell, Tooby, and Cosmides (2009), explains a potential additional adaptive advantage of anger.

Bonding Emotions

From an evolutionary standpoint, survival is only important when it leads to reproductive success. Without reproductive success, genes are not propagated. Traits that promote procreation are paramount, and emotions that facilitate this process are what move life forward.

Bonding emotions such as erotic, romantic, and maternal love are often not included in a discussion of emotions, but they clearly qualify (Al-Shawaf et al., 2015). They are strong feelings in response to external events, and they have a physiological response, an expressive reaction, and a behavioral response. Empathy, which we discussed in detail in the last chapter, and which is an emotion in itself, facilitates shared feelings between individuals and is an essential component of these three bonding emotions.

Erotic love, a deep feeling of sexual desire and attraction, evolved as a fundamental emotion to solve arguably the most important adaptive problem of animal existence—the coordination of reproduction. Erotic love initiates the cooperation of a diverse array of behavioral algorithms in pursuit of and culminating in sexual intercourse.

Erotic love differs from **romantic love**, and they serve different adaptive purposes. While erotic love evolved to promote sexual reproduction, romantic love, the long-lasting relationship between two people whose lives are deeply intertwined and who trust and care for one another, evolved for another purpose. Most psychologists believe human romantic love evolved as a form of pair-bonding to aid in child-rearing (Fletcher et. al, 2014). The adaptive advantages are obvious. Creating children has little benefit in propagating parental genes unless children can be nurtured until they are independent and able to parent offspring of their own.

No other species' offspring are so dependent for so long—more than a decade. This creates a burden of childcare that is too onerous for the mother alone and requires the help of the father. Maternal-paternal pair-bonding evolved to provide cooperative child-rearing and ensure the survival and success of offspring. Romantic love, which so brightens and gives meaning to our lives, is the legacy of this evolution.

Maternal love has obvious survival advantages for offspring and helps to ensure that paternal and maternal genes are passed to subsequent generations. As we discussed in the last chapter, bonding between mother and offspring may have originated in early mammals as a precursor to empathy and maternal love. Parental care is nearly ubiquitous in animals, but this behavior may not always equate with love. Social insects display elaborate forms of care for offspring, but they seem to be the result of complex instincts, and most of us would doubt they convey love. Love as we define it requires a cognitive component and an emotional relationship with shared empathy (Allott, 2019). We cannot access the cognitive component and shared empathy of animals, so we cannot know for sure if animals experience maternal love as humans do, but most evolutionary psychologists believe maternal love, with feelings and empathy, is experienced by nonhuman primates and some other mammals (de Waal, 2005). Maternal love remains one of the essential emotions that bind humans together and help our species survive and propagate.

Social Emotions

We *Homo sapiens*, more than any other animal, spend a good portion of our lives reacting to the behavior of other members of our social group. Many of our emotions are related to these social interactions and are triggered by the thoughts, feelings, and behavior of other people (Hareli & Parkinson, 2008; van Kleef et al., 2016). These social emotions dictate how we relate to one another and how we cooperate with one another. They can only be experienced by organisms with advanced cognitive capacity and a high sense of self-reflection, and they are believed to be distinctly human (Simons, 2009). The social emotions include the negative emotions of guilt, shame, embarrassment, jealousy, envy, and contempt and the positive emotions of gratitude, admiration, and pride. These self-conscious emotions are a response to how we imagine our behavior, or the behavior of others, conforms to society's norms (Simons, 2009).

Guilt and **shame** are self-conscious emotions, in which individuals have negative feelings about themselves in response to their behavior (Image 3.4). Guilt embodies negative feelings caused by actions or failures to act for which one bears responsibility. For example, if a stranger gives up a bus seat for an elderly person, and you do not, you feel guilty. Shame is slightly different. Shame embodies a negative feeling about some aspect of who we are as a person. If I see a homeless man on the street suffering, and I fail to help him, I may feel shame about lacking empathy. Guilt is a negative feeling about one's behavior. Shame is a negative feeling about one's self. Guilt is "I did something bad." Shame is "I am bad." Both guilt and shame facilitate prosocial behavior. They are crucial for the maintenance of interpersonal relationships because they encourage a balance between selfish interests and the needs of others. Feelings of guilt lead people to exhibit more prosocial behaviors in future acts and future relationships. Feelings of shame can sometimes cause irreparable damage and lead to avoidance and antisocial behavior, but when shame is reparable, it can also lead to prosocial behavior in future relationships.

Image 3.4 Shame. Guilt and shame are self-conscious emotions, in which individuals have negative feelings about themselves in response to their behavior

Embarrassment is a feeling of humiliation or distress, often triggered by a public display in which the individual is clumsy or forgetful or behaves in a socially awkward way. It impacts future behavior but not nearly to the extent of guilt and shame. Embarrassed individuals are incented to conform, curry favor, and be conciliatory to win approval from others in future interactions (Tangney et al., 2007).

Most of us have felt **envy** when someone else has something we think we deserve or wish we had. When we experience envy in its strongest form, we feel hostility toward the advantaged person, wish them ill will, and hope they will lose their advantaged position. **Jealousy** and envy are closely related and often used interchangeably, but jealousy is generally a stronger emotion and is often used in a sexual context (Ramachandran & Jalal, 2017). I'm jealous of my classmate because he is handsome, and my girlfriend has shown affection for him. Envy is regarded as a negative emotion—a self-destructive emotion that breeds unhappiness. But if envy has become part of our innate human nature, it must have had some benefits for it to have survived natural selection (Collins, 2011). Envy may motivate individuals to achieve greater status, wealth, and power, which may lead to greater reproductive success. This trait may have been valuable to our ancient ancestors but appears to be counterproductive in today's societies, where prosocial traits are so highly valued.

People are often profoundly influenced and moved by the virtue or skill of others. When this happens it often elicits the emotions of **elevation** (a feeling of warmth and appreciation for conduct that exhibits moral excellence) or **admiration** (a feeling of respect and strong approval for extraordinary displays of skill, talent, or achievement). The results of several studies suggest that elevation motivates prosocial behavior, and admiration motivates behavior aimed at self-improvement (Algoe & Haidt, 2009; Haidt, 2003). These adaptive advantages likely explain why these emotions have survived natural selection and are part of our innate human nature.

Pride is the feeling of deep pleasure or satisfaction from one's own achievements or the achievements of others with whom one is closely associated. We feel pride from qualities and accomplishments that are widely admired. We feel pride in a job well done. We feel pride in our children's accomplishments. As *Homo sapiens* formed large social groups, behavior that contributed value to the group provided important adaptive advantages. Evolutionary psychologists have postulated that pride may have evolved to promote such behavior. Cosmides and Tooby believe that pride motivates us to perform activities and exhibit behaviors that are valued by society and enhance our reputation (Estrada, 2017; Sznycer et al., 2017; Cosmides & Tooby, 2008). Accomplishments with the greatest social value result in the greatest pride.

Greed and Hate

Greed is an intense, selfish desire for power, wealth, status, or material goods. Unlike pride, which fosters behavior that society values, greed encourages selfish and unscrupulous behavior to reach personal goals (Jarrett, 2011). Greed may have provided adaptive advantages in our ancient hominin ancestors' struggle for survival but may be counterproductive in today's diverse societies, which value prosocial behavior. Any short-term benefits to the individual may be outweighed by damage to the individual's reputation within the group.

Hate and hate crimes appear to be on the rise in the United States. On June 17, 2015, for example, 21-year-old White supremacist Dylann Roof attended Bible study at the Emanuel AME Church in Charleston, South Carolina, where he was welcomed by the parishioners. He then drew his pistol and opened fire, killing nine African Americans, including the senior pastor (Shapiro, 2017). During the rampage he ranted, "I have to do this because y'all raping our women and taking over the world."

Such violence has become all too common. What is the motivation? Why would evolution preserve such a powerful, evil emotion as hate? The actions of suicide bombers and mass murderers clearly do not appear to support the survival and reproductive success of the perpetrator. But there must be some benefit. Evolutionary psychologists believe that hate may have evolved as part of our tribal instincts, which embody hostility toward those outside the tribe. In today's societies, those outside the tribe may include those of a different race, religion, sexual orientation, or political party. Hate crimes against individuals in out-groups often arise to curb perceived infractions of cultural norms or rising inequity (Fels, 2017). Perpetrators of hate crimes against the LGBTQ community, for example, may feel their acts are retribution against practices they believe are violations of cultural or religious norms. The perpetrators may feel a sense of satisfaction or accomplishment because they believe their actions enhance the values of their tribe (Fels, 2017).

Hostility and hate toward groups outside the tribe may have provided a survival benefit for the tribes of our ancient hunter-gatherer ancestors, but such behavior is detrimental in today's diverse societies. We must overcome our tribal instincts and mitigate the hostility and hate we feel toward those who are different from us. This is one of society's greatest challenges today.

Conclusion

Our goal in this book is to assess how our innate human nature will impact our ability to cooperate with one another in our struggle to save our democracy from rising autocratic forces. Most of our emotions, especially our social emotions, have survived natural selection because they promote social interaction and cooperation between members of our social group. In the next chapter we will explore how cooperation evolved as the driving force of evolution.

CHAPTER 4

COOPERATION: THE DRIVING FORCE OF EVOLUTION

There can be no doubt that the tribe, including many members who are always ready to give aid to each other and to sacrifice themselves for the common good, would be victorious over other tribes. And this would be natural selection.

—Charles Darwin, *The Descent of Man, and Selection in Relation to Sex*

When an *Escherichia coli* bacterial colony invades a host, the bacteria freely multiply and begin to release molecules that lock onto receptors of similar bacteria. When the bacteria sense that they have reached a critical number (a mechanism called **quorum sensing**), they act in unison to release a toxin strong enough to overwhelm the host (Bassler, 2009). If each bacterium released toxin on its own, there would not be enough toxin to harm the host, and the results would not be effective. Such synergistic cooperation provides a strong selective survival advantage for the bacterial colony.

Darwinian evolution has been characterized as a battle for survival of the fittest, pitting individual against individual, with natural selection acting at the level of the individual. But as the bacterial colony illustrates, organisms acting together and cooperating within a group may have a much better chance of survival. Natural selection then acts at the level of the group, choosing more cooperative groups over less cooperative ones. Cooperation, more than competition, becomes the driving force of evolution.

He Ain't Heavy—He's My Brother

Millions of years ago, in the Pleistocene epoch, our ancient hominin ancestors formed clans of 25 to 100 individuals, comprised mostly of kin. These relatively small groups cooperated in many essential activities of daily life, such as hunting, preparing food, child-rearing, and protecting the group. Members of the group often put themselves at risk to perform altruistic acts to help other members. Altruists help others but, in doing so, sacrifice themselves by jeopardizing their survival and reproductive advantage. Evolutionary biologists wondered how such self-sacrificing behavior could survive natural selection. English evolutionary biologist William Hamilton provided some answers, which form the basis of **kin selection**, a term made popular by evolutionary biologist John Maynard Smith (Hamilton, 1964; Maynard Smith, 1964; Rubenstein & Kealey, 2010).

To understand kin selection, we need to understand how genes are selected for transmission to the next and subsequent generations. If a gene codes for a trait that helps an individual adapt to an environment such that the individual is better able to survive and reproduce, this gene has a better chance of being passed to the next generation. We say the gene has been selected. So how does kin selection work? We share many of our genes with our relatives. If I have an altruistic gene that makes me inclined to sacrifice myself to help a relative, say my brother, this sacrifice will help select my brother's genes to pass to the next generation. Since my brother and I share about 50% of our genes, he likely shares my altruistic genes, and my altruistic act toward him will increase the likelihood of passing altruistic genes to the next generation. If my sacrifice is not too great, there is still a good chance that I too may survive, reproduce, and pass my altruistic genes to the next generation. The net effect is an increased likelihood of altruistic genes being selected and passed to subsequent generations, and over time these genes will become prevalent. Kin selection is believed to be responsible for the beginnings of altruistic and prosocial behavior in social animals, including *Homo sapiens.*

In a famous remark that has become a hallmark of kin selection, renowned twentieth-century biologist J. B. S. Haldane, partly tongue in cheek, declared that "he was willing to lay down his life to save two brothers or 10 cousins." (Smith & Szathmary, 1999, p. 125). Haldane's conclusions are based on the knowledge that we share about 50% of our genes with our siblings and about 12.5% of our genes with our cousins. The spirit of kin selection is captured by the title of the 1969 ballad recorded by multiple artists: "He Ain't Heavy, He's My Brother" (Image 4.1).

Image 4.1 He Ain't Heavy, He's My Brother. Altruistic behavior toward kin helps transmit shared altruistic genes to the next generation

Payback: Reciprocal Altruism

If kin selection were the only selective force influencing human cooperation, our society would be very different. We would only exhibit altruistic behavior in small groups composed mostly of kin. Clearly there is some reason why cooperation is favorable even outside the family. If it were not, we might not have the large cooperative societies we have today, and we might consider all people outside our families as potentially hostile. Most members of human social groups are not genetically related kin, and yet we humans still direct altruistic helping behavior toward each other. How could altruistic behavior toward someone who's not related to us, potentially at high cost to our own survival and reproductive success, persist through natural selection?

Part of the answer lies in **reciprocal altruism**. Evolutionary biologist Robert Trivers (1971) described this social system in which individuals do favors for other *non-related* individuals with the expectation that these favors will be returned in the future.

This system should benefit both parties if the benefits of the altruistic act outweigh the costs. Consider the situation in which a man, Steven, is drowning, with a 50% chance he will die if not rescued. And consider that an unrelated bystander, Joseph, can rescue the drowning man with a 5% chance he will die in the attempt. Now suppose that Joseph successfully rescues Steven. Two years later the situation is reversed, and Steven returns the favor and saves the drowning Joseph. Both men's lives were saved through reciprocal altruism.

But clearly there are defects in the system. Suppose Steven did not want to take a risk and did not return the favor. For reciprocal altruism to work, several conditions must be met. A society built on reciprocal altruism requires individuals with complex psychological machinery. Individuals must to be able to assess costs and benefits, store favors and paybacks in memory, and detect those who might be cheating and taking advantage of others' altruism. For all of this to work, groups must be small enough for individuals to know and trust one another and for there to be a good chance that there will be opportunities for paybacks by the recipients of altruistic acts. Because of these constraints, reciprocal altruism is less common than kin-directed altruism. Cultural anthropologist Christopher Boehm (2012, p. 61) believes reciprocal altruism works primarily when pairs, including married couples, close partners, and very close friends, cooperate over the long term.

Are Humans Innately Good?

Altruism evolved through kin selection and reciprocal altruism, but many have argued that these are not "true" altruism. Behaving nicely to someone to procure benefits in return seems instead to be delayed self-interest (Okasha, 2013). But many anecdotes from everyday life show us that people are biased toward selfless behavior even on behalf of non-kin individuals and even with no reasonable expectation of anything in return. Certainly, some of this behavior may be motivated by a desire to enhance one's reputation, but there are many examples of selfless acts performed without any shared knowledge of the act. A gentleman may help an elderly lady across the street with no one around to watch or praise him and no expectation of anything in return. We often see donors provide anonymous gifts to charities, which provide no benefit to the donor in terms of enhanced reputation and provide no payback. This type of altruistic behavior has been called true altruism or psychological altruism, in contrast to altruism based on kin selection or reciprocal altruism. So, how could such acts of selflessness, which may bring harm to the altruist with no potential benefit, survive natural selection?

Philosopher Elliott Sober and biologist David Sloan Wilson (1998) in their thought-provoking book *Unto Others* make the case that true altruism is part of our human nature and has evolved through Darwinian natural selection by acting at the level of the group. They reject the dogma that natural selection must act solely at the level of the individual and that all selfless deeds have hidden selfish motives. As Darwin advocated in the epigraph to this chapter, groups with altruistic individuals who really do care about each other may have a distinct survival advantage over less caring groups, and the survival of caring groups will propagate true altruistic traits of its individual members to subsequent generations (Okasha, 2013; Taylor, 2010). The capacity to care for others as a goal is closely tied to our innate human trait of empathy. As we have seen, empathy, which is hardwired in our genes, allows us to share the emotions of others and want to help and relieve those in distress.

Recent evidence has shown that true altruistic behavior appears to be part of our genetic makeup and may be mediated, at least in part, through the hormone oxytocin, which we discussed in Chapter 2. There are numerous studies documenting that oxytocin facilitates prosocial and altruistic behavior (Campbell, 2010). Investigators have identified genes that code for oxytocin receptors in the brain, and slight variations in these genes have been associated with greater generosity, greater engagement in supportive behavior, and higher levels of self-reported prosocial temperament (Poulin, 2012; Poulin et al., 2012). This suggests there is a genetic basis to our altruistic behavior. We humans do appear to have an innate goodness.

Indirect Reciprocity

Altruism based on kin selection applies only to kin, and reciprocal altruism depends on knowing and trusting all members of a relatively small group. But over time, social groups simply became too big for us to keep track of everyone. And yet, we still act with kindness—even toward perfect strangers whom we may never see again. Why does this happen?

Evolutionary biologist Richard Alexander (1987) in his transformative book *The Biology of Moral Systems* championed the concept of **indirect reciprocity**. Unlike reciprocal altruism, which is based on the principle, "I'll scratch your back if you scratch mine," indirect reciprocity is based on the concept "I'll scratch your back, and I don't expect you to scratch mine, but I expect someone else will scratch mine when I need it." If everyone, or almost everyone, in society buys into this idea, it could provide tremendous adaptive advantages for both individuals and the group. But the potential for cheating is a big issue. How can we prevent others from cheating? The answer is through reputation. Cheaters are discovered, are either punished or gain a tarnished reputation, and are no longer eligible for favors. Darwin appreciated the fundamental role of reputation in human cooperation. In *The Descent of Man, and Selection in Relation to Sex*, he wrote, "The motive to give aid is likewise somewhat modified in man: it no longer consists solely of a blind instinctive impulse but is largely influenced by the praise or blame of his fellow men" (Darwin, 1871).

We all continually judge the behavior of one another through daily observation. But observation alone is not enough to provide widespread information about reputations. The powerful tool of language allows the spreading of reputations and facilitates the process of indirect reciprocity and cooperation between individuals. The advantages of cooperation through indirect reciprocity, in turn, may have accelerated the evolution of language (Dunbar, 1998).

The importance of reputation cannot be overemphasized. Reputation is paramount to what Christopher Boehm (2012, Chapter 7) calls social selection. Those with good reputations are more likely to be chosen for cooperative efforts and as sexual partners, both of which enhance survival and reproductive success or fitness. Those with poor reputations are left behind. This social selection is analogous to Darwin's sexual selection. And in fact, sexual selection may be considered a subcategory of social selection. Remember Darwin's peacock? The bird had a flamboyant eye-spotted tail that made him a likely target for predators. Darwin could not understand how such an extravagant appendage could have evolved until he realized the tail helped the peacock to attract female mates. It made him a target of sexual selection. This gave him a reproductive advantage that outweighed the survival disadvantage. Similarly, individuals who perform altruistic acts may disadvantage themselves in terms of survival but greatly enhance their reputation. And a boosted reputation will make them candidates for social selection by potential mates and other cooperative partners. The desire to obtain a strong positive reputation provides great incentives to enhance prosocial behavior and suppress antisocial behavior. The extensive cognitive abilities required for developing and appreciating reputations make indirect reciprocity a uniquely human trait.

Societies' moral fabric and laws can also greatly influence behavior. If society rewards cooperators with favors and punishes cheaters with penalties or incarceration, individuals will be incentivized toward prosocial behavior and against antisocial behavior. Rewards from society may improve a cooperator's ability to survive, reproduce, and pass altruistic genes to the next generation; punishment from society may impair a cheater's ability to survive, reproduce, and pass on antisocial genes. These processes promote prosocial cooperative behavior by classic Darwinian evolution through individual selection. We create a culture that values and rewards cooperation, and this provides an environment in which we must evolve prosocial traits to enhance our survival and reproductive success within our society. This simultaneous biological and cultural evolution is a strong driving force for collaborative behavior.

Synergistic Cooperation

Altruistic behavior, by definition, is behavior that sacrifices the altruist while providing help or benefit to a recipient. But there are many cooperative behaviors that are synergistic—they benefit both parties. Let's suppose a friend and I wish to pick oranges from a very tall orange tree. I have a ladder, but I'm still not tall enough to reach the oranges. My friend is much taller than I, but he does not have a ladder. Together with my ladder and his height, we can reach and pick the oranges. Through synergistic cooperation we both benefit.

Recently, evolutionary biologist Peter Corning (2018) has advocated the importance of synergistic cooperation in the evolution of complex societies. He explains how this behavior provides huge adaptive advantages for both the individuals and the group. Natural selection acts at the level of the individual and the group, selecting those that work together best and passing the cooperative genes to subsequent generations. Evolution, which has historically been driven by competition and conflict in battles for individual survival, is now driven by cooperation between members of a group. Complex human societies are the pinnacle of these processes.

Abstract Thinking and Cooperation

Historian Yuval Noah Harari (2015) argues in his best-selling book *Sapiens: A Brief History of Humankind* that the evolution of humans' ability to engage in abstract thought is an essential factor in facilitating our capacity to cooperate in huge numbers. He calls our abstract thoughts "imagined realities" or "myths." Only humans possess the ability to think in this way. Our imagined realities can be shared by many and provide a common vision and purpose that allow for large groups to work together toward shared causes, even with people they do not know and have never met. For example, shared laws enable large societies to live in peace and order. Monetary policy and the imagined reality that the dollar bill has value allows us to exchange goods and services, which greatly facilitates trade and commerce. And shared patriotism and love of country can unite peoples in a march to war.

Cooperation: The Driving Force of Evolution

British evolutionary biologist Richard Dawkins (1976) was a strong advocate that competition and conflict were the major driving forces of evolution, as individuals struggled against individuals in battles for survival of the fittest. He believed that selfish behavior evolved to promote the survival and reproductive success of individuals and that natural selection, acting at the level of the individual, selected those who were best adapted to their environments. Dawkins argued that altruistic behavior only existed to the limited extent that it provided some secondary benefit to the altruist. He and evolutionary biologist John Maynard Smith (1964) described the problem of "subversion from within" (Dawkins, 1976). They argued that altruists would be exploited by selfish free riders who refrained from altruistic behavior. They argued that it only takes a few free riders, who have a relative survival and reproductive advantage over altruistic members of the group, to grow in numbers, overwhelm the altruists, and dominate the group.

This paradigm was widely accepted in the 1970s and for many decades after. It was not until early this century that perspectives changed when legendary Harvard biologist E. O. Wilson got into the fray. He and his colleagues were studying the social behavior of ant colonies dominated by a queen with the support of worker and soldier ants (Hölldobler & Wilson, 2008). The worker ants take care of the colony and forage for food, and the soldier ants, with their large mandibles and bulky bodies, protect the colony from predators (Ortiz & Swinderman, 2012). Both the worker and soldier ants cooperate for the good of the colony and sometimes sacrifice their lives. Wilson was puzzled. Why would these ants cooperate and sacrifice themselves with no hope of payback? This did not seem to fit with Dawkins' model of evolution dominated by individual competition and conflict.

Wilson proposed a new model for biological evolution. He believed that animals and insects, by joining together and cooperating with one another, could create larger, more complex social units that were much better adapted to their environments. He proposed that natural selection acted not only at the level of the individual but also at that of the group—what has been called **multilevel selection** (Nowak et al., 2010). Groups with cooperative members would prevail over less cooperative groups and would survive and pass their cooperative genes to subsequent generations. Wilson (2012) published his findings and ideas in his landmark book *The Social Conquest of Earth*. He advocated that cooperation within groups, rather than conflict, and selection at the group level have become the major driving forces of evolution. Human societies and groups of eusocial insects are the best examples of how cooperation and selection at the group level have produced complex social units well adapted to their environments.

The problem of Richard Dawkins and John Maynard Smith's "subversion from within," in which a few cheaters can multiply and overwhelm altruistic members of the group and drive them to extinction, has recently been revisited. A team of evolutionary biologists and mathematicians created computational models to predict the evolutionary paths of colonies of microorganisms populated by cooperators (who sacrifice their reproductive success to produce enzymes to make food available) and cheats (who use up resources but don't contribute) (Constable et. al, 2016). Unlike prior models, they incorporated changes in population size due to random fluctuations in birth and death rates—a process called demographic stochasticity. Their models showed that if, by chance, there are a sufficient number of cooperators to produce enough food, the population grows larger. However, if, by chance, there are fewer cooperators and more cheats, food will be scarce, and the population will decrease and become extinct. In this way, groups with enough cooperators are able to survive and pass their cooperative genes to subsequent generations, while groups with too few cooperators will perish. So, altruistic behavior in sufficient numbers favors survival of the group, and with it, propagation of altruistic genes that lead to a stable, cooperative population. The problem of "subversion from within" by cheaters is not an inevitable outcome.

The concept of natural selection operating at the level of the group as well as at the level of the individual—multilevel selection—is now a mainstream concept and well accepted by most evolutionary biologists and anthropologists (Wilson & Wilson, 2007; Wilson et al., 2008). As we discussed above, synergistic cooperation between individuals within a group provides adaptive advantages to the individuals and is propagated by natural selection at the level of the individual. Cooperative behavior between individuals within the group also provides adaptive advantages for the group, and these cooperative groups prevail by natural selection at the level of the group. Cooperative traits are passed to subsequent generations through multilevel selection, and over time cooperation has become the major driving force of evolution, resulting in complex organisms and societies. The evolution of multicellular organisms from single-celled organisms is an early example of this. The creation of eusocial insect colonies and human societies are more recent complex examples.

CHAPTER 5
HIERARCHICAL AND EGALITARIAN INSTINCTS

Before twelve thousand years ago, humans basically were egalitarian. They lived in what might be called societies of equals, with minimal political centralization and no social classes. Everyone participated in group decisions, and outside the family there were no dominators. For more than five millennia now, the human trend has been toward hierarchy rather than equality. But the past several centuries have witnessed sporadic but highly successful attempts to reverse this trend.

—Christopher Boehm, *Hierarchy in the Forest: The Evolution of Egalitarian Behavior*

If an unacquainted group of hens is put in an enclosed area, there will be a rustling commotion and combat until things settle down. After that, if there is a dispute over food or space, it will be settled with a quick peck. Close observation shows that the pecking is not random but indicative of a hierarchy among the hens—a pecking order. The higher ranked hens will get the best food, water, and roosts, while the lower placed hens will get what is left. The layered social order ensures there is order between members of the flock with few petty squabbles.

All social animals require hierarchy. Without it there would be continual conflict between individuals, damaging both the individuals and the group, and the group might degenerate into anarchy. Although our societies demand hierarchy, we humans have strong egalitarian instincts—we desire to be treated as equals and to have equal respect and opportunities. How did these traits evolve, and how do we achieve some balance between our hierarchical and egalitarian instincts?

Origins of Hierarchical and Egalitarian Societies

Our ancient hunter-gatherer ancestors lived in tribes of a few dozen individuals in the late Pleistocene epoch, over 100,000 years ago. They obtained their food by hunting, fishing, scavenging, and gathering wild plants, moving from place to place as supplies ran low. Each member of the tribe contributed in some way—in hunting big game, in preparing the kill for consumption, in child-rearing and parenting, and in defending the tribe. The culture was characterized by sharing, cooperation, and consensual decision making, and it emphasized individual autonomy and equality. There were no strong leaders. If abusive alpha males tried to dominate the group, coalitions formed to resist such attempts and ostracize the abuser. Our ancient ancestors had a truly egalitarian society.

Much of our knowledge about these societies comes from research by American anthropologist Christopher Boehm (1999), who studied isolated nonliterate hunter-gatherer tribes that exist today and are believed to have changed little from the Pleistocene epoch. Boehm believes hunter-gatherer societies, in the Pleistocene and today, have maintained an egalitarian society because they have strongly resisted domination by bullies and alpha males and because they have worked vigilantly against inequality.

Harvard primatologist Richard Wrangham and Dale Peterson (1996) in their enlightening book *Demonic Males: Apes and the Origins of Human Violence* analyzed the hierarchical and egalitarian nature of our closest relatives—gorillas, chimpanzees, and bonobos (Pinchbeck, 1996). We *Homo sapiens* descended from a common ancestor with gorillas about 10 million years ago and from a common ancestor with chimpanzees and bonobos about 6 to 7 million years ago. Our three relatives are believed to have changed little over millions of years and can be viewed as a "time machine" to give us a look at the origins of their behavior.

Gorilla societies are highly hierarchical and male dominated. The troop usually consists of an alpha silverback male, sometimes two or three subordinate adult males, several breeding females, and their offspring. The alpha male has exclusive rights to mate with the females. When the male offspring reach adulthood, they may break off from the group to form a bachelor group or may challenge the male leader. Breeding females have hierarchy among themselves based on when they joined the troop.

Chimpanzee societies are also highly hierarchical male dominated societies. The alpha male is the dominant male. He forms alliances with male subordinates, but these subordinates are in a continual struggle, jockeying for status and power and frequently plotting to overthrow the alpha male. The alpha male has his choice of mates, but other males also dominate females through violence and rape (Cohen-Brown, 2018). Chimp societies are violent not only internally but also against members of neighboring troops. Males will organize raiding parties to seek out, maim, and kill isolated members of rival chimpanzee bands. In 1974, eminent primatologist Jane Goodall witnessed a disturbing scene of violence (Wayman, 2012). A gang of male chimpanzees on a hunting raid invaded their neighbors' territory and attacked a male chimp sitting by himself in a tree. The gang pulled the rival chimp to the ground, pinned him to the earth, and bit him all over his body, finally hurling stones at him as he lay limp and helpless. After the gang left, the victim died from his wounds. The victim was not a stranger. He had previously been part of the same group as the murderous gang. Since this report, researchers have documented similar episodes of violence and warfare among chimpanzees. These stories have led many anthropologists to suggest that the instinct for warfare may be a grisly trait that we inherited from a common ancestor with the chimps seven million years ago. Violence against our own kind may be part of our human nature, stamped in our DNA.

Image 5.1 Bonobos. Bonobos (pygmy chimpanzees) are a smarter, gentler type of ape. Bonobos' female-dominated societies are less violent and more egalitarian that those of gorillas and chimpanzees

Bonobos are a smarter, gentler brand of ape (Image 5.1). They have quite a different social order than the male-dominant, hierarchical society of chimpanzees (Angier, 1997; de Waal & Lanting, 1997). Bonobos are not as aggressive or hot tempered as chimpanzees. They are less prone to physical violence and less obsessed with power and status. The female is the dominant sex, but not in an abusive way. Females are slightly smaller than their male counterparts, but by forming alliances and banding together, they can maintain control over males (Saini, 2017). For example, females have priority in eating. Should a bigger, muscular male try to butt in, females band together to put him in his place. One unique feature of bonobos' social life is the use of sex in mending and molding relationships. This comes in all kinds and combinations—male to male, male to female, female to female, intercourse, oral sex, and mutual masturbation. But as primatologists Frans de Waal and Frans Lanting (1997) explain in their book *Bonobo: The Forgotten Ape*, sex is different for bonobos. It is not driven by orgasm or reproduction. It is casual and used like any other social interaction. De Waal explains that understanding bonobo societies, which are female dominated, less violent, less hierarchical, and more egalitarian than gorilla and chimpanzee societies, may change the stereotypes we have about the aggressive nature of our ancestors. We may have a kinder, gentler side in our ancient roots.

While bonobos have a predominantly egalitarian society, and chimpanzees and gorillas have a predominantly hierarchical society, they each have a blend of both characteristics. Some abusive male bonobos seek to dominate the group, just like a gorilla or chimpanzee. Similarly, while chimpanzees and gorillas have strong hierarchical societies, they sometimes have egalitarian insurgents who rebel against authority (de Waal, 1998).

We humans have inherited a hybrid of hierarchical traits, which evolved to help maintain order within complex societies, and egalitarian traits, which evolved to maintain individual liberty and social parity. Human history is filled with the conflict between our attraction to power and hierarchy and our desire for social equality. This conflict continues today.

The Transition from Egalitarian to Hierarchical Societies

Homo sapiens first appeared in Africa about 300,000 years ago. Our ancestors were hunter-gatherers, living in bands or tribes of 25 to 100 individuals hunting, foraging, and gathering nuts and berries. All individuals shared in the chores, and all had pretty much equal status, including the women. There were no social hierarchy, hereditary leaders, or central government. Our ancient *Homo sapien* ancestors maintained these egalitarian tribes for hundreds of thousands of years.

About 12,000 years ago, things began to change. The climate was warming, and rainfall was plentiful. *Homo sapiens* began to abandon their hunter-gatherer lifestyle and learned how to farm and domesticate animals. They no longer had to venture out in search of food—they could produce all they needed at home. They built permanent dwellings and came together in communities and villages. The Agricultural Revolution was underway.

The Agricultural Revolution brought great social and cultural change. Farming and the domestication of animals ensured that food was plentiful. Populations soared. People had time to learn new skills, becoming toolmakers, carpenters, weavers, merchants, and soldiers. Innovation, enhanced communication, and cooperation led to great cultural and technological progress. The Agricultural Revolution resulted in perhaps the most profound social transformation in human history. But there was an underappreciated downside. With division of labor came division of classes. A new class of merchants emerged, some of whom became enormously wealthy and powerful, while the working class toiled. Women, weakened by more frequent pregnancies, were relegated to menial tasks. Economic and social hierarchies became a necessary part of the Agricultural Revolution. Life for the elites was certainly better, but life for the peasants was assuredly worse.

The Industrial Revolution, which began in eighteenth-century England, extended and expanded the hierarchical structure in human societies. Populations transitioned from farming in rural societies to manufacturing in factories in newly formed cities. A new economic system emerged as people became factory owners, bankers, and financiers. In 1776, Adam Smith published *The Wealth of Nations*, which outlined the foundations for modern capitalism. The Industrial Revolution accelerated our cultural evolution but also had a downside. Manufacturing brought further division of labor and, in turn, further division of classes. Merchants, businessmen, and bankers became tremendously wealthy, while the working class labored for minimal wages and had dangerous and monotonous working conditions. Urban life was crowded and living conditions were poor. Life for those at the bottom was often filled with despair. The Industrial Revolution further degraded the egalitarian aspects of our societies and created greater hierarchy.

Most anthropologists believe the transition from egalitarian to hierarchical societies has been an inevitable consequence of the increasing size and complexity of human societies, driven by the Agricultural and Industrial Revolutions. Large, complex human societies require hierarchy, but we yearn for our egalitarian heritage. We are engaged in an ongoing struggle to preserve our liberty and independence and to achieve equal rights and opportunities for all. Can we balance our need for hierarchy and still maintain an egalitarian society? Sociologists, anthropologists, humanists, and politicians are searching for an answer. The future of our democracies may depend upon it.

Hierarchies: Good and Bad

Western societies have placed a high value on equality. Equal rights are enshrined in our constitution and laws, and hierarchies of social class have been challenged and to a great extent dismantled. But our societies have remained highly hierarchical, stratified by wealth and status in countless ways. Most agree that purely egalitarian societies void of hierarchies are both unrealistic and unwanted (Hains, 2017). We all agree that some people are more qualified or more skilled than others for specific roles in society. In medicine, patients defer to the authority and hierarchy of experienced physicians; in law, we accept the recommendations and know-how of an accomplished lawyer; and when we need our car fixed, we take the advice and work of a trusted mechanic. Good hierarchies in areas of expertise abound.

It is important to make distinctions between justified hierarchies and those that are exploitative and serve only the interests of those in authority (Hains, 2017). Bureaucratic hierarchies in a democratic society can have value and can promote equality. Consider the United States Department of Justice and the federal and state judicial systems guided by our Constitution and the rule of law. These hierarchical institutions are responsible for enforcing federal, state, and local laws, which are designed to help safeguard equal rights for all.

There are many types of hierarchical relationships embedded in our social structure that we take for granted. The relationship between parents and children may be the most important. Parents provide protection, supervision, support, and instruction for their children, and this is made possible by an authority-dependent relationship. This is a healthy form of hierarchy for two reasons: (1) the dominant party cares deeply about the interests of the dependent party, and (2) this is a temporary arrangement—the dependent party will graduate to a less dependent or a dominant position in time.

There are many other similar authority-dependent relationships. Teachers have authority over students, who learn over time and graduate to more authoritative positions. Employers have authority over employees. Certainly, these can be abusive and exploitive relationships, but in an ideal world, and at least in many circumstances, they meet the two healthy criteria above. An employer may care about the welfare of their employees, and employees may have the opportunity to advance to positions of more authority in the company or in their chosen profession. Inequalities of authority and power are accepted if they are based on relationships of mutual concern and as long as there is opportunity for the advancement of the dependent party.

To protect against abuse, hierarchies should also be domain specific. Harvey Weinstein and the Me-Too movement provide a good example of abuse of this principle. Weinstein had authority in the realm of film production, but he abused his position by extending his authority to sexual domination. Societies need to guard against the extension of power and authority from a legitimate domain to an illegitimate one.

We acknowledge that some individuals acquire excellence and excel over others in specific fields. Since excellence is comparative, skilled individuals will be ranked over less skilled individuals in their specific field. This establishes hierarchy, and the concept of equality is put aside. Deference associated with this type of hierarchy is usually positive. When one individual defers to the authority of another who has expertise in a specific field, and the dependent person has an openness to learning and growth, the result is a productive relationship. This is part of our cultural evolution and is how we pass knowledge and skills from generation to generation.

A more difficult balance between hierarchical and egalitarian relationships occurs between the government and its citizens. Today, our nation-states fall under two broad categories of governance. At one extreme are autocratic, centralized governments run by dictators and controlled by the military and police. These governments are often corrupt and abusive and have little regard for equality and human rights. At the other end of the spectrum are egalitarian democracies, which believe that all humans have equal worth and should be treated with dignity and respect. They believe all individuals should have basic human rights, equal justice under the law, and equal opportunity. Today there is an ideological struggle between hierarchical and authoritarian forces supporting autocracies and egalitarian forces supporting democracies.

Are Hierarchical/Authoritarian and Egalitarian Traits Hardwired in Our Genes?

We know that our genes predispose us to be tall or short, to have blue or brown eyes, and to be able to run fast or slow. And we saw in Chapter 2 that our genes also shape our behavior. In contrast, most of us believe our opinions and social perspectives are shaped by our culture and environment—but this may be only part of the story. New research has challenged this viewpoint and suggests our social views may have a strong genetic component.

A team of investigators studied 596 pairs of identical and fraternal twins from the Minnesota Twin Registry to evaluate a possible genetic component to our social views (Funk et al., 2012). In one sub-study, the investigators asked the twins to record their level of agreement on a scale of 1–7 with statements about hierarchical and authoritarian principles. Here are some examples: "Our country needs a powerful leader to destroy the radical and immoral currents prevailing in society today" and "Our country needs free thinkers, who will have the courage to stand up against traditional ways, even if this upsets many people" (Morin, 2013). A twin supporting strong hierarchical and authoritarian principles would strongly agree with the first statement and strongly disagree with the second statement. The investigators found that scores supporting hierarchical and authoritarian views correlated much greater between identical twin pairs than fraternal twin pairs. Since the influence of environment on these views should be similar between both identical and fraternal twins, this suggests there is a strong genetic contribution to these beliefs. The investigators estimated that about half (48%) of the variability in hierarchical and authoritarian traits are due to genetic differences (Funk et al., 2012).

The investigators also evaluated possible genetic contributions to egalitarian traits (Funk et al., 2012). They found that scores supporting egalitarian views on questionnaires correlated much greater between identical twin pairs than fraternal twin pairs, indicating a strong genetic contribution to egalitarian views as well.

Social dominance orientation (SDO) is a personality trait defined by psychologists that reflects the degree to which one is predisposed to support hierarchically organized social structures in which some groups dominate and have power over others (Sidanius & Pratto, 2001). Individuals who score high in SDO questionnaires believe in a competitive world of survival of the fittest and often have strong authoritarian and racist beliefs and right-wing politics. People who score low in SDO questionnaires believe society should be structured such that all people are equally valued, with no single group dominating others (Kleppesto et al., 2019).

Psychologists at the University of Oslo found that scores assessing the strength of SDO personality traits correlated better in identical than fraternal twins, indicating a strong genetic contribution to SDO personality traits (Kleppesto et al., 2019). Men generally have significantly higher SDO scores than women, and those with a higher position within the societal hierarchy also have higher scores. We can conclude from this that our views about a hierarchical versus an egalitarian society have a strong genetic component, but they are also influenced by our position in society (Lee et al., 2011).

The Minnesota Twin Registry investigators also used twin studies to evaluate a possible genetic contribution to political ideology. The investigators found that conservative and liberal political views, like hierarchical and egalitarian views, do have a significant genetic component (Funk et al., 2012).

A word of caution. Twin studies have limitations and are not necessarily the final word. They have been criticized because of the "equal environments" assumption: it is assumed that identical twin pairs are raised in similar environments and that fraternal twin pairs are raised in equally similar environments, but it is possible that identical twins may stick closer together and thus may experience more identical environments. Consequently, environmental factors rather than genetics could in part be responsible for the better correlation of scores measuring psychological traits between identical twins and between fraternal twins.

Astonishingly, there appear to be differences in brain anatomy associated with different political opinions. British neuroscientists evaluated a large number of young adults and asked them to self-assess their political attitudes as liberal or conservative and then evaluated their brain anatomy with structural MRIs (Kanai et al., 2011). Those with liberal views had a greater volume of brain tissue in the anterior cingulate cortex, while those with conservative and hierarchical views had a greater volume of brain tissue in the right amygdala (Image 5.2). These structures are both part of the limbic system, which is associated with emotional traits.

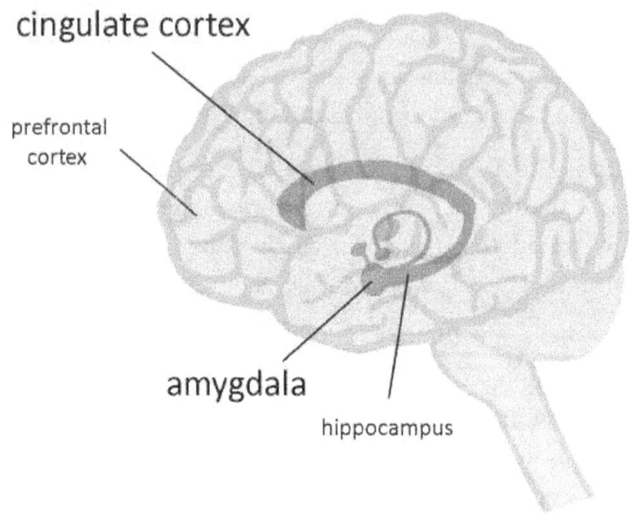

Image 5.2 Brain Anatomy and Psychological Traits. Astonishingly, human brain anatomy correlates with political and hierarchical traits. Liberal views have been correlated with a greater volume in the anterior cingulate cortex, while conservative and hierarchical views have been correlated with a greater volume in the amygdala, which governs emotions and survival instincts (Kanai, 2011; Nam, 2018)

In a separate study, psychologists at New York University evaluated the relationship between brain anatomy and hierarchical traits. The investigators evaluated 138 adults and asked them a series of questions to see if they had a mindset that supported social hierarchy and favored social inequality between groups as legitimate and necessary (Goldhill, 2018; Nam et al., 2018). The investigators then evaluated the brain structure of each participant with structural MRIs and found that those with stronger hierarchical beliefs had larger bilateral amygdalae—the paired structures in the brain governing emotions and survival instincts. This and the previous study document there are clear correlations between brain structures and psychological traits that influence political and social attitudes.

While the results of these studies indicate that genetics play a significant role in our personality traits and views on social and political issues, this does not mean that we inherit attitudes on specific issues—rather, we inherit predispositions. These predispositions are modified by our cultural environment and our life experiences, and together they shape our attitudes on issues of the day and help us to navigate our social and political worlds (Funk et al., 2012).

Is Hierarchy Our Default Mode?

We all have a mixture of innate, contrasting hierarchical and egalitarian traits that have been handed down to us through evolution. These traits, combined with cultural and environmental influences, shape our behavior. We learn a sense of hierarchy early in life. Our early years are dominated by hierarchical relationships with our parents, our teachers, our coaches, and others. As teenagers and adults, we devote a substantial portion of our lives perceiving status, seeking dominance, and offering submission when necessary. These experiences with hierarchy during our early, formative years may build on a genetic bias in support of hierarchy and shape deeply ingrained hierarchical behavior that persists into adulthood (Van Berkel et al., 2015).

We harbor innate egalitarian traits, but egalitarian behavior does not usually emerge until late childhood and correlates with the development of theory of mind—the ability to appreciate and relate to the mental states of others (Fehr et al., 2008). Prosocial and egalitarian behavior require sophisticated cognitive function. Before helping others, one must be able to understand and appreciate others' needs. Once children understand the mental states of others, they begin to empathize with them and comprehend egalitarian values of equality and fair resource allocation.

We all have a combination of competing hierarchical and egalitarian traits. Some of us are more hierarchical and some more egalitarian. Children learn hierarchy early in life, and some children suppress this trait later in favor of socially preferred egalitarianism. Some have argued that when cognitive capacity is high, people exhibit more egalitarian behavior, but when cognitive capacity is limited, they revert to their default hierarchical behavior (Van Berkel et al., 2015).

Psychologists at the Universities of Kansas and Arkansas sought to test this hypothesis. They postulated that hierarchical behavior is our default mode, and egalitarian behavior only overrides it through cognitive effort. They performed several experiments evaluating the effect of temporary cognitive impairment on support for hierarchical and egalitarian values (Van Berkel et al., 2015; Khan, 2016). The investigators subjected volunteers to alcohol consumption and stressful conditions that impaired cognitive abilities and then surveyed them regarding their feelings about hierarchical and egalitarian values. They found that under conditions of cognitive impairment, the subjects had greater support for hierarchical values and less support for egalitarian values. Hierarchical values may be our default mode, and egalitarian values may require intense cognitive effort.

Hierarchies are an essential part of all modern societies. We have hierarchy in our families, our schools, our businesses, our places of worship, and our governance. Many of us long for an egalitarian society in which all persons are guaranteed equal rights under the law, are treated with respect, and are provided equal opportunities, but a pure egalitarian society void of hierarchies is neither realistic nor desirable. Our goal should be to create democratic societies that embrace egalitarian principles and encourage healthy constructive hierarchies but discourage exploitative hierarchies. History has shown us that egalitarian democracies are very fragile and can easily morph into autocratic, hierarchical, exploitative regimes. Given the basic tendency of human nature to exhibit hierarchical authoritarian traits that may be stronger than our egalitarian traits, this may not be surprising. Our historical past helps us understand the great challenge we face in strengthening and preserving our egalitarian democracy.

CHAPTER 6
TRIBAL INSTINCTS

A basic element of human nature is that people feel compelled to belong to groups and, having joined, consider them superior to competing groups.

—E. O. Wilson, *The Social Conquest of Earth*

On Monday, September 20, 2004, Islamist militants in Iraq executed an American construction contractor named Eugene Armstrong. Four men, masked and clothed in black, tensely clutched their automatic weapons while the bound and blindfolded Armstrong knelt in front of them. 'God's soldiers from Tawhid and Jihad were able to abduct three infidels of God's enemies in Baghdad,' the leader intoned. 'By the name of God, these three hostages will get nothing from us except their throats slit and necks chopped, so they will serve as an example.' The long knife sliced through Armstrong's flesh. He screamed. Blood gushed from his neck. His body shuddered and became limp. (Smith, 2007, p. 1)

To the Islamic militant tribe, Eugene Armstrong was a member of an outgroup of infidels and got what he deserved. This horrific account shows the dark side of **tribal instincts**.

Origins of Tribal Instincts

As we have seen, our ancient hunter-gatherer ancestors evolved prosocial altruistic traits that enhanced cooperation between individuals within the tribe because this provided great adaptive advantages to both the individuals and the group. Groups with cooperative members can out-compete and triumph over less cooperative groups and can pass their members' cooperative genes to subsequent generations. As Darwin (1871) explains in *The Descent of Man, and Selection in Relation to Sex*, "[Groups with] a greater number of courageous, sympathetic, and faithful members, who were always ready to warn each other of danger, to aid and defend each other … would spread and be victorious over other tribes."

But along with altruistic, kind behavior toward those within the tribe, our ancestors evolved traits of hostility and xenophobia toward outsiders, who were typically seen as enemies. Humans and other animals have learned to quickly recognize and categorize individuals from outside groups. Is this individual a friend, a foe, or a possible mate? Is this group hostile or friendly? Quick assessment is an important adaptation for survival. In most cases, our hunter-gatherer ancestors found that outside groups were competing with them for territory and resources and represented hostile adversaries. Archaeological records have documented numerous instances of deadly conflict between tribes of our late Pleistocene hunter-gatherer ancestors (Bowles, 2009). Hostility toward these outside groups provided adaptive advantages for survival and has persisted as part of our genetic makeup.

This combination of prosocial, altruistic, and cooperative traits toward members of our own tribe and hostile, xenophobic traits toward outsiders has been referred to as **tribal instincts**. Tribal instincts have promoted survival of the group over rival groups but have left us innately nepotistic, ethnocentric, and xenophobic. These traits promote what we consider today to be both moral and immoral behavior.

Tribal instincts are not uniquely human behaviors. They appear to have roots dating back to long before our species appeared on the planet. Animal species form social groups for mutual protection, cooperative hunting, and other adaptive advantages, and they often display hostile behavior toward outside groups of the same species. Conflict between disparate groups within a species has been documented in a number of species, including hyaenas, wolves, lions, and most social primates (Wrangham & Peterson, 1996). We saw in the last chapter how groups of male chimpanzees set out on hunting raids seeking to harm vulnerable members of rival chimpanzee groups (Wayman, 2012).

Tribal instincts are hardwired in our brains and persist as part of our human nature today. We all still belong to tribes. Most of us prefer to associate with people of the same race, religion, politics, and nationality. We automatically feel more comfortable around people who look, act, speak, and think like we do. In contrast, we often regard those outside our groups in a hostile way, finding them less honest, less competent, and less likable. If racism is the belief that members of another ethnicity possess characteristics that are inferior to ours, we are all instinctively racist. Fortunately, we have the capacity to override these built-in prejudices through cultural learning, although our tribal instincts frequently resurface.

The Male Warrior Hypothesis

Conflicts between human groups have occurred since the origins of our species. Whenever violence, injury, and death characterize these conflicts, men are almost always the perpetrators. Men's participation in coalitional aggression is manifest across all cultures, spans the entire timeline of human existence, and can be considered a human universal (McDonald et al., 2012). Men's involvement in these conflicts can be partly explained by physical and psychological differences between the sexes. Men generally have greater size and strength and are more aggressive than women, making them better candidates for fighting. These traits are driven in large part by the hormone testosterone. Women are smaller, less muscular, and have responsibilities to bear and raise children, making them less suited for intergroup conflict.

Conflicts between groups have large potential costs, yet they have been widespread across time and cultures, so they must provide adaptive advantages. It turns out that men stand to benefit much more than women from intergroup conflict (McDonald et al., 2012). If the conflict is successful, men may gain reproductive advantages by taking new territories and acquiring new mates from their vanquished foes. Brave warriors return home as heroes, receiving reputational benefits and more opportunities for mates and reproduction. Women, on the other hand, are at risk of sexual attack by warriors from outside groups.

The human propensity for intergroup conflict may also have been enhanced through the selection and propagation of warrior-like traits in males (Smith, 2007). Historically, after killing most of the men in an enemy settlement, conquering armies often engaged in mass rapes of the women that remained. Some of these women survived, delivered offspring, and assimilated into the victors' societies, propagating warrior-like genes in the population. Additionally, returning victorious warriors were sought after by the women of their own society. They became objects of sexual selection and as such had a reproductive advantage in passing on their warrior-like genes. Warrior-like self-sacrificing behavioral traits may also have evolved through group selection. Groups with a high proportion of self-sacrificing fighters would survive over rival groups with fewer such warriors and would pass warrior-like genes to the next generation through group selection (McDonald et al., 2012).

Dutch evolutionary psychologist Mark van Vugt introduced the male warrior hypothesis based on many of these considerations (McDonald et al., 2012). He posited that human psychology has been shaped by the long history of intergroup competition and that men and women have evolved different perspectives on outside groups and conflicts with those groups. Such conflicts have afforded men many adaptive advantages, while women gain little and incur significant risks. Consequently, men have evolved psychological traits to initiate these conflicts, while women have evolved traits to avoid them. Men also have stronger tribal instincts than women— they are more xenophobic, more ethnocentric, and have greater hostility toward outside groups than women (van Vugt, 2009).

Although there may have been benefits to intergroup conflict in the days of our hunter-gatherer ancestors, today the social and economic costs of armed conflict are immense and possibly existential. The male warrior hypothesis provides a novel theory of how the long history of intergroup conflict may have shaped the different social psychologies of men and women. In today's complex societies, the empowerment of women may have a pacifying influence and may help to promote the decline of hostilities (Pinker, 2011, pp. 684–689). A number of studies have shown that nations with greater gender equality have consistently experienced less domestic and international violence (Caprioli, 2000; Crespo-Sancho, 2018). Understanding these sex-specific psychologies may provide a start to improving intergroup relations and preventing conflict in our current environment (McDonald et al., 2012). We will come back to this in Chapters 16 and 17.

Tribal Instincts, War, and Genocide

We humans have strong universal codes of morality, but no other species organizes violence, plans brutality, and develops weapons of war like we do. Violence against our own kind through intergroup conflict has been our species' birthright dating back to *Homo sapiens'* likely extermination of the Neanderthals 44,000 years ago. Such conflicts are usually based on tribal differences in ethnicity, religious beliefs, and nationality. In the last century alone, genocides have killed more than 30 million people (Image 6.1). Here is a list of the largest of these massacres (Smith, 2007, pp. 217–218):

- 1915–16: Muslim Turks slaughtered 1.5 million Armenian Christians.

- 1931–32: The Soviet Union forged a famine that killed 5 million Ukrainians.

- 1940s: Nazi Germany exterminated 11 million Jewish, Romani, Polish, and gay people in brutal concentration camps.

- 1970s: The Khmer Rouge massacred 1.7 million Cambodians.

- 1971: The Muslim Pakistani army in East Bengal killed 2.5 million Hindus.

- 1994: The Hutu majority in Rwanda murdered 1 million Tutsis.

- 2007: The government of Sudan killed 2 million black Sudanese in Darfur.

Image 6.1 Genocide. Stacked human skulls at the Killing Fields in Cambodia, where the Khmer Rouge regime killed and buried more than a million people from 1975 to 1979

While not on the list of massacres in the last century, our American ancestors committed some of the worst acts of genocide. European colonists massacred, raped, and committed numerous atrocities against millions of Native Americans over hundreds of years. The spread of infectious diseases wiped out millions more. In North America, the Indigenous population shrank from an estimated 5 to 15 million people when European explorers first arrived in the fifthteenth-century to less than 300,000 by the late nineteenth-century (Fixico, 2021).

War is sanctioned premeditated violence, pitting one group—usually a nation—against another. The key word here is "sanctioned"—war is killing that culture condones. Violence against an outside group is considered a prosocial action. A person can leave their family, go off to war, butcher and murder scores of enemy combatants, and return as a loyal patriot and hero, welcomed back into society with open arms. We have inherited behavioral traits that inhibit us from murdering people within our own social groups, so we might expect that we would also have constraints against killing those outside our group—after all, they're people like us. But this is simply not the case. Morality is tribal.

History has shown that we have been able to overcome our aversion to killing our enemies by engaging in a process of self-deception called dehumanization. In war, we convince ourselves that the enemy is not quite human and undeserving of our empathy, making it easier for us to commit murder and other atrocities. For example, the Hutu ethnic majority in Rwanda characterized the Tutsi ethnic minority as "cockroaches" as they set about to exterminate them.

The deception of others has promoted individual advancement and survival and has become part of our moral—or immoral—fabric. Self-deception, paradoxically, has evolved to enhance the deception of others (von Hippel & Trivers, 2011). If you do not think you are deceiving, you will not give away cues that might reveal deceptive intent. And if you do not think you are deceiving, you can avoid the cognitive challenge of deceiving and can minimize retribution if the deception is discovered. Self-deception also enhances one's belief in self-righteousness and allows greater self-confidence, which has a host of social advantages. We detest dishonesty and deceit and value truth and honesty above all, yet we all have an innate trait of self-deception to some degree or another. It is not hard to understand that evolution would want to wire our brains with such a tool that would give us an evolutionary advantage over our competitors.

The implications of self-deception are profound. Evolutionary biologist and anthropologist Robert Trivers describes it well:

If (as Dawkins argues) deceit is fundamental in animal communication, then there must be strong selection to spot deception, and this ought, in turn, to select for a degree of self-deception, rendering some facts and motives unconscious so as to not betray—by the subtle signs of self-knowledge—the deception being practiced. Thus, the conventional view that natural selection favors nervous systems which produce ever more accurate images of the world must be a very naive view of mental evolution. (von Hippel & Trivers, 2011)

If we can better understand why we are predisposed to making war, it may be possible to learn how to constrain the tendencies that have caused so much suffering over the course of human history. A big part of the problem is our tribal instincts. If we can expand our tribal boundaries beyond our race, religion, and national boundaries to include others who are different from us, we may be able to contain our warlike behavior. If we understand the male warrior hypothesis and men's innate, warlike psychology, we may be able to mitigate war by empowering women. If we can eliminate or modify the process of self-deception that dehumanizes the enemy and makes killing bearable, we may be able to deter war (Smith, 2007). However, if left unchecked, these tendencies, combined with a growing arsenal of weapons of mass destruction, may well lead to our extinction.

Tribal Instincts in America Today

Tribal instincts are part of us all and play a major role in our social interactions. We all need to belong to groups—families, communities, clubs, sports teams, fraternities. We all establish tribal identities based on race, religion, politics, nationality, and many other factors. Some tribal loyalties, such as loyalties to a sports team, are benign, and some, such as blind political partisanship, can be very malignant.

America is unique. We have forged a nation composed of diverse ethnic groups that have transcended tribal politics and created an identity that does not belong to any single group. This has been accomplished through shared values that transcend religious, racial, ethnic, and other groups. It has been a hard-won journey and a very fragile accomplishment. The American mosaic is unique among the major powers. In his "I Have a Dream" speech at the 1963 March on Washington, Dr. Martin Luther King Jr. captured this vision:

When the architects of our republic wrote the magnificent words of the Constitution and the Declaration of Independence, they were signing a promissory note to which every American was to fall heir. This note was the promise that all men, yes, black men as well as white men, would be guaranteed the unalienable rights of life, liberty, and the pursuit of happiness. (King, 1963)

King's ideals were universal and transcended group divisions. "Unalienable rights of life, liberty, and the pursuit of happiness" were the birthright of all men and all women. These were part of America's shared values. This was a time when the idea of universal human rights proliferated and served as the foundation of a just international order. Liberals advocated ideals that were group blind and called for transcending ethnic, racial, gender, and even national boundaries (Chua, 2018).

Barack Obama at the 2004 Democratic Convention in Boston famously advocated for transcending group divides: "There is not a black America and white America and Latino America and Asian America; there is the United States of America" (Obama, 2004). **Identity politics** based on tribal instincts and group-based rhetoric was not yet the mainstream in America, but times were changing.

Liberals became aware that conservatives were using color blindness to oppose policies, such as affirmative action, intended to redress longstanding and persistent racial inequities. To liberals, blindness to group identity began to mark a continuation of group hierarches and oppression. Identity politics, involving exclusive political alliances, was born out of necessity. We are no longer part of one tribe. Identity politics has moved us away from inclusion and toward exclusion and division. We now have multiple tribes, largely defined by identity politics aligned with the left or the right. A broader American identity that transcends and unites the country's many subgroups based on common values has lost its voice and power (Chua, 2018).

Working-class White people, who have emerged as a tribal group on the political right, feel threatened by the loss of jobs due to outsourcing and advanced technology, by immigration, by profound demographic changes in the country, and by the affirmative action championed by the left for underrepresented groups at their expense. There is a long tradition of White tribalism in America, but White racial pride generally dared not speak its name, instead defining itself primarily through cultural clues (Chua, 2018). This has changed with the ascendency of Donald Trump. The extreme wing of White tribalism has surfaced and is no longer lurking in the shadows.

Can We Overcome Tribalism?

Recall that oxytocin has been called the love hormone for its role in facilitating bonding and promoting trust, cooperation, and empathy between human individuals (Barraza & Zak, 2009; Kosfeld et al., 2005). While oxytocin aids bonding and trust between members of the same group, it is not known whether it might enhance positive feelings toward outsiders. Could it be the hormone that promotes universal brotherhood?

Psychologists at the University of Amsterdam sought to answer this question with a series of experiments using Dutch student volunteers (de Dreu et al., 2011; Wade, 2011). In one of these experiments, students were faced with a number of moral dilemmas. In one famous example, a runaway trolley is running toward five people who will be killed if nothing is done. Hitting a switch will divert the trolley to another track, where it will kill only one person. The five people are anonymous, but the single person was given an in-group Dutch name, such as Luuk, or an out-group name, such as Helmut (German) or Ahmad (Arab). These names were chosen because Dutch people generally have a negative image of Germans and Arabs. The student volunteers were randomly assigned to receive nasal oxytocin or placebo before deciding whether to divert the trolley. We might expect the Dutch students during the control phase of the experiment (in which they did not receive oxytocin) to be less likely to pull the switch if the individual sacrificed was Dutch rather than German or Arab, but surprisingly, there was no difference. However, when the students received nasal oxytocin, they were less willing to throw the switch and sacrifice their countryman and more willing to sacrifice the German or Arab individuals.

The psychologists' experiments suggest that oxytocin either enhances feelings of loyalty and affinity toward members of one's own group, motivates negative feelings toward members of outside groups, or both. The authors could not distinguish between these possibilities, but the results did suggest that oxytocin may enhance ethnocentrism—the view that one's group is centrally important and superior to others. These findings refute the idea that oxytocin is a universal "love drug" and suggest that oxytocin may exacerbate tribalism and intergroup division by enhancing feelings of loyalty and affinity toward members of the in-group while possibly intensifying feelings of hostility toward outsiders. Lost is the hope for a pharmaceutical solution to the dichotomy of tribalism.

But there still is hope that tribal boundaries may be expanded. Remember the studies evaluating empathy in rats by investigators at the University of Chicago, which we discussed in Chapter 2? The investigators showed that when rats observed the distress of fellow rats confined in cages, they showed empathy and attempted to release them to relieve their distress (Bartal et al., 2014). The free rats demonstrated empathy only for rats of the same strain. However, if rats were raised alongside rats of another strain, they attempted to free those of another strain. This demonstrates that if previously exposed to outside strains, rats expand their empathy to include those outside strains.

Humans also show more empathy and tolerance to outside groups when they have had prior exposure to members of outside groups (The Century Foundation, 2019). Students who participate in socioeconomically and racially integrated schools and classrooms, for example, have dramatically less discriminatory attitudes and prejudices toward outside groups and more respectful treatment of these groups (The Century Foundation, 2019). Exposure to outside groups appears to expand our tribal boundaries.

Human nature is evolving, and we are gradually becoming a more cooperative species as we come together in large societies. But evolution is a slow process. Changes in behavioral traits, including tribal instincts, may require centuries to millennia to become established in our DNA (Hawks et al., 2007; Pritchard, 2012). Our hope is that we may be able to modify our tribal behavior through changes in our cultural environment, such as exposure to outside groups at a young age as described above. We will discuss some of these possibilities in Chapter 16.

CHAPTER 7

THE MORAL ANIMAL

I fully subscribe to the judgment of those writers who maintain that of all the differences between man and the lower animals, the moral sense or conscience is by far the most important.

—Charles Darwin, *The Descent of Man, and Selection in Relation to Sex*

"In a world without God, all things become permissible," Ivan Karamazov famously cautioned in Dostoevsky's (1880) *The Brothers Karamazov*. For most of our history, morality has been the realm of theologians and philosophers. But times have changed. Religion no longer has a monopoly on our thinking about human good and evil. In 1975, E. O. Wilson suggested in *Sociobiology: The New Synthesis* that evolution could explain moral behavior in humans. He believed morality evolved because it provided essential adaptive advantages. He elaborated, "The time has come for ethics to be removed temporarily from the hands of the philosophers and biologicized," (Wilson, 1975, p. 562). It was the beginning of a new era in which social behavior and morality were viewed through the lens of Darwinian evolution. Wilson's sociobiology later morphed into the field of evolutionary psychology.

Our morality is our sense of what behavior is right and what is wrong. There has been a great deal of controversy about the origins of morality, but evolutionary biologists and evolutionary psychologists have provided convincing evidence that much of our morality is innate, a product of Darwinian evolution and natural selection (Boehm, 2012; Tomasello, 2016). Like our other social behavior, human morality is based on our inherited innate morality traits, but it is also shaped by our cultural environment. Let's see how it all may have started.

Origins of Morality

We humans spent more than 95% of our evolutionary past as hunter-gatherers in the late Pleistocene and early Holocene epochs. Anthropologists have learned much of what we know about how our ancestors lived by studying the few remaining hunter-gatherer societies that exist today. We believe these societies are little changed from ancient times and can give us a glimpse of our evolutionary past (Boehm, 2012; Burkart et al., 2018). Our ancestors lived in highly interdependent, egalitarian societies. They were "cooperative breeders," meaning parents obtained a significant amount of help in rearing their offspring. Both the growth and survival of offspring depended on help from other members of the tribe. Our ancestors became big game hunters, tracking bison, mammoth, deer, and other megafauna, which required that they develop rules of conduct about how to share a kill between large groups of people. Such sharing was vital because hunters often returned empty-handed and would otherwise have been without food for extended periods. Major decisions were usually made collectively. Smaller groups within the tribe ostracized and punished males who tried to dominate the group. These dominant males learned to tone down or cease their controlling behavior to avoid punishment, and they evolved rules of behavior that allowed them to survive. This preserved the egalitarian nature of the group.

Anthropologists and psychologists believe that human morality likely had its origins in these ancient egalitarian societies (Boehm, 2012; Burkart et al., 2018; Smith, 2015; Tomasello, 2016). They view human morality as an adaptation that enabled cooperative behavior between individuals in these highly interdependent hunter-gatherer groups. Collaborative hunting and food sharing were critical for survival and required high levels of cooperation. This behavior led to rules of conduct and norms that facilitated cooperation. Individuals began to feel "shared intentionality." They began to think of themselves as part of a larger group working toward a common goal. Individuals in these ancient societies evolved an innate sense that prosocial behavior was virtuous and selfish behavior was contemptuous.

This sense guided their day-to-day activities (Burkart et al., 2018). This was the beginning of human morality.

Evolution of Morality

Evolutionary biologists and evolutionary psychologists have accumulated strong evidence that much of our morality is innate (Pinker, 2003; Wilson, 1975). There are three major sources of data that support this position (Burkart et al., 2018).

First, although morality varies widely across diverse contemporary cultures, there is a common core of moral values across the world. Almost all cultures extol the virtues of love, respect for human life, honesty, fairness, empathy, compassion, and altruism, and almost all cultures condemn murder, theft, dishonesty, deception, corruption, and hypocrisy (Burkart et al., 2018). This commonality of belief in what is moral and immoral behavior provides strong evidence that much of our basic moral compass has been handed down through natural selection, embedded in our genes.

Second, experiments have shown that infants appear to exhibit moral traits before culture can influence their thinking and behavior. Psychologists at Yale University performed experiments suggesting that babies are capable of identifying with cooperative traits at a very young age (Bloom, 2010; Hamlin et al., 2007). In one experiment, two-month-old babies watched a puppet show in which a cat is trying to open a big plastic box but just can't seem to get the lid off. A "good" bunny in a green T-shirt comes along and helps the cat open the box. In a second scenario, the cat is having difficulty opening the box, but is making some progress, when a "bad" bunny in an orange T-shirt comes along and slams the box shut. After watching these puppet shows several times, the infants were presented with the two bunnies, and they almost always reached for the bunny in the green T-shirt—the good guy.

Other studies suggest that infants are capable of judging fairness. In one experiment, 15-month-old infants observed a person distributing crackers to two recipients. In one scene the distributor gave two crackers to each recipient, and in another the distributor gave one cracker to one recipient and three crackers to the other. The investigators then showed the movies repeatedly to the infants and found the infants spent more time watching the unequal distribution of crackers, suggesting that they found this behavior abnormal or different (Schmidt & Sommerville, 2011).

A third piece of evidence suggesting that much of our morality is innate is that nonhuman animals share some of the building blocks of moral behavior (Decety & Cowell, 2016). One of these building blocks is a prosocial concern for the well-being of others. Primatologist Frans de Waal has observed that rhesus monkeys are very consoling. One infant rhesus monkey was severely punished and rejected by her elders, and as she cowered in the corner, another infant monkey embraced, groomed, and comforted her. The other monkey seemed to genuinely share her peer's discomfort (Van Wolkenten, M., Brosnan, S. F., & de Waal, Frans B. M., 2007).

Another building block of morality is an aversion to unfair treatment. De Waal showed that monkeys have a sense of fairness in a famous experiment called the "fairness study," in which capuchin monkeys were placed in adjoining cages where they could see and interact with one another. (van Wolkenten, Brosnan, and de Waal, 2007) A keeper at the center gave one monkey a piece of cucumber, which he readily took and ate. Then the keeper gave the second monkey grapes—a much tastier treat than a cucumber. Of course, the second monkey eagerly took and ate the grapes. But then, when the keeper went back to the first monkey and gave him another piece of cucumber, the monkey took the cucumber, threw it at the keeper, and violently shook the cage, as if in protest. The monkey sensed the unfairness of its treatment and seemed to be demanding that he, too, should receive grapes.

Many nonhuman animals have building blocks of morality, but this does not mean they have morality in the same sense as us. Most animals simply do not have the cognitive ability required for high-level morality. But the commonality of these building blocks across a wide range of animal species does suggest that morality is a product of evolution (Decety & Cowell, 2016).

These traits have been preserved by natural selection because they have provided incremental adaptive advantages, and they created the foundation for the evolution of human morality.

Why Morality?

Why would we evolve a moral compass? There must be an evolutionary advantage. The short answer is our morality evolved because it helped promote cooperation within our societies (Curry, 2016; Curry et al., 2019). As *Homo sapiens* came together in large societies, they learned to cooperate with one another because it benefited both the individuals and the group. We have seen how humans cooperating in societies have huge adaptive advantages over individuals acting and coping alone. As we evolved the ability to cooperate with one another through kin selection, reciprocal altruism, and indirect reciprocity, we evolved a sense that behavior beneficial to the group is moral and righteous and that behavior that is selfish and often destructive to the group is immoral and dishonorable. Our morality allows us to recognize and choose appropriate behavior, which greatly promotes cooperation within the group.

Our conscience is our "inner" self that helps us choose between moral and immoral behavior. Having a conscience requires identifying with and internalizing society's values. One must connect with these values emotionally—feel ashamed when breaking them and proud when living up to them. Having a moral compass and a conscience does not mean that one will always choose moral behavior. Many times, one will choose selfish behavior. Sometimes this will be done impulsively, and sometimes this will be done with the calculation that the individual benefits of such behavior outweigh the negative impact on one's reputation within society. Or sometimes this is done believing the selfish behavior can be hidden from others.

As our morality and conscience evolved, we also developed social emotions that added intense feelings to moral and immoral behavior. We feel guilt, embarrassment, or shame at our own misbehavior, which incents us to improve in future interactions. We feel disdain toward others when they exhibit selfish or antisocial behavior, and this incents them to do better. We feel pride when we have done a good job or helped a friend in need, and we feel admiration toward a colleague who has performed a selfless act. Our social emotions reward us when we choose prosocial, cooperative behavior and punish us when we choose selfish, antisocial behavior. Our morality, conscience, and social emotions promote prosocial behavior that benefits the group. Moral, prosocial behavior enhances individual reputation, and a good reputation promotes survival and reproductive advantages.

The ability to assess moral and immoral behavior and have a conscience to help choose between the two requires great communicative skills, including language, and high cognitive ability. Our closest relatives—chimps, bonobos, and apes—do not have the language or cognitive skills required for morality (Boehm, 2012). Morality and a conscience appear to be uniquely human traits. As Darwin (1871) wrote in the epigraph to this chapter, human conscience and morality may be the most important differences between us and other animals. We *Homo sapiens* are the moral animal (Wright, 1994).

Culture Shapes Morality

While much of our morality is innate and has been formed by the long process of evolution, culture plays a major role in shaping it. Moral values vary across cultures and change over time. Contemporary society plays an important role in determining what each of us consider moral and immoral behavior. Consider the words of the Declaration of Independence, written in 1776: "We hold these truths to be self-evident, that all men are created equal, that they are endowed by their Creator with certain inalienable Rights, that among these are Life, Liberty and the pursuit of Happiness" (Jefferson et al., 1776). At the time these words were written, "all men" did not refer to all men and all women. Black people were enslaved, and women did not obtain equal rights, including the right to vote, until the twentieth-century. Today we interpret these words much more broadly, although ethnic minorities and women are still struggling for equal opportunity.

There are innumerable examples of differences in morality across contemporary cultures. Being gay is considered highly immoral in many countries and punishable by death in a few, while many other countries, including the United States, have accepted same-sex relationships and legalized gay marriage (Byrnes, 2019). Subordination of women's rights is common in many countries and varies greatly across cultures. Many societies condone polygamy, though it is outlawed in most. Female genital mutilation is practiced and considered part of the moral code in several African, Middle Eastern, and Asian countries. The list goes on.

So, if we ask whether our moral compass is inherited and embedded in our genes or is learned behavior derived from our culture, the answer is clearly both. Culture influences our morality in two ways.

From the time we are born, we learn society's moral code and incorporate it into our own. If we live in Spain or Colombia, we may regard bullfighting as a valued sport and spectacle. If we live in North America or most European countries, we probably see it as a cruel form of entertainment promoting animal torture and suffering.

Our culture also shapes our morality in a more fundamental way that represents a new paradigm for evolution. The classic model of evolution holds that random genetic mutations create new traits, and those traits that promote survival and reproductive success in the existing environment will be selected and passed to subsequent generations. In this model, we do not control the existing environment. In the new paradigm, we shape the existing cultural and social environment and consequently affect which genes and traits are selected. If we create a cultural and social environment that rewards prosocial behavior and punishes antisocial behavior, individuals with prosocial traits will be selected over those with antisocial traits, and over time genes that support prosocial traits will become prevalent in the population. Since we control the cultural environment, the biological evolutionary process is no longer "blind" (Boehm, 2012). We shape our culture, and our culture helps shape the innate or genetic component of our morality. Our culture and biology coevolve (Richerson & Boyd, 2005).

This coevolution has implications for our future. If we can create a culture and an environment that favors prosocial behavior, we can help make human nature and morality more prosocial. We do have some control—and this should give us hope.

Can We Achieve a Universal Morality?

When we look across the many cultures of the world, we find a number of diverse, contradictory, and sometimes bizarre moral codes. Each culture believes in the truth of its own morality. Some philosophers have taken the position that there is not an inherently right or wrong moral code—the principle of **moral relativism**. Some have advocated this principle because of the untenability of identifying any objectively valid universal moral code. Others have supported it by arguing we should be tolerant of other moral codes, even if we disagree with their philosophy. This position has gained popularity because it promotes peace, tolerance, and understanding of other cultures. But it has been criticized because it allows for certain behaviors that may destroy human rights and lives. Indeed, it seems unacceptable to permit such acts as slavery, beheadings, female genital mutilation, and the deprivation of women's rights, to name a few, simply on the premise of having an "open mind" to behaviors based on alternative moralities.

Can we find a universal morality? The call for a universal moral code has echoed through history and is even more urgent today. Many feel that achieving a common morality or common values may be a prerequisite for the survival of our species. As we have seen, we have an innate common morality that evolved through natural selection and became part of our genetic makeup because it promoted cooperation within our societies. Could this innate part of our morality be a substrate for a universal morality?

A team of anthropologists at Oxford's Institute of Cognitive and Evolutionary Anthropology may have found an answer to this question

(Curry et al., 2019). They agree with the prevailing view that human morality evolved because it promoted cooperation within social groups, and they set out to prove the theory of morality-as-cooperation. This theory holds that behavior that enhances cooperation is universally considered moral, and behavior that degrades cooperation is universally considered immoral.

The anthropologists examined behavior across 60 diverse cultures to determine whether behaviors that improved or harmed cooperative efforts were regarded as moral or immoral. The investigators examined seven areas of cooperation, and in each case, across all cultures, behaviors that boosted cooperation were universally regarded as morally good, and behaviors that hurt cooperation were universally regarded as morally bad. To provide one example, behaviors related to helping one's family included being a protective father, helping a brother, caring for a frail relative, and engaging in incest. The first three behaviors enhanced cooperation and were regarded as moral behavior, and the last behavior, engaging in incest, degraded cooperation and was regarded as immoral behavior in all 60 cultures. The authors concluded that this may help us to define a new universal morality—morality-as-cooperation.

As globalization marches forward through expanded trade, greater communication, and shared ideas, there will be expanded opportunities for collaboration between diverse cultures. An expanded global morality may evolve to facilitate this cooperation. This process has already started. Today's companies are outsourcing much of their manufacturing and production to countries where the protections for workers' health and safety are weak, with little enforcement. Tragedies such as the Rana Plaza factory collapse in Bangladesh in 2013, which was due to blatant disregard for building codes and killed more than 1,000 workers, illustrate the problem (Yardley, 2013). Many companies that outsource labor to developing countries have hired staff to focus on labor conditions in overseas supply chains, and they often incorporate human rights and environmental protections into their contracts. Over time, the human rights of workers may become a shared moral principle hopefully of all societies. As globalism causes societies to merge, and as cooperation becomes increasingly necessary, a common moral code may evolve to facilitate this cooperation. This may be the pathway to a universal shared morality and improved global cooperation.

CHAPTER 8
SOCIAL DARWINISM

A drunkard in the gutter is just where he ought to be. ... The law of survival of the fittest was not made by man, and it cannot be abrogated by man. We can only, by interfering with it, produce the survival of the unfittest.

—William Graham Sumner, *What Social Classes Owe to Each Other*

Charles Darwin's theory of evolution revolutionized our understanding of biology and impacted every aspect of the life sciences. Darwin intended that his theories be applied to biology alone, but not long after the 1859 publication of *On the Origin of Species*, his ideas were extended to the fields of sociology, economics, and politics. **Social Darwinism,** as the new ideology was called, was used to justify specific and often radical social, economic, and political views, which ultimately tarnished Darwinism's legacy. Social Darwinism is widely discredited today, but its values are still alive and influential. An understanding of this ideology will provide meaningful perspectives as we try to shape our societies to be compatible with the hybrid character of our human nature.

Origins of Social Darwinism

Darwin's theory of evolution through natural selection challenged religious beliefs and stirred great controversy. In an attempt to explain his theories to the larger British public, Darwin borrowed popular terms such as "survival of the fittest" from sociologist Herbert Spencer and "struggle for existence" from economist Thomas Malthus. Darwin himself rarely discussed the social implications of his theories, but Spencer, Malthus, and others used his ideas to advance their own agendas.

Image 8.1 Herbert Spencer (1820–1903). A radical and influential English sociologist and philosopher, Spencer founded the movement that came to be known as social Darwinism

Herbert Spencer (1820–1903), a radical and influential English sociologist and philosopher, was a contemporary of Darwin and an early advocate for Darwin's theories (Ruse, 2017; Image 8.1). He championed libertarian principles the preeminence of the individual over society and of science over religion. Spencer applied Darwin's theories to his own ethical and social thought and founded the movement that came to be known as social Darwinism. Social Darwinists believe in competition and survival of the fittest: strong and fit individuals will prevail over poor and weak individuals and, in the end, will create a stronger society. Competition establishes the social order, and there is no need for government social programs or intervention. Social Darwinism is used to justify laissez-faire capitalism, in which businesses are allowed to operate with little regulation. Advocates of social Darwinism believe the fit inherit traits such as industriousness, intelligence, and the ability to create wealth, while the unfit are innately lazy and stupid. nineteenth-century titans of capitalism in the United States used Spencer's doctrine to oppose social reform and government intervention and justify the fates of the rich and the poor.

Social Darwinism holds that nations and races that are superior and more adaptable will survive and dominate through natural selection. This idea was used throughout the nineteenth-century to justify European colonialism, imperialism, and the inequities of capitalism. The dominant nations were dominant because they were the most fit and most adaptable, and their colonies were subjugated because their inhabitants were less fit and "naturally" inferior (Skagit Valley College, 2017). Natural selection created this order.

As we will see, Spencer's work gained popularity outside of Great Britain and had a great influence in the United States. Later, as social Darwinism fell into disfavor, Spencer, to his credit, renounced many, if not most, of its applications (Ruse, 2017).

English political economist Thomas Robert Malthus (1766–1834) in his treatise *An Essay on the Principle of Population* (1798) prophesized the inevitability of what was later called a Malthusian catastrophe (Shermer, 2016). He proposed that the combination of accelerating human population growth and an inability to provide food supplies to meet its needs would result in famine and starvation that would wipe out much of the world's population. Malthus' ideas of a "struggle" for existence laid the foundation for Darwin's concepts of natural selection, and sometime later his ideas influenced English philosophers and policy makers to embrace social Darwinism. The English Poor Law, which was enacted to provide food for the poor, was curtailed in 1834 based on Malthusian reasoning that the law encouraged the poor to have more children and exacerbated poverty. In another example, the British government took a hands-off approach during the Irish potato famine of the 1840s, with the British assistant treasury secretary citing the disaster as an "effective mechanism for reducing surplus population" (Shermer, 2016). While there is currently still great concern about population growth because of its impact on climate change, depletion of natural resources, and damage to our planet's biodiversity, a Malthusian catastrophe is no longer on the immediate radar. Fertility rates have declined in developed nations, population growth has slowed, and technological advances have greatly increased food production.

The Eugenics Movement

As we have seen, British anthropologist Sir Francis Galton was greatly influenced by Darwin's work. A disciple of social Darwinism, he argued against social institutions such as welfare programs and mental asylums that allowed "inferior" humans to survive and reproduce at higher levels than their "superior" counterparts. He also launched the controversial new science of **eugenics**, which sought to improve the "quality" of human populations through selective breeding to increase the frequency of desirable heritable traits. Galton's ideas never took hold in his native Great Britain, but they became popular early in the twentieth-century in the United States, where the eugenics movement rapidly gained strength.

The United States has dark chapters in its history—slavery, war atrocities, and the decimation of Native Americans, to name a few—but most Americans are unaware of the shameful eugenics movement. The movement took root in the early 1900s, led by biologist Charles Davenport and Harry Laughlin (Bouche and Rivard, 2014). They established the Eugenics Record Office at Cold Spring Harbor Laboratory on Long Island with the goal of improving the quality of the human population by applying classic genetics to breeding better citizens. Regrettably, the focus of the office's activities was the collection of data from "unfit" families in Manhattan and New Jersey slums, identifying negative traits such as mental disability, dwarfism, promiscuity, and criminality (Bouche & Rivard, 2014). This led to forced sterilization efforts to prevent "unfit" individuals from having children (Norrgard, 2008).

Indiana passed the first eugenics sterilization law in 1907, requiring the mandatory sterilization of criminals, rapists, and "idiots" in state custody. An additional 29 states passed similar laws by 1931. More than 64,000 people underwent sterilizations, which were focused first on disabled persons but later included people who were simply poor (Bouche & Rivard, 2014). The U.S. Supreme Court gave its blessing to these sterilization programs in its 1927 ruling of *Buck v. Bell*, when it ruled in favor of forced sterilization of Carrie Buck because of her promiscuity in having a child out of wedlock. Supreme Court Justice Oliver Wendell Holmes wrote:

> It is better for all the world if, instead of waiting to execute degenerate offspring for crime or to let them starve for their imbecility, society can prevent those who are manifestly unfit from continuing their kind. …Three generations of imbeciles are enough. (Black, 2003)

Adolph Hitler is probably the world's most well-known and notorious eugenicist. He studied social Darwinism and eugenics while he was imprisoned after a failed coup attempt against the Weimar Republic in 1923. He believed the German master race had been weakened by breeding with non-Aryans, and he targeted groups for extermination that he proclaimed were "inferior"—including Jews, Poles, gypsies, gay people, and people with disabilities. The horrors of the Holocaust are written in history.

Eugenics and social Darwinism have fallen from favor in the United States and Europe, in large part due to their association with the eugenics movement in Nazi Germany. But remnants are still part of the social, economic, and political dialogue.

Social Darwinism in America

The **Gilded Age** of American history (1870–1900) was a time of dramatic change. Industrialization spread rapidly, unregulated capitalism flourished, and the United States appeared as a dominant force on the world stage. But greed, corruption, and huge disparities in income and wealth between rich and poor have marred the period's legacy.

At the time, industrialists infamously known as "robber barons" dominated the American economy. John D. Rockefeller and Andrew Carnegie were the most notable of these. They built massive empires and accumulated great wealth by establishing monopolies and paying minimal wages. Their businesses ran free with minimal regulation in the era's laissez-faire economy. The robber barons viewed their success through the lens of social Darwinism: the smartest and most industrious people would outcompete those with lesser talents and would rise to the top. They believed they were entitled to their wealth, power, and influence.

John D. Rockefeller in 1882 founded the Standard Oil Company, which grew to a huge monopoly that controlled over 90% of the country's oil refineries. Because of his firm's size, he was able to drive his competitors out of business, and with an influx of European immigrants, he was able to pay very cheap wages. He became the wealthiest man in the country, amassing over one billion dollars in personal assets. He is quoted as saying, "The growth of a large business is merely a survival of the fittest … the working out of a law of nature" (Bergman, 2001). Rockefeller was widely criticized for his ruthless practices, but like other industrialists of the time, he generously supported a number of philanthropies, many of which continue to make important contributions today.

Andrew Carnegie, a Scottish-born American industrialist, led the expansion of the American steel industry in the late nineteenth-century and founded what became the Carnegie Steel Company. He too became one of the richest men in American history. He was a leading advocate of social Darwinism and was convinced that competition sorted people according to their abilities and that huge wealth disparities were justified. He deplored charity for the poor, advocating that every person maintained by charity was a source of moral infection (DeSantis, 1988; Hall, 2020). Yet, paradoxically, he gave almost all of his wealth to numerous charitable organizations by the time of his death.

Social Darwinism was widely disseminated and was accepted in academic circles such as Harvard, Yale, and Johns Hopkins during the Gilded Age and early twentieth-century. Yale sociologist William Graham Sumner (1840–1910), who held the nation's first professorship in sociology, advocated strong social Darwinist views and was widely respected. He argued that "humans must stop 'sentimentalists' and allow unfit people to die, or at the very least not reproduce" (Thomas, 2011). Social Darwinism continued to have great influence on social, economic, and political life in the United States, peaking in the 1920s and 1930s, but fell from favor after the Great Depression and World War II.

Social Darwinism Today

Ask someone today about social Darwinism, and you are likely to get an answer like, "Oh, social Darwinism, wasn't that used to justify ruthless capitalism, militarism, imperialism, and racism, using Darwin's 'survival of the fittest'?" Such answers are commonplace and show that social Darwinism has a dim legacy. But while social Darwinism is less often cited today to justify political, social, and economic views, its ideas are still very much with us and remain part of our dialogue, especially on the political right.

Many conservatives embrace many of the principles of social Darwinism. They argue that human beings are essentially selfish, greedy, competitive, and individualistic, and our economic, social, and political systems need to accommodate those traits. They believe in laissez-faire capitalism with minimal regulation that rewards the strong and talented with success and wealth. They value capitalist entrepreneurs as change agents who shape the future by relying on their own instincts, intuition, and knowledge and by taking risks. In their view, entrepreneurs drive the economy by creating businesses and providing jobs. Conservatives value self-reliance and individualism and deplore welfare for the poor, which they view as demeaning and counterproductive. They believe in low taxes and fiscal responsibility and endorse only a minimal social safety net. They support a hierarchical society and value respect for authority and tradition. An understanding of the historical background of social Darwinism provides perspectives on these principles and the conservative movement today.

PART II
STRUCTURAL RACISM AND SOCIOECONOMIC INEQUITIES

CHAPTER 9
THE TOXICITY OF STRUCTURAL RACISM

Few societies in history have managed to be both multiracial and genuinely democratic. That is our challenge. It is also our opportunity. If we meet it, America will truly be exceptional.

—Steven Levitsky and Daniel Ziblatt, *How Democracies Die*

Our country's history of slavery and the Jim Crow South have left a stain on our nation that we have not been able to overcome. Despite progress through the civil rights movement, Black people and other ethnic minorities are disadvantaged in every institution of our society. Our innate tribal instincts have caused hostile and racist behavior toward ethnic minority groups and have left us with a racial divide that polarizes our country. Large democracies with great ethnic diversity are very fragile due to the potential for ethnic strife. For all that is good about us, part of us is rotten, and this may be the greatest threat to our democracy.

Origins of American Slavery

In 1619, a Portuguese ship carrying 20 kidnapped Black Angolans arrived at the British colony of Jamestown, Virginia, where the Africans were sold as slaves to the English colonists. This marked the beginning of the transatlantic slave trade. The trade accelerated near the end of the seventeenth-century, and historians estimate that during the eighteenth-century alone six to seven million Africans were shackled in the holds of ships, transported to the Americas, and sold into a lifetime of forced labor, violent abuse, and dehumanization, leaving an indelible stain on our nation (Schermerhorn, 2018). Enslaved Africans initially worked mostly on tobacco, rice, and indigo plantations on the southern coast, but during the late eighteenth-century the textile industry in England expanded rapidly, creating a huge demand for American cotton. Southern plantation owners transitioned from the production of tobacco to the large-scale farming of cotton, a change that reinforced their dependence on enslaved labor. The domestic slave population grew quickly and by 1860 had reached nearly four million.

By the mid-nineteenth-century, enslaved Black people constituted about one-third of the southern population, most of whom lived on large plantations or small farms (Schermerhorn, 2018). Most plantation owners and farmers sought to make their slaves completely dependent upon them by prohibiting them from learning to read or write and by restricting their movement. Owners brutally punished rebellious slaves and often raped enslaved women. They established a strict hierarchy among the slaves, ranging from privileged house workers and skilled artisans to lowly field hands. This system was designed to keep the slaves divided and less likely to rebel against their masters. There were no legal marriages among enslaved people, but they did often raise large families, which provided additional slaves for the owners. Spouses were often separated from one another, and parents were often separated from their children following their owner's death or business failures.

Renowned novelist and abolitionist Harriet Beecher Stowe brought unprecedented light to the plight of enslaved people in the South with the publication of her best-selling novel *Uncle Tom's Cabin*. The highlighted awareness of the oppression of southern Black slaves fanned the flames of the abolitionist movement in the North and served as a prelude to the Civil War. When Republican presidential candidate Abraham Lincoln, who was a staunch abolitionist, was elected and inaugurated as president in 1861, the South reached a breaking point, and seven southern states seceded from the Union to form the Confederate States of America, launching the Civil War. Four more southern states followed suit after the onset of the fighting. The war ended four years later, with an estimated 620,000 people dead, when Robert E. Lee surrendered to Ulysses S. Grant at Appomattox Court House on April 9, 1865 (Schermerhorn, 2018). Three million slaves in rebel states had been freed during the conflict when President Lincoln issued the Emancipation Proclamation in 1863.

On the evening of April 14, 1865, just five days after General Lee had surrendered, Abraham Lincoln was assassinated by a Confederate sympathizer, John Wilkes Booth, at Ford's Theatre in Washington, DC. Sadly, Lincoln did not live to see the fulfillment of his dream with the passage of three constitutional amendments that transformed American society. The 13th Amendment, ratified in 1865, abolished slavery; the 14th Amendment, ratified in 1868, granted citizenship to all former slaves; and the 15th Amendment, ratified in 1870, granted voting rights to all African American men. There was hope for the future.

Reconstruction (1865–1877)

The Civil War brought the end of the shameful, deplorable practice of slavery, but its aftermath marked one of the most difficult times in American history (Foner, 2014). During **Reconstruction**, the U.S. faced the daunting task of reincorporating the eleven states that had seceded from the Union and of ensuring the rights of newly freed Black Americans. Andrew Johnson, who became president following Lincoln's assassination, opposed any protection for Black people. But the Republican-controlled Congress, overriding President Johnson's veto, passed the Reconstruction Act of 1867, which created military districts in the South to enforce Black people's voting and civil rights. Southern Black people won elections to state governments and the U.S. Congress. The South's first public schools were established, and laws against racial discrimination in public transportation and accommodations were passed. This was an experiment in interracial democracy not seen before in human history, offering Black people a brief glimpse of hope (Foner, 2014). But the honeymoon was short lived.

Southern White people turned to violence in response to the revolutionary changes of Reconstruction. The Ku Klux Klan and other White supremacist groups targeted local Republican leaders and Black people who challenged White authority with violent attacks. Racism remained a potent force in both North and South, and Republican enthusiasm for Reconstruction waned. Reconstruction had perpetuated a deep, virulent, and often violent divide between North and South, Republicans and Democrats, that was only resolved with the infamous **Compromise of 1877**. With this Compromise, Republicans agreed to remove federal troops from involvement in the politics of the South in exchange for votes that would put Republican candidate Rutherford B. Hayes in the White House. The Compromise reduced polarization between the two parties and may have saved our democracy for the time, but it came at the expense of Black people, who were again subjected to segregation, servitude, and violent abuse for the next hundred years in the Jim Crow era.

The Jim Crow Era

Free of military control, the Southern states passed a series of what were called Jim Crow laws that legalized segregation (Packard, 2002). The laws required segregated waiting rooms, water fountains, building entrances, elevators, and cemeteries (Image 9.1). Restrooms came in threes—men, women, colored. In the **Jim Crow era**, there were legal limits to where Black people could work and for what compensation and where they could travel. Violators who were convicted of crimes were incarcerated in camps where they were treated as enslaved people, with long sentences and grueling labor (Image 9.2). Southern states instituted poll taxes, literacy tests, property requirements, and complex ballots to suppress the African American vote. Black voter turnout in the South fell from 61% in 1880 to 2% in 1912. White Democrats remained in power in the region for nearly a century.

Image 9.1 Segregated Water Fountain in the Jim Crow South

Violence was common, and danger was a regular part of the lives of southern Black Americans (Packard, 2002). Black schools were vandalized, and Black families were attacked and forced off their land. Discrimination worked not only through Jim Crow laws but also through racial "etiquette." Deviations were rigidly enforced not only by police and courts but by ordinary citizens who took the law into their own hands. The Ku Klux Klan and other White supremacist groups attacked, tortured, and lynched Black citizens at night for the most minor infractions. The Klan permeated White Southern culture, and its members reached the highest levels of government.

The early twentieth-century did not bring much relief. Lynchings of Black people in the South became more prevalent, and with them came a series of violent protests across the U.S. With continued oppression and few opportunities in the South, the 1920s saw a Great Migration of Black people to the North. But the North was not immune to Jim Crow–like laws. Schools and neighborhoods were segregated, voting rights were suppressed, and businesses displayed WHITES ONLY signs.

Image 9.2 Four Black Youths in a Southern Chain Gang. Southern jails made money leasing convicts for forced labor in the Jim Crow South. Circa 1900

Following World War II, the U.S. reached new milestones. In 1948, President Truman ordered integration of the military, and in 1954, the Supreme Court in *Brown v. Board of Education* ruled that segregation in schools was unconstitutional. In the 1950s and 1960s the civil rights movement under the leadership of Martin Luther King Jr. began the struggle for equal rights and equal justice for Black Americans. President Lyndon B. Johnson and the Democrat-controlled Congress passed the Civil Rights Act in 1964 and the Voting Rights Act in 1965, overriding state-sponsored Jim Crow laws and assuring civil and voting rights for Black people and other people of color (Image 9.3). This marked the end of the Jim Crow era.

Image 9.3 Signing of the Civil Rights Act, 1964. President Lyndon Johnson signs the law as Dr. Martin Luther King Jr., Senator Barry Goldwater, and others look on

Structural Racism in the Twenty-first Century

While the civil rights movement and the passage of the Civil Rights Act and the Voting Rights Act marked an end to the Jim Crow era, the march toward the "promised land" has not been fulfilled for most Black Americans. Today, **structural racism** deeply divides our country. People of color face a litany of discriminatory laws and policies in labor, housing, education, voting, healthcare, justice, and more (Costigan et al., 2020). America is still, to a very large extent, geographically segregated by race. Most White Americans are insulated from the obstacles and lack of opportunities that predominantly Black communities face, and most do not have a single close relationship with a Black individual outside the workplace. Lack of economic resources and discrimination in obtaining home loans have made home ownership an unreachable goal for most Black people. Neighborhood school funding relies heavily on property taxes, and schools in predominantly less affluent Black neighborhoods have less money to pay for teachers, facilities, and opportunities for students. Consequently, Black children are more likely to attend inferior schools.

Black people have long suffered from widespread voter suppression, which has recently grown more severe in many states. Black people more frequently lack health insurance and have reduced access to quality healthcare. Black women are three to four times more likely to die in childbirth than White women, and Black people have a life expectancy six years shorter than White people. The average Black family has an income that is about half that of the average White family and a net worth of only one-tenth of that of the average White family. Black people are six times more likely to be incarcerated than White people and make up 33% of our prison population while comprising just 12% of the general population. The list goes on. Jeh Johnson, Homeland Security Secretary under President Obama, put it bluntly: "Defined broadly enough, one could say that there's structural racism across every institution in America" (Worland, 2020).

The concept of structural racism is distinguished from racism. Racism is an individual's belief that people of another race or ethnic group have traits or characteristics that make them inferior to individuals of one's own race. In contrast, structural or systemic racism is present when laws, customs, and institutional policies disadvantage and reduce opportunities for racial and ethnic groups. We may not know if another person is racist because we cannot always know what they believe, but we can document structural racism by the measurement of differences in opportunities and outcomes of racial groups in various social institutions, such as education, policing, healthcare, or economics.

Structural Racism Undermines Democracy

Structural racism is fundamentally antithetical to the values of egalitarian democracy. When Black people and other underrepresented groups are deprived of equal opportunities and equal justice under the law, the basic principles of democracy are violated, and democracy is weakened.

Many Black people and other people of color have lost faith in a government and political parties that have done little to repair the inequities suffered for so long. When there is a lack of trust, there is little involvement in community and political affairs, and many Blacks and other ethnic minorities have dropped out of participation in the democratic process. This is reflected in lower voter turnout for African Americans (59.6%), Asian Americans (49.3%), and Hispanic Americans (47.6%) compared with European Americans (65.3%) in the 2016 election and most earlier elections (Ray & Whitlock, 2019).

The Civil Rights Act and the Voting Rights Act strengthened our democracy by including Black people and other ethnic minorities in our governance, but this resulted in political polarization deeper than at any time since the Civil War and Reconstruction. African Americans migrated to the Democratic Party in appreciation of its support for their rights, while White southern Democrats defected in mass to the Republican Party.

Today, the Republican Party, which once was the party of Lincoln that championed the end of slavery, has become the party of White Christian America. The party is now a coalition of rural White Americans, the White working class, Evangelical Christians, small business owners, and plutocrats, while the Democratic Party is made up of Black people, other people of color, feminists, the LGBTQ community, and well-educated liberal elites. The Democratic Party has also become increasingly secular. The two parties now differ not just on policy issues but on the more fundamental issues of race and religion. This has made the divisions between them deeper and more indelible and has contributed to the intense political polarity that threatens our democracy today.

Maintaining a functioning democracy at a time of increasing racial, ethnic, and religious diversity requires the creation of an inclusive America with shared values to which members of all identities can feel connected. This is a great challenge. Large democracies with great ethnic diversity, such as the United States and the United Kingdom, lack the shared experiences and shared values of smaller, less diverse democracies, such as the Nordic states. Throughout human history, large democracies with great ethnic diversity have been less successful and more fragile than smaller, mono-ethnic democracies (Fish & Brooks, 2004). Harvard professor and political scientist Danielle Allen (2017) puts it well:

> The simple fact of the matter is that the world has never built a multiethnic democracy in which no particular ethnic group is in the majority and where political equality, social equality and economies that empower all have been achieved.

Structural racism in the setting of our substantial ethnic diversity may be the greatest threat to our democracy. As Harvard professors Steven Levitsky and Daniel Ziblatt (2019) conclude in *How Democracies Die*, if we can heal our large, diverse democracy and save it for posterity, we will truly be exceptional.

Critical Race Theory

Critical race theory (CRT), once an obscure academic concept, is now making national and international headlines as a major player in America's political culture wars. It has turned school boards into battlegrounds, has been a major issue in state and national politics, and has been branded as "activist indoctrination" by conservatives and dozens of U.S. senators (Fortin, 2021).

As a scholarly movement, critical race theory began in the 1970s with the early writings of Derrick Bell, a civil rights lawyer and the first Black person to teach at Harvard Law School. Bell was part of a growing group of scholars who realized that the gains of the civil rights movement had stalled and that new approaches were needed to address the racial biases of our institutions (Delgado & Stefancic, 1998). Critical race theorists hold that the law and legal institutions of the United States are inherently racist and function to create and maintain social, political, and economic inequalities between

White and non-White people, especially Black Americans. CRT rejects the philosophy of color blindness, advocating that it has not corrected the many racial biases in our institutions that have been present since the founding of our country (Fortin, 2021). Due to its complexity, CRT is primarily taught in colleges, universities, and law schools, although aspects of CRT are part of the curriculums of some public high schools.

Teaching history in K–12 schools has always been a balance between patriotism and American exceptionalism on the one hand and the country's history of exclusion and violence against Indigenous peoples and its enslavement of African Americans on the other. Unfortunately, the teaching of CRT and the history of racism in America has become highly politicized. Liberals regard CRT as a way of understanding how America's history of racism has shaped current public policy and created our current state of structural racism, while conservatives view it as a divisive discourse that pits people of color against White people. The right-wing media have turned CRT into a catchall buzzword for any teaching in schools about race and American history, and Republicans have used it as a weapon in culture wars against Democrats (Smith, 2021).

Republican governor Glenn Youngkin used CRT as a major issue in his 2021 race against Democratic candidate Terry McAuliffe. Youngkin preached, "What we won't do is teach our children to view everything through the lens of race. On day one, I will ban critical race theory" (Smith, 2021). Anti-CRT rhetoric resonated with Republican voters and appeared to contribute to Youngkin's win.

By late 2021, nine Republican state legislatures had passed legislation curbing how teachers can teach about race (Ray & Gibbons, 2021). Under such laws, teachers are not able to discuss racial discrimination and racial inequities. Idaho governor Brad Little signed into law a measure banning the teaching of CRT in public schools, claiming that teaching CRT would "exacerbate and inflame divisions on the basis of sex, race, ethnicity, religion, color, national origin, or other criteria in ways contrary to the unity of the nation and the wellbeing of the state of Idaho and its citizens." (Smith 2021). This puts a chilling effect on teachers' ability to discuss American history and race relations in the United States. Teachers in K–12 schools are often asked to respond to students who ask about Black Lives Matter protests and why so many Black people have been killed by police, yet they are unable to discuss and teach related issues. This has fueled a fierce debate about how to teach children about race relations and their role in our country's history.

Progress Against Structural Racism

The slow-motion death of George Floyd at the hands of the Minneapolis police galvanized the Black Lives Matter movement and triggered nationwide protests involving people of all races, genders, and ages. People from all over the world came together to protest police brutality against Black people. This brought new hope for meaningful change. In the weeks that followed George Floyd's death, police choke holds were banned in 20 cities, with more to come. Confederate monuments were toppled by protesters and removed by officials. People considered changes to the mission of police departments. Maybe our police had been asked to do too much. Maybe the police were not the appropriate authorities to deal with disturbances related to homelessness and mental illness.

An NBC/*Wall Street Journal* survey taken shortly after George Floyd's murder showed that Americans' views about race were changing. Many were more likely to appreciate that Black people experience discrimination, to view the Black Lives Matter movement as a positive force, and to support the removal of Confederate monuments in public places (Dann, 2020). These results may inspire some optimism that attitudes about racism are improving, but still only 46% of the American voters interviewed believed that structural racism was built into society, while 44% believed there was no structural racism and it was only individuals who held racist views. Our society remains deeply polarized on this issue: a majority of Democrats (70%), Black voters (65%), and young voters (59%) believe racism is structural, while a majority of Republican voters (66%) and a plurality of White voters (48%) attribute racism solely to individual behavior.

Joe Biden in his 2021 presidential inaugural address prioritized dismantling structural racism as one of his administration's primary goals. He chose Kamala Harris as his running mate, who became the first woman and first person of African American and Asian American descent to win a nationally elected office, and he chose the most diverse cabinet in our nation's history. He nominated Ketanji Brown Jackson to the Supreme Court, where she became its first female Black justice. On the day he took office, Biden signed an executive order establishing a government-wide initiative to address diversity, racial inequity, and systemic racism in all government agencies. He acted to curb the U.S. government's use of private prisons, bolstered enforcement of anti-discrimination policies in housing, and strengthened the sovereignty of Native American tribes. All this has provided hope for positive change, but there are many strong forces aligned in opposition. Racism and White supremacy grew bolder during the Trump administration, and the directors of the FBI and National Intelligence have identified the White supremacy movement as our greatest domestic terror threat.

Can We Become Less Racist?

We have all inherited tribal instincts that make us feel adversarial and often hostile toward those who are not like us. In this sense, we are all innately racist. Can we change this part of our human nature? Can we become less tribal, less racist?

As we came together in larger diverse societies, our culture rewarded individuals who exhibited cooperative, prosocial behavior and tolerance toward diverse groups. The most cooperative, prosocial, and tolerant individuals were provided with advantages that helped them to survive and reproduce and pass their cooperative, prosocial genes to the next generation. On the other hand, selfish individuals with antisocial traits and little tolerance for diverse groups were punished or incarcerated by society and were less likely to survive and pass their antisocial genes to the next generation. As this cycle has repeated itself generation after generation, our human nature has become more cooperative, more prosocial, and less tribal. This has been evidenced by the growth of today's large, diverse societies.

The coevolution of culture and biology represents a new paradigm in evolution (Richerson & Boyd, 2005). Evolutionary theory has taught us that change is brought about by random genetic mutations. If genetic mutations lead to genes with traits that promote survival and reproductive success in the current environment, these genes and their traits will be passed to the next generation. The process is random, and we have no control over it. But if we are able to shape and control our cultural environment, we can control the forces that drive evolution. This gives us some control over our evolution, including the evolution of our human nature.

While human nature may be evolving to become more cooperative, less tribal, and less racist, the process is too slow to provide us with much benefit over the short term. Our best hope is that we may be able to modify our tribal and racist behavior in the short term through changes in our cultural environment. We will discuss this further in Chapters 16 and 17.

CHAPTER 10

THE GROWING CRISIS OF SOCIOECONOMIC INEQUITY

The test of our progress is not whether we add more to the abundance of those who have much; it is whether we provide enough for those who have little.

—Franklin D. Roosevelt, inaugural address

Christine Lagarde, managing director of the International Monetary Fund, spoke of her concern about growing income and wealth inequities before the 2014 World Economic Forum in Davos, Switzerland: "Business and political leaders at the World Economic Forum should remember that in far too many countries the benefits of growth are being enjoyed by far too few people. This is not a recipe for stability and sustainability" (Giles, 2014).

Income and wealth inequities in this country and abroad have become the subject of great concern. The very rich have become much richer, while wages for the middle and working class have stagnated. At the lower end, millions have struggled to pay the rent, put food on the table, and live in dignity. The Great Recession of 2008 and the COVID-19 pandemic and subsequent recession have magnified these inequities and heightened the crisis. Income and wealth disparities have separated us into adversarial tribes that can no longer cooperate. These inequities have stoked social discontent, political polarization, and divisive right-wing populist nationalism. They are morally wrong, the antithesis of democratic values, and they have become a great threat to our democracy. In the United States, politicians, economists, sociologists, and ordinary citizens are asking: can we reverse these trends and salvage our democracy so that we can once again be, as President Ronald Reagan (1989) described, a "shining city upon a hill"?

Inequity Versus Inequality

The terms inequity and inequality are sometimes confused, but they are not the same. It might be helpful for our discussion here to clarify the differences between them. Inequity refers to disparities that are unfair or unjust, while inequality refers to differences that may or may not be unfair or unjust. When we talk about income and wealth inequities, we mean extreme differences in income and wealth that arise from unequal opportunities, unfair government policies and regulations, deregulated capitalism whose rules favor one part of our society over another, and other social conditions that favor one group over another. Not all income and wealth differences are inequitable. Some individuals may achieve greater income and wealth due to hard work, perseverance, and superior mental or physical abilities without having better opportunities.

Growing Income and Wealth Inequities

The years following World War II were filled with hope and promise. Capitalism was thriving and global economies were expanding. Workers and owners alike shared the growing wealth and prosperity as income inequalities fell from prewar levels across the developed world. Unions provided strong advocacy for workers and were able to secure fair wages, substantial benefits, and safe working conditions. The United States and European democracies expanded social safety nets to provide for and protect their citizens. Democracies and capitalism were flourishing as synergistic partners. These were good times for working- and middle-class Americans. But this was about to change.

The 1970s ushered in an era of globalization, international trade, and deregulation of capital markets. Ronald Reagan took office in 1981 with the slogan "Government is not the solution to our problem; government is the problem." Supply-side economics cut taxes and slashed government regulations and investment to free up private capital for investment in a growing economy. Conservatives argued this would trigger global economic growth, lower prices for consumer goods, and stimulate innovation to create new products that would benefit all. There was great enthusiasm for the growing global economy, but unfortunately, most economists had underestimated a tragic downside for the working- and middle-class in developed countries. Many manufacturing jobs were outsourced to China, Mexico, and other developing countries where labor costs were so much cheaper. As manufacturing plants shut down, there was a ripple effect as supporting services—restaurants, retail stores, schools, churches—closed, and entire areas dependent on the manufacturing base became ghost towns.

Technological advances over the past several decades also contributed to the rise in income inequality. Automation of low- to middle-skilled jobs shifted labor demand toward higher-level skills, displacing and hurting wages for lower-skilled workers. Firms with large capital and advanced technology achieved dominance in the market and replaced many low-skilled jobs with higher paying, high-skilled jobs. This shifted income from labor to capital and widened the income gap between labor and capitalists (Qureshi, 2020). Unfortunately, the hope that workers in low-skilled jobs could be trained and transitioned to high-skilled jobs has fallen far short of expectations.

Government-supported safety nets for low-income citizens were weakened over the past several decades and contributed to the rising inequity. Government fiscal redistribution to offset market inequalities has shrunk because of less progressive income tax rates, lower taxes on capital gains, and limited spending on social programs (Qureshi, 2020).

The steady growth in the income and wealth gap between the rich and the middle and working classes in the United States over the past several decades has now reached a critical level. In 2017, the average income in the top quintile of households was \$309,400 and in the bottom quintile \$21,300. The income for the top 1% was \$1,961,500 (Congressional Budget Office, 2020; Image 10.1). In 2018, the wealth of the top 10% comprised 77% of the nation's assets, compared with that of the bottom 90% making up only 23% (Stewart, 2018).

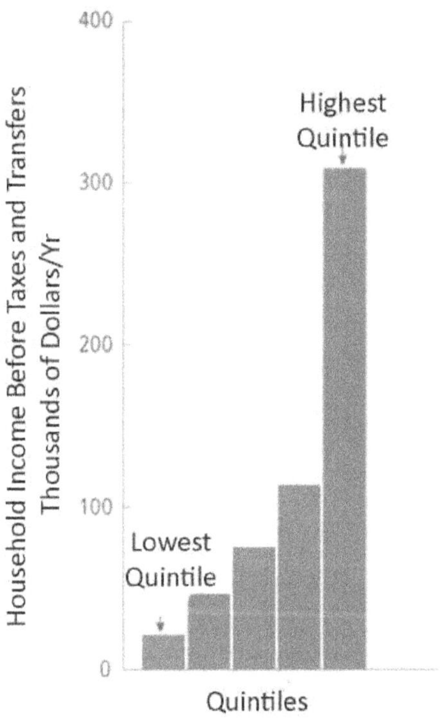

Image 10.1 Income Inequality. In 2017, the average income for the top quintile of households was \$309,400 and for the bottom quintile was \$21,300. The average income for the top 1% was \$1,961,500

The financial crisis and Great Recession of 2008 and the COVID-19 pandemic and recession of 2020–21 widened the income and wealth gap between the rich and the poor. These crises have thrown into stark relief the high and rising economic inequities in the United States and elsewhere. During the pandemic, the stock market soared, and those at the top profited while the middle and working classes risked their lives working on the front lines, frequently losing their jobs or housing. These effects have been even more concentrated for poor ethnic minorities (Inequality.org, 2021). Today, economic and health inequities have reached crisis levels that appear unsustainable.

Corporate Elites Bear Responsibility

Pulitzer Prize–winning author Hedrick Smith (2013) in his impactful book *Who Stole the American Dream?* argues that greedy business elites bear a great responsibility for the financial divide and the loss of the **American Dream**. Following World War II, the corporate business model and mantra were to share the wealth. When corporate profits rose due to growth and increased productivity, employees shared in the profits. High employment and healthy salaries created greater consumer demand and stimulated "the virtuous circle of growth," which allowed businesses to grow and hire more. This was an era of stakeholder capitalism.

Beginning in the 1970s, things began to change. It was a new era of globalization, international trade, and government deregulation to stimulate business growth. This marked the beginning of the New Economy, in which businesses abandoned stakeholder capitalism and focused almost solely on profits. The share-the-wealth ethic was abandoned as employee pay was dissociated from profits—worker wages were treated as an expense to be minimized. Smith acknowledges the role of globalization and automation in contributing to the huge and growing inequities in income and wealth between the business elite and the working class, but he offers a stinging indictment of Wall Street and the corporate elite for their selfish greed.

In early 2022, in the midst of the COVID-19 pandemic, the annual inflation rate reached 8.5%, the greatest since 1981. This was partly explained by pent-up demand from savings during the pandemic and impaired supply lines. But economist Robert Reich (2022) explains that a great part of the inflation problem is related to corporate greed. Corporate profits were at a 70-year high, and in this environment, we would expect corporations to absorb most of the increasing costs of supplies and labor, but they did not. Instead, they raised prices beyond what was needed to absorb their growing costs, padded their profits, and added to inflation. They could do this because corporations have grown bigger and face little or no competition. We would expect that with record profits corporations would also pay higher wages, but this has not happened. Instead, they are buying back their own stock. This diminishes the number of shares outstanding and raises the price of the stock, which benefits stockholders and CEOs but not workers. The result is that income and wealth are being distributed upward from workers to CEOs and shareholders, the wealthiest people in the world.

Reich outlines the solutions to these inequities, which seem evident but are difficult to achieve. We need tougher antitrust enforcement to promote better competition. We need campaign finance reform to get big money out of politics. We need stronger unions, a ban on corporate buybacks, and higher taxes on corporations and the wealthy. And we need a return to stakeholder capitalism.

Income and Wealth Inequities Are Self-Perpetuating

Columnist Matthew Stewart (2018) of *The New Yorker* describes an alarming phenomenon in detail: when income and wealth inequities reach a certain level, they become self-perpetuating. The wealthy provide their offspring with a good education, often sending them to private schools, elite colleges and universities, and graduate schools, leaving them with no debt. They help provide contacts and connections to land high-level jobs. The children, now young adults, often meet and marry connected partners at elite schools or in the workplace, adding to their wealth—a process called assortative mating. In contrast, those at the lower levels of society have few of these advantages. They have fewer educational opportunities and often do not go to college, and if so, accumulate large debt. They have fewer mentors, less support, and fewer contacts to attain better jobs. They often marry partners who have no job outside the home or have similar low-paying jobs. Today, they are much less likely to achieve the American Dream than their parents.

Economic immobility in any country appears to occur when income and wealth inequalities reach a certain critical level. Alan Krueger, past chairman of Obama's Council of Economic Advisers, described the linkage between income inequality and economic immobility in a speech given in 2012 just before Obama's State of the Union address. Krueger introduced the Great Gatsby Curve, which shows that countries with the greatest income and wealth inequalities also have the greatest economic immobility (Image 10.2). Human societies under capitalism have a natural tendency for growing income and wealth divisions, and once the divide is great enough it tends to crystallize, making it difficult for those at the bottom to move upward (Stewart, 2018).

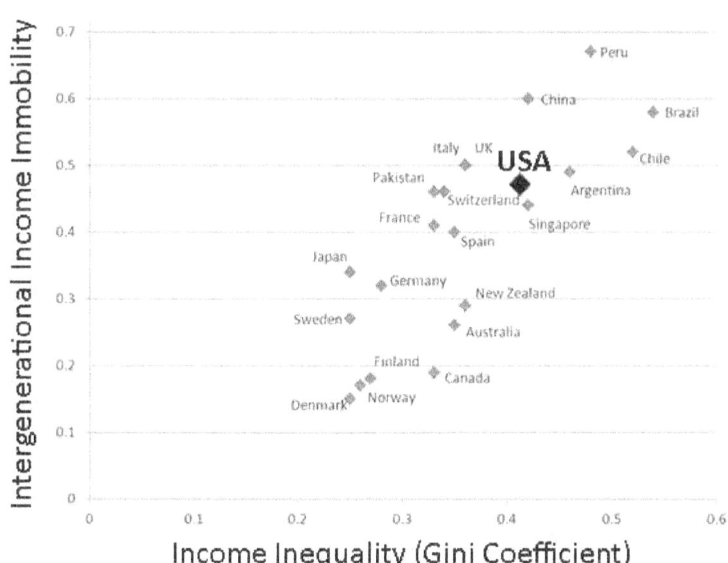

Image 10.2 The Great Gatsby Curve. The relationship between income inequality (measured by the Gini Coefficient) and intergenerational income immobility (a measure of the extent to which parental earnings determine children's earnings: 0 = no influence; 1 = complete influence) across countries is relatively linear. Nations with high income inequality, like the U.S., have high intergenerational income immobility. This means parents with high incomes will usually produce children with high incomes, and parents with low incomes will produce children with low incomes. Once income inequality reaches a certain point, it tends to perpetuate itself, and there is little chance for upward mobility (Stewart, 2018)

The Great Gatsby Curve got its name from F. Scott Fitzgerald's novel *The Great Gatsby*, which highlights the inequality and class distinctions in America during the Roaring Twenties (Corak, 2016). The U.S. currently ranks high on the list of nations with income inequality and economic immobility. Children of high-income parents tend to have high incomes, and those of low-income parents tend to have low incomes. These latter children have few opportunities for the economic and social advancement that used to be part of the American Dream, which has unfortunately faded. As President Barack Obama (2011) put it, "Over the last few decades, the rungs on the ladder of opportunity have grown farther and farther apart, and the middle class has shrunk." The middle class decreased from 50% of all families in 1970 to 42% in 2010 (Krueger, 2012; Image 10.3).

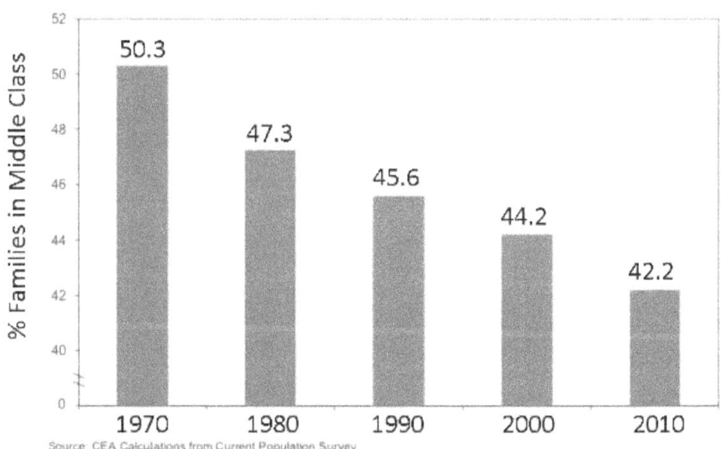

Image 10.3 The Declining Middle Class. The middle class, defined as families with incomes between 50% and 150% of the median family income, comprised 50% of all families in 1970 but only 42% in 2010 (Kreuger, 2012)

Consequences of Income and Wealth Inequities

The data are clear. Countries and states with the greatest income and wealth inequities have more teenage pregnancy, obesity, addiction, violence, and imprisonment and shorter lifespans (Wilkinson & Pickett, 2009). Societies with wider inequities, such as the United States and the United Kingdom, score poorly on almost every metric of quality of life and sense of well-being, while societies with less socioeconomic inequality, such as the Nordic countries and Japan, score well.

Working- and middle-class Americans who have been left behind by the tide of socioeconomic change feel an intense resentment and alienation toward those they feel are responsible. These include the government and governmental institutions, politicians of both political parties, big businesses that sent their jobs overseas, immigrants who may be coming to take their jobs, and ethnic minorities who have been shown favors, especially by the Democratic Party. Working-class White males, who work hard to provide for their families, attend church services regularly, participate in community activities, and cherish their patriotism, see their value system disappearing. Lost jobs and economic inequity have resulted in lost self-esteem and a sense of detachment from society. For many workers, their social and economic environment has collapsed, and there seems little hope for the future.

Income and wealth inequities undermine democracy. Those who have been left behind either drop out of the democratic process entirely, or they follow the promises and divisive rhetoric of opportunistic populist leaders. As the politics of resentment unfolds, we may reach a point of instability—unreasonable people tend to be ungovernable. Witness the refusal to get vaccinated and wear masks by many populists on the right in the United States during the COVID-19 pandemic. The growing inequities in income and wealth make our democracy more brittle. Historians have made the case that these inequities usually end with catastrophic events—wars, revolutions, plagues, and, as we will see, the replacement of democracies with authoritarian rule (Mason, 2017; Piketty, 2014; Scheidel, 2017).

The American Social Divide

When we think about inequality in societies, we usually think about wealth, income, and power. But we also need to think about inequalities in social status—how much we, as individuals or as a group, are valued and respected by society. American journalist Thomas Edsall (2020) emphasizes in a *New York Times* opinion piece the importance of social status as a motivator of human behavior and its role in American politics. Social changes over the past few decades have threatened the status of working-class and rural White Americans, who used to feel they held a secure, respectable, middle-class position in American society. They felt they were part of the core of American life—part of "Main Street" America. Times have changed. Many in this group have been left behind by the loss of jobs through outsourcing and automation, and many more, who are still employed, are working in lower-paying jobs or feeling that their jobs and positions in society are in jeopardy. They feel they are a shrinking majority, threatened by immigration, growing demographic diversity, advancing technology, and urbanization of the population. They feel an intense alienation and resentment toward the establishment and liberal and corporate elites. Hillary Clinton's referring to Trump supporters as "deplorables" during the 2016 presidential campaign has left a deep scar and caused intense resentment—resentment fueled more by a perception of reduced social status than by declining income and wealth.

Berkeley sociologist Arlie Hochschild (2017) in her compelling book *Strangers in Their Own Land: Anger and Mourning on the American Right* provides a vivid and empathetic picture of the people left behind in rural Louisiana (DeParle, 2016). She tries to understand the "Great Paradox"— why people who can benefit from federal help and programs are so opposed to a government that endorses policies that can help them. Many of these rural Louisianans have been marginalized by flat or falling wages, rapid demographic change, and a liberal culture that mocks their faith and patriotism. Hochschild provides a compelling story that explains their plight:

You are patiently standing in a long line for something you call the American dream. You are white, Christian, of modest means, and getting along in years. You are male. There are people of color behind you, and in principle you wish them well. But you've waited long, worked hard, and the line is barely moving.

Then Look! You see people cutting in line ahead of you! Who are these interlopers? Some are black, others are immigrants and refugees. They get affirmative action, sympathy, and welfare—checks for the listless and idle. The government wants you to feel sorry for them.

And who runs the government? The biracial son of a low-income single mother, and he's cheering on the line cutters. The president and his wife are line cutters themselves. The liberal media mocks you as racist or homophobic. Everywhere you look, you feel betrayed.

Hochschild points out that none of her characters appear to have been directly hurt by people of color. Their economic decline lies in corporate power, outsourcing of jobs, and technological transformation. Still, it is clear that demographic and cultural change cheated these White men of the status they once enjoyed, and Hochschild can feel their pain.

Stanford sociology professor Cecilia Ridgeway (2014), viewed as a leading expert on the importance of social status in society, describes an exchange that puts status in perspective:

An airport shoe-shine man once asked me what I did. When I told him, he said, "My daughter wants to go to Stanford and be a physician. What I do is just for her; I want her to *be* someone." Now, what was that about? Power? Not so much. Money? Yes, a bit. But above all it is about public recognition of his daughter's social worth. It is about social status.

The desire for elevated social status, the desire to be someone, is a major motivator of human behavior. We all want to be valued and respected. We all want to have a good reputation. This is part of our human nature. As we discussed in Chapter 4, reputations facilitate cooperation through indirect reciprocity and, as such, provide great adaptive advantages that have allowed them to survive natural selection. The displaced White working class, which has lost much of its self-esteem, is highly motivated to regain its diminished social status. Danish political scientists have outlined two major pathways to acquire or regain social status: prestige and dominance (Edsall, 2022; Peterson et al., 2020). Prestige is achieved by acquiring skills that are beneficial to society, and dominance is acquired through intimidation and fear. Individuals who have lost status and are in pursuit of dominance are more likely to engage in online vitriolic dialogue and political violence and more likely to play a major role in political destabilization. The working-class White people who have lost or are losing their social status form the core of the populist movement and pose a great risk to American democracy.

Joan Williams (2016), professor at the University of California, Hastings College of the Law, and author of *White Working Class: Overcoming Class Cluelessness in America*, describes several misconceptions about the working class. They are not the poor. The poor are the bottom 12% of American families by income. The working class are the middle 50% of families, whose median income was $64,000 in 2008—they call themselves the working class or the middle class, although their relative incomes are not what they were in the 1950s and 1960s.

Progressive Democrats offer policies, such as paid sick leave and an increase in the minimum wage, that are meant to help the working class. But for members of the working class, paid leave does not support a family, and they are not interested in working at McDonald's for $15 per hour instead of $9.50. They want a solid, stable, full-time, middle-class job with a salary that will provide for their family, enable them to own a house in the suburbs, and give them the ability to fund their children's educations.

The working class often have great resentment for the poor. Progressive Democrats have supported programs that benefit the poor, but almost all of these are means tested and don't benefit the working middle class. The Affordable Care Act and childcare subsidies are two examples. Working-class men pride themselves on hard work, thrift, and self-discipline. They often see the poor as having different values. In their minds, many of the poor do not work and live on government handouts. Some poor succumb to alcohol, drugs, and despair. It is a different culture (Williams, 2016).

The Plight of Poverty

Poverty inhabits the very low end of the socioeconomic scale. The U.S. government defines it as a household income of $24,858 or less, and by this criterion there were 37.2 million Americans (11.4%) living in poverty in 2017 (Shrider et al., 2021). Poverty has been a persistent problem in the United States, with consequences that can span lifetimes and generations. From the uncounted population of people who are homeless, to unemployed Americans looking for low-wage service jobs, to single parents working multiple jobs to try to get by, poverty can take many forms (Image 10.4). Poverty is associated with poor nutrition, poor health, mental illness, addiction, and premature death. Households in poverty experience more than double the rate of violent crimes, including murder, rape, sexual assault, robbery, and aggravated assault (Bureau of Justice Statistics, 2014). Even after controlling for other factors that influence violent behavior, such as substance abuse and poor family functioning, poverty has been shown to have a direct effect on young peoples' likelihood to engage in violence (Chowdhury, 2018).

Poverty and inequality breed low self-esteem, which may be an important root cause of violent behavior. While some disputes may seem trivial, the feeling of being seen as inferior and unworthy of respect is not trivial to those who have been left behind. When someone bumps into a young man passing in the hallway, looks flirtatiously at his girlfriend, or makes a derogatory remark, it may not threaten his self-respect if he has status and high self-esteem, but such acts could trigger a violent reaction if he perceives his own inequality. When inequality strips men of the usual markers of status—a good job and the ability to support their family—self-esteem plummets, and signs of respect and disrespect take on enhanced importance (Szalavitz, 2017). Inequality and poverty breed poor self-esteem and bring out the inner demons of our human nature.

Image 10.4 American Poverty. In 2020 there were 37.2 million Americans (11.4%) living in poverty (Shrider et al., 2021)

New York Times columnist Nicholas Kristof and former *Times* business manager Sheryl WuDunn (2020) take us deep into the lives of "Other America" in their book *Tightrope: Americans Reaching for Hope.* They take a trip to the rural Oregon town of Yamhill where Kristof grew up. Yamhill was a solidly blue-collar town through most of the twentieth-century but fell on hard times over the past several decades as jobs disappeared. Kristof tells the stories of his childhood friends and classmates, many of whom have succumbed to "deaths of despair"—deaths due to alcohol, drugs, crime, and suicide.

One of Kristof's (2021) columns is about his childhood buddy, Mike Stepp. Mike and his brother, Bobby, lived just down the street from Kristof, and every school day the three of them would walk together to the bus stop in the morning and to home in the afternoon. Mike was fun to be around—

good natured and a ham. Mike and Bobby's dad had a well-paying union job in the sawmill when the timber industry was robust. Their family was not much into education and had no books in their home. The brothers were not good students, and both dropped out of high school, thinking they could get good jobs in the lumber mills like their dad. But jobs were disappearing. The environmental movement ended the old-growth logging industry in much of Oregon, and many manufacturing jobs were lost due to automation and outsourcing.

The loss of good jobs had a devastating effect on the social fabric of families in Yamhill. When Mike and Bobby's dad lost his job, he drifted into alcoholism and became abusive to his wife and kids. Mike dropped out of high school and declined into "male idleness." He bounced around from one low-paying job to another and began to find escape in alcohol and drugs. His high school sweetheart and wife, Stephanie, with whom he had two kids, could no longer tolerate his drug abuse and kicked him out of the house. Mike ended up homeless in the nearby town of McMinnville.

Despite his downward spiral and homelessness, Mike always seemed upbeat. When Kristof came back to visit, Mike told him, "I like it out here. This is the great outdoors." As he walked the streets collecting returnable cans to make a few dollars, he would always greet passers-by with a friendly hello. One night, Mike was found on the sidewalk stricken with a heart attack, from which he died in the hospital a few days later. A local newspaper headline read "Beloved Downtown Homeless Man Dies," and a remembrance at a bus shelter where Mike often slept drew 30 people, who recalled his good cheer.

Kristof was able to escape the declining environment of Yamhill because his parents valued education and were invested in his welfare and future. He graduated from Harvard University and became a Pulitzer Prize–winning columnist at *The New York Times*. Like many liberals with a university degree and a reliable paycheck, he had been enthusiastic about globalization and unaware of its toll. But he and WuDunn, his wife, gained a greater perspective from their travels back to Yamhill and other disadvantaged areas. Kristof explains that the problem with those who have been left behind is not that they are weak-willed and irresponsible. The problem is they are walking a tightrope. They live paycheck to paycheck, and their lives are one small step from catastrophe. If they lose their job, incur catastrophic medical bills, or get caught up in addiction, they don't have the support, resources, or money to buy a second chance.

Mike was abused during childhood and had mental illness that was never diagnosed and treated, and these certainly contributed to his problems. But he had little support and few resources. Once he got derailed by losing his job and succumbing to alcohol, he had little chance of getting back on track. Mike's crisis is not isolated but is shared by an entire generation of low-educated workers.

The narrative that anyone can succeed with the right attitude and hard work, regardless of the circumstances, is part of the American Dream. This doctrine of social Darwinism is not only held by many at the top but has been absorbed by many at the bottom, leading them to believe their condition is their own fault. They are left with a sense of poor self-esteem, which is difficult to overcome. Some pundits talk about the role of personal responsibility in helping the disadvantaged rise from the depths of poverty. While personal responsibility may play some role, Kristof and WuDunn believe the plight of people like those in Yamhill, Oregon, is primarily the collective responsibility of our society and government. Their views are supported by the data that show that in countries with wide income and wealth inequities, there is little economic mobility. Children of low-income parents are usually trapped and invariably also have low incomes. The American Dream is seldom achieved.

Kristof and WuDunn's primary mission in *Tightrope* is to help us understand and appreciate the precarious circumstances under which those at the margins of society live. They list some solutions society and government can offer—high quality early childhood education, expanded internet access, expansion of drug treatment programs, a childhood allowance, and a higher minimum wage—but they write primarily to increase awareness of the problem. The hope is that greater awareness may be a call to action.

The Nordic Model

The growing gap between the rich and poor has become a political hot button in developed nations. Many have argued that capitalism, as presently structured, fosters economic inequality and may not be compatible with egalitarian democracies. Scholars have questioned whether Western capitalistic democracies can achieve long-lasting equality. (We'll discuss this in more detail in Chapter 12.) Experts looking for answers have focused on the Nordic countries of Sweden, Norway, Finland, Denmark, and Iceland (Image 10.5). These countries have achieved high living standards and low income disparity and may serve as models of economic opportunity and equality.

Image 10.5 Nordic Nations. The democracies of Sweden, Norway, Finland, Denmark, and Iceland have achieved high living standards and low income disparity. They may serve as models for egalitarian democracies with economic opportunity

The Nordic model combines free market capitalism with comprehensive social safety nets, including free education, free universal healthcare, and generous retirement pensions (Hodgson, 2018). The state enforces regulatory statutes and plays a strategic role in the economy but preserves capitalistic incentives of economic autonomy and enterprise. This makes the economy competitive with that of other Western developed nations. The social safety net is funded through redistributive taxation that reduces the gap between the rich and poor. High taxation is accepted because there is social solidarity, and the citizenry has a high degree of trust in the government. All five countries are democracies with checks and balances to prevent drift into authoritarian rule. Gender equality is a hallmark of the cultures and results in high participation of women in the workplace and high participation of fathers in childcare.

The Nordic countries are among the leaders in income equality, all ranking within the top 18 nations, while the United States ranks 108th and the United Kingdom 43rd (World Bank, 2019). These rankings are based on the Gini coefficient, which measures how much a country's income distribution differs from a totally equal distribution. Four of the five Nordic countries rank among the top 5 in gender equality, and all rank above the United States, which is in 49th place (World Economic Forum, 2017). Norway, Denmark, and Iceland are ranked as the three happiest countries in the world, and Finland and Sweden are in the top 10. The U.S. is ranked 15th (Hodgson, 2018). Norway is ahead of the U.S. in economic output (GDP per capita). The other four countries are behind the U.S., but all are ahead of the U.K., France, and Japan (Hodgson, 2018). Four were among the 6 least corrupt countries in the world, and all were ahead of the U.S., which was ranked 18th (Transparency International, 2020). These metrics highlight the success of these countries as egalitarian democracies.

Why does the Nordic model work? Part of its success may be due to the nations' small size and the fact that they are more ethnically and culturally homogeneous than most large, developed countries. Their citizens have a shared history and shared values. This gives them a collective mentality and a belief that citizens seeking beneficial solutions to problems lead their government (McWhinney, 2020). Norway has the added benefit of revenues from vast oil reserves discovered in 1969. Unlike so many other countries with oil, Norway has invested the revenues for the public good by supporting government programs and creating a pension fund for its citizens.

Despite their success, the Nordic states face major obstacles (McWhinney, 2020). With low fertility rates and little immigration (until recently), the population is aging. This leaves a smaller base of young taxpayers and a larger population of senior citizens receiving services and pensions—an economic formula that is usually unsustainable. The second problem is immigration. New immigrants into the European Union from the Middle East and elsewhere with different ethnicities and religions do not share history and values with the Nordic population. The new immigrants may come to expect generous public benefits but do not have the high participation in the workforce that the Scandinavians expect. The new arrivals could pose a significant burden to the system.

Many critics of unbridled American capitalism see the Nordic model as an attractive alternative to the winner-take-all American system that has fostered wide socioeconomic inequities, lack of affordable healthcare and education, and a deteriorating social safety net. But the United States, United Kingdom, European Union, and other Western democracies may be too large and too diverse and may lack the shared experiences and values needed for a system like the Nordic models to work (McWhinney, 2020). We may need to work harder to overcome the obstacles of size and diversity, or we may need to look for alternative solutions to revitalize our egalitarian roots.

What Can Be Done?

The growing socioeconomic inequities in nations across the world are morally unacceptable and threaten our democracies. They unleash our tribal instincts and stoke hostility and resentment among the working class toward the establishment and the economic elite. It is not surprising that these inequities have fomented right-wing populist movements in the United States and elsewhere that could very well become violent and challenge our democracies.

Because of the size and diversity of most Western democracies, the challenge of reversing our growing socioeconomic inequalities is immense. The solution requires government intervention and a change in attitudes and culture. Transfer payments through tax reform will not be enough. We must provide genuine equal opportunity for all. We must rewrite the rules of capitalism, as we will discuss in Chapter 12, so that the economy no longer preferentially benefits corporations and wealthy individuals but provides a fair distribution of income, wealth, and opportunity for all. Those of us who are the momentary winners and whom columnist Matthew Stewart (2018) calls "the new aristocrats" must look beyond our own success and think about what we can do for the people who are not our neighbors. He advises, "We should be fighting for opportunities for other people's children as if the future of our own children depended upon it. It probably does."

PART III

THE CONFLICT BETWEEN AUTOCRACY AND DEMOCRACY

CHAPTER 11

THE SEDUCTIVE LURE OF AUTHORITARIANISM

However sugarcoated and ambiguous, every form of authoritarianism must start with a belief in some group's greater right to power, whether that right is justified by sex, race, class, religion or all four.

—Gloria Steinem, *Outrageous Acts and Everyday Rebellions*

After the collapse of the Soviet Union and the fall of the Iron Curtain in 1989, a fresh new wave of democracies emerged in Eastern Europe and beyond. There was great hope for a better world. Over the past decade or two, things have changed. Authoritarian regimes have begun to replace democracies across the globe. The list includes Hungary and Poland in Eastern Europe, Turkey and Egypt in the Middle East, the Philippines and Myanmar in southeast Asia, Venezuela and Brazil in South America, Russia, China, and more. Russia's invasion of democratic Ukraine accentuates the conflict between autocracy and democracy. This may be the most treacherous time for democracies since the 1930s, when fascism spread across Europe. Donald Trump's drift toward an authoritarian government in the United States highlighted this movement and triggered a cottage industry of commentary about the decline of democracy and the rise of authoritarian regimes.

Poland's Drift into Autocracy

Poland's slide from democracy to autocracy provides an illustrative example of an all too familiar theme. This transition has been chronicled in detail by columnist and historian Anne Applebaum (2020) in her enlightening book *Twilight of Democracy*. In the 1980s, Lech Wałęsa, leader of the Solidarity union of shipyard workers, negotiated Poland's transition to democracy from the collapsing Soviet Union. Wałęsa and his blue-collar shipyard union members were staunch allies at the time, but little did they know that years later they would be on opposite sides of the country's political rift. Following Poland's independence, Wałęsa endorsed the Kaczyński twins, Lech and Jarosław, as candidates for Parliament. When Wałęsa was elected Poland's first president in 1990, Jarosław became his chief of staff (Mounk, 2019).

The honeymoon was short-lived. Jarosław Kaczyński turned against Wałęsa, organizing protests against his presidency and accusing him of complicity with the Communist regime. He and his brother Lech formed the far-right Law and Justice Party built on a series of conspiracy theories arguing that liberals, gay people, and Communists were undermining the nation from within. Surprising to many, this paranoid fearmongering proved successful, and the Law and Justice Party gained power. In 2005, Lech was elected president, with Jarosław serving as prime minister. Lech died in a tragic plane crash in 2010, and the party's hold on power slipped, but in 2015 Jarosław staged a successful comeback as the party won the presidency and a majority in Parliament (Image 11.1).

After coming to power, Kaczyński, as head of the Law and Justice Party, staged a massive attack on Poland's democratic institutions. He turned state television into a purveyor of government propaganda, gained control of the country's court system through imposed term limits and new appointees, restricted free speech, and initiated high-profile trials against political opponents. The country became extremely polarized, with well-educated urban elites, grateful for the opportunities of democracy, pitted against mostly rural blue-collar populists who felt they had been left behind. In the 2019 elections, the Law and Justice Party remained in control over weak opposition. The country, which fought so valiantly for its liberty against Communist oppression, seems apathetic in face of the grave threat to its democracy (Mounk, 2019).

Image 11.1 Jarosław Kaczyński. The former Polish prime minister and current head of the right-wing Law and Justice Party has been the major leader responsible for Poland's transition from a democratic government to an authoritarian regime

Poland, like most democracies that have transitioned to authoritarian rule, has adopted the illiberal one-party state as a means for holding power (Applebaum, 2020). Lenin's Bolshevik one-party state is the prototype for this type of autocracy, and there are many other examples—Hitler's Nazi Germany may be the most famous. Apartheid South Africa also had a one-party system, the Nationalist Party, that eliminated Black people from political life and promoted Afrikaners. In present-day Europe, Viktor Orbán's Fidesz party has consolidated authoritarian, one-party rule in Hungary, like the Law and Justice Party in Poland.

In modern Western democracies, competition determines the right to rule. Political parties compete with one another on a level playing field, and the politicians who are the most appealing and competent and who have the support of the majority of citizens will prevail and rule. Positions in government and society are ideally based on competition, skill, and merit.

In one-party autocratic rule, most members of the party have authoritarian personalities and strong tribal instincts (Altemeyer, 2006). The party is your tribe, and you treat your tribe and its members with loyalty. Positions in government and society are based on loyalty, not competition and competence. If your party believes in a conspiracy theory, you also believe in that conspiracy theory. If your party adopts a policy, you support that policy. If you are loyal to the Party, you will be rewarded with upward mobility, both within the party and society. In line with tribal instincts, those outside the party are regarded as inferior and treated with hostility. To party loyalists, the one-party state is fairer than a competitive democracy because, as Jarosław Kaczyński describes it, society is run by a "better sort of Pole" (Applebaum, 2018).

The Authoritarian Personality

Following World War II and the Holocaust, there was great interest in understanding the root causes of the rise of fascism and identifying those who were susceptible to anti-democratic and authoritarian ideologies. The mass genocide of the Jews raised grave questions about the origins of racism and prejudice. Scientists realized that prejudice and anti-democratic, authoritarian ideologies were not characteristic of any single group, and they began looking for ways to explain these phenomena. German sociologist Theodor Adorno believed there was a characteristic personality that was common among people who fall victim to authoritarianism. In his highly influential book *The Authoritarian Personality*, he introduced a questionnaire to identify those individuals with an **authoritarian personality**—individuals who were predisposed to antidemocratic and authoritarian beliefs (Adorno, 1950). Although the book was strongly criticized for its bias and methodology, it triggered an explosion of research and publications in social psychology.

In the early 1980s, Bob Altemeyer (2006), psychology professor at the University of Manitoba, refined Adorno's work and renamed the authoritarian personality **"right-wing authoritarianism (RWA)."** He defined RWA as an authoritarian personality characterized by three traits: (1) extreme obedience and submission to authority figures, (2) a hierarchical viewpoint of society with prejudicial and aggressive behavior toward outside groups, and (3) a high level of conforming to old traditions and values. Altemeyer created a 20-element questionnaire spanning a variety of social issues that assessed an individual's tendency toward an authoritarian personality. A recent survey using Altemeyer's questionnaire found that 26% of Americans had scores corresponding to high RWA (Venaglia & Maxwell, 2021). More Americans scored in this category than individuals from any of the other seven nations studied, and by a wide margin.

People with an authoritarian personality who have extreme obedience to a leader or father figure also have tolerance for any of that leader's illegal and immoral acts. In democracy, no one is expected to be above the law, but authoritarians put that restriction aside for their leader. Authoritarians also harbor anti-scientific dogmatic beliefs and are frequent participants in conspiracy theories. Their ferocious dogmatism makes it difficult to impossible for anyone to change their minds with evidence or logic. For example, at the end of World War II, many Germans refused to believe Hitler ordered the extermination of millions of Jews. In America many Trump followers bought in to his "Big Lie" that the 2020 presidential election was a fraud and was stolen from him. Authoritarians believe in a hierarchical society in which their own group is superior to other groups and should be the dominant group. They harbor extreme hostility toward out-groups—"If you are not with us, then you're against us." Trump's authoritarian followers have been quick to berate and censure those who have not shown loyalty to their leader and their cause.

Authoritarian Leaders

Individuals with authoritarian personalities tend to be followers of authoritarian leaders, but not necessarily leaders themselves. Individuals with personalities characterized by social dominance orientation (SDO) are similar to those with authoritarian personalities in many ways, but they long to control others and strive to be authoritarian leaders and dictators (Altemeyer, 2006; Sidanius & Pratto, 2001).

Psychologists use the social dominance questionnaire to create an SDO scale that classifies the personalities of respondents. Here are a few sample queries from the questionnaire (Altemeyer, 2006):

- This country would be better off if we cared less about how equal all people are.

- Some groups of people are simply not the equals of others.

- Some people are just more worthy than others.

Social dominators would agree with these statements. They believe in a competitive world of survival of the fittest and often have strong authoritarian and racist beliefs and right-wing politics. Typically, they are dominant, driven, and tough, and they seek power. They are inclined to be intimidating, ruthless, and vengeful and would rather be feared than loved. They love power and are willing to take casualties in their rise to the top. In contrast to these social dominators, people who score low on the SDO questionnaire have predispositions for an egalitarian society and believe society should be structured such that all people are equally valued, with no single group dominating others (Kleppesto et al., 2019).

The Genetic Basis of Authoritarianism

Where do authoritarian traits come from? Are these traits a product of our culture and experience, or are they inherited? Political scientists Albert Somit and Steven Peterson (1997) put forth an unpopular thesis in their provocative book *Darwinism, Dominance, and Democracy: The Biological Bases of Authoritarianism*. The authors hypothesize that the most important reason for the rarity of democracy and the ascendency of authoritarian regimes throughout human history is that evolution has endowed humans with the predisposition for hierarchically structured social and political systems. Humans have a genetic bias toward hierarchy, dominance, and submission. Authoritarianism is in our genes (Corning, 2000).

The authors make their case with several pieces of evidence. First, dominance hierarchies are the most common social order in most of our primate relatives. We saw in Chapter 7 that gorilla and chimpanzee societies are highly hierarchical, with dominant alpha males. Bonobos are an exception and have a female dominated society that is egalitarian in nature. Secondly, authoritarian regimes have been the most frequent governing systems of the past 6,000 years of human history, while democratic governments have shown great fragility. And finally, there is a wealth of research in social psychology supporting the hypothesis that many humans have a genetic predisposition to hierarchy and authoritarianism. In Chapter 7, we reported the results of several twin studies that found a strong hereditary component to hierarchical and authoritarian personality traits (Funk et al., 2012; Kleppesto et al., 2019; Morin, 2013).

Psychologists at the University of Minnesota performed similar twin studies to assess the genetic contribution to authoritarian traits, but they also looked at how authoritarian traits changed over time (Ludeke & Krueger, 2013). The investigators used RWA questionnaires to assess the presence and strength of authoritarian traits at baseline when the twins were approximately 50 years old and 15 years later. The correlation of scores from the RWA questionnaires for identical twins was significantly greater than for fraternal twins at baseline and at the 15-year follow-up, indicating a strong genetic component to the trait. Follow-up RWA scores at 15 years had not changed greatly from baseline scores, indicating that authoritarianism is a relatively stable personality trait during the latter years of life.

But culture does influence our hierarchical and authoritarian traits. Children raised by authoritarian parents or Christian Fundamentalists are more likely to have authoritarian attitudes. This may be partly due to heredity, but culture surely plays a big role (Altemeyer, 2006). Although the authoritarian personality is a relatively stable personality trait, it can change over time in young adults. Altemeyer found that University of Manitoba students' RWA scores fell 10% from the time they entered as freshmen until they graduated four years later (Altemeyer, 2006). Those with the highest RWA scores as freshmen had the greatest drop. Following graduation, participants had a modest 5–11% drop in their RWA scores over a follow-up period of 12 to 27 years. While the change in the strength of these traits over time was modest, it should not be trivialized. The identification of cultural contributors to changes in authoritarian traits has great implications for society and remains a high priority for continued research.

Genetics play a major role in determining our predispositions to both authoritarian and egalitarian personality traits. We all inherit a blend of both traits, but some of us are more authoritarian, and some are more egalitarian. These predispositions interact with cultural experiences to determine our behavior. Understanding that these traits have a genetic basis and understanding how they may be modified by culture and life experiences may help us understand, explain, and perhaps mitigate society's drift toward authoritarian rule.

Conspiracy Theories and Authoritarian Rule

Conspiracy theories are used by authoritarian regimes as propaganda to denounce enemies and silence political opponents (Giry & Gürpınar, 2020). We saw how Jarosław Kaczyński and the Law and Justice Party of Poland used conspiracy theories to denigrate their political opponents as gay people and Communists to facilitate their rise to power. Hungary's authoritarian leader Viktor Orbán has targeted and maligned Jewish Hungarian American billionaire George Soros for decades as an evil drug smuggler, conspiracist, profiteer, and Nazi. Conspiracy theories are also used as a test of loyalty to authoritarian regimes. Trump's Big Lie that the 2020 presidential election was stolen has become a requirement for good standing in the Republican Party. Such theories also can silence the debate so essential to the democratic process. If parties cannot agree on facts, how can they have rational discourse?

Authoritarian leaders use conspiracy theories for political gain, but do they and their followers really believe in these theories? The answer is often yes. Deception of others has promoted individual advancement and survival and has become part of our moral—or immoral—fabric. As we discussed in Chapter 6, self-deception, paradoxically, has evolved to enhance the deception of others (von Hippel & Trivers, 2011). Understanding why so many succumb to conspiracy theories may help us understand the challenges we face as authoritarians continue to use conspiracy theories to gain power.

Conspiracy theories are not harmless rumors. Climate change denial has thwarted attempts to mitigate the disastrous consequences of global warming. Anti-vaccination conspiracy theories that vaccines contain microchips or alter the recipient's DNA have caused additional COVID-19 deaths. Trump's Big Lie has threatened our democracy.

The Milgram Experiments

Stanley Milgram (1933–1984) was an American social psychologist best known for his controversial experiments on obedience performed while he was a professor at Yale. Milgram sought to examine and understand the claims of those accused of genocide at the Nuremberg trials. Their defense was based on obedience—they were just following orders. Milgram's experiments began in 1961, a year after Adolf Eichmann's trial in Jerusalem, and they focused on the conflict between obedience to authority and personal conscience (McLeod, 2017).

In a famous learning experiment, Milgram recruited and assigned participants as teachers or learners (Altemeyer, 2006; Milgram, 1963). The teachers and learners were in adjacent rooms, but they could see one another through a window, and the rooms were wired so they could hear one another. The teacher asked the learner preselected questions, and if the learner was unable to answer correctly, the teacher administered an electric shock. Each time the learner failed to correctly answer a question, the intensity of the shock was increased. The teachers were instructed to continue delivering shocks even though they were able to witness the increasing discomfort of the recipients. Unknown to the teachers, the learners were not volunteers but members of the experimental team who were only pretending to receive shocks. Milgram found that two-thirds of the volunteer teachers, with encouragement from authorities administering the experiment, delivered the highest intensity shocks despite the screams and perceived distress of the recipients. After many sessions, the study concluded that people are strongly inclined to obey orders given by an authority figure if they believe the authority is morally or legally right (Milgram, 1963). Since our early childhood, we have been taught that obedience is a virtue and disobedience is wrong and damaging.

Milgram added another variant to his experiment. In addition to the volunteer teachers, he had members of the experimental team serve as fake teachers administering shocks to fake learners. These fake teachers were dispersed among the volunteer teachers and served as a peer group. When the volunteers saw the fake teachers deliver shocks at higher and higher levels, they were much more likely to continue delivering high energy shocks. The volunteer teachers almost invariably did what the fake teachers around them did. This modified experiment shows the importance of peer pressure in achieving compliance (Milgram, 1963).

This was one of social psychology's great discoveries. We are profoundly affected by peer pressure and the social circumstances surrounding us. Most of us do not realize the full strength of these forces. Milgram's experiments show us how hard it is to say no to a malevolent authority and how difficult it is to resist when peers are following an authority's orders (Altemeyer, 2006). Perhaps we should not be so self-righteous when judging others. Perhaps we can better understand what was happening in Germany during the Holocaust. (Milgram's experiments have been criticized based on methodology, but the influence of peer pressure on behavior has been documented in numerous subsequent studies (Simons-Morton and Farhat, 2010)).

Our scores on the RWA and SDO scales do not tell us how authoritarian we are—only how authoritarian we are inclined to be. Our behavior is the true gauge. Individuals with low scores on both scales require more pressure to act shamefully in situations like the Milgram experiments than individuals with higher scores. But with enough pressure from a malevolent authority and the crowd, most of us will cave (Altemeyer, 2006). This does not paint a pretty picture, but it does emphasize the importance of keeping malicious leaders from power.

Right-Wing Populism: Pathway to Autocracy

Right-wing populism is on the rise. Economic hardship and growing unease with globalization, automation, immigration, corruption, and the elite establishment have led to widespread support for leaders promising to hold the forces of cultural and social change at bay. The growing list of populist parties emerging across the globe include Austria's Freedom Party, the Dutch Party for Freedom, the UK Independence Party, Hungary's Fidesz, Poland's Law and Justice Party and, yes, Trump's Republican Party, to name a few (Democracy Digest, 2016).

The right-wing populist movement extols the virtues of strong, decisive leadership and shows disdain for established institutions, distrust of experts and scientists, and resentment of liberal elites. It favors nationalism over globalism, closed borders over liberal immigration, and traditionalism over progressive social values. Right-wing populism has historically been susceptible to demagogues who pit virtuous but downtrodden peoples against privileged elites who deprive them of their rights, prosperity, values, and voice. Resentment is a key driving force. Populist demagogues frame themselves as the voice of the people, and they claim, with anti-expert rhetoric, that the people know what is right and wrong intuitively. Professor Ruth Wodak (2015) in *The Politics of Fear: What Right-Wing Populist Discourses Mean* labels this "the arrogance of ignorance."

Political scientist Erica Frantz (2018) in her informative book *Authoritarianism: What Everyone Needs to Know* has called the all-too-frequent transition from democracy to authoritarian regimes **authoritarianization**. Populist leaders are elected in free democratic elections, but they then gradually erode democracies by undermining institutional constraints on their rule, weakening those who oppose them and splintering civil society. The gradual transition to authoritarian rule frequently has a telltale trajectory: placement of loyalists in positions of power (especially the judiciary), seizing control of the media, manipulating electoral rules to favor the incumbent, and passing constitutional amendments that empower the incumbent. Populist strongmen such as Venezuela's Hugo Chávez, Russia's Vladimir Putin, and Turkey's Recep Tayyip Erdoğan provide instructive examples (Image 11.2).

Image 11.2 Recep Tayyip Erdoğan. Over more than a decade, the president of Turkey has transformed its government from a constitutional democracy to an authoritarian regime. He and his Justice and Development Party (AKP), after being democratically elected, consolidated power by prosecuting political opponents, packing the courts with sympathetic judges, and seizing control of the media. This type of transition from democracy to authoritarian rule has become increasingly common

Military coups have been the greatest threat to democracies since World War II, but authoritarianization is on the rise and is becoming the most common pathway to autocracy. Populist leaders come to power with broad public support and a mandate for change. They run on a platform to challenge the liberal elite and existing institutions, and because of these expectations, efforts to expand their control are dismissed as necessary to implement ambitious reforms.

Once populist democracies transition into autocracies, they often give rise to dictatorships, in which power is highly concentrated in the hands of one individual (Kendall-Taylor & Frantz, 2016). Dictatorships, which lack accountability, lead to risky behavior and the worst outcomes of any political regime. They espouse xenophobic views, are abusive of citizen's civil rights, and are riddled with corruption. They are less likely to engage in international cooperation and are more likely to invest in nuclear weapons and engage in war. Russia's Putin is the best contemporary example, particularly in light of his invasion of Ukraine. Today's populist movements could be fueling the proliferation of the world's most problematic regimes (Kendall-Taylor & Frantz, 2016).

Human Nature and Authoritarianism

Throughout this chapter we have seen how human nature may facilitate our drift toward authoritarian rule. Many of us have a genetic predisposition to authoritarian personality traits, which predisposes us to support a hierarchical society and authoritarian rule. Tribal instincts, which we have inherited from our hunter-gatherer ancestors, are an integral part of our human nature and have shaped much of our politics. Most of us belong to political parties and have become members of a political tribe. We steadfastly remain loyal to our own political tribe, we often blindly support its policies and positions, and we regard the opposing political tribe with contempt and hostility.

The Milgram experiments have taught us that we human beings are strongly inclined to obey orders given by authority figures, and we are greatly influenced by peer pressure. History shows us how hard it is to resist a malevolent leader, especially when the crowd is following the leader's orders. If we were to put ourselves in the place of citizens in Nazi Germany during World War II and the Holocaust, we would like to think we would speak up and resist such horrific acts. But none of us knows for sure how we would respond.

Authoritarian regimes have dominated human societies throughout our long history, and egalitarian democracies have shown great fragility over the past centuries and especially the last two decades (Freedom House, 2022). Creating and maintaining egalitarian democracies in the face of our strong hierarchical traits and the seductive lure of authoritarianism is a great challenge. But there is hope. Egalitarian traits are also a part of our human nature—most of us carry an innate belief in the equality and dignity of all human beings. To translate our egalitarian traits—which may be less dominant than the hierarchical and authoritarian traits in many of us, into egalitarian behavior, we must create a social and political environment that encourages and facilitates the egalitarian part of our human nature.

CHAPTER 12

CAN DEMOCRACY SURVIVE CAPITALISM?

How does one put together a democracy based on the concept of equality while running an economy with ever greater degrees of economic inequality?

—Lester Thurow, *Shifting Fortunes: The Perils of the Growing American Wealth Gap*

Following the collapse of Soviet-style socialism in 1989 and the transformation of China's economy, capitalism has become the almost universal economic system around the world. Democracy has been the most cherished political system, but it is far from universal—only 60 countries out of about 200 can be classified as true rule-of-law liberal democracies (Merkel, 2014).

Capitalism and democracy are strange bedfellows. Capitalism's mantra is "survival of the fittest." Capitalism embodies a hierarchical society with corporate executives and owners of capital at the top and workers at the bottom. With profit as the primary motive, capitalism has created great inequalities in wealth, income, and power. In contrast, democracy is egalitarian and lives by the mantra "all men are created equal." All citizens should have equal rights and opportunities, should have the right to participate in choosing those who govern them, and should be provided with a social safety net to supply their basic needs. Given the divergent nature of capitalism and democracy, there has been widespread debate about whether they are compatible.

Democracy and Capitalism in Nineteenth- and Twentieth-Century America

The **Gilded Age**, the period between the Civil War and the end of the 19th-century, saw rapid growth in the U.S. economy, but it was characterized by political and corporate corruption and industrialists' accumulation of great wealth. State institutions adopted a laissez-faire attitude toward capitalism, largely refraining from interfering with capital and labor markets. Government taxes and expenditures were low, there was little protection of workers' rights, and the government did not do much to provide for the social welfare of its citizens. This was the era of massively wealthy robber barons such as John D. Rockefeller and Andrew Carnegie, whom we discussed in Chapter 8. Recall that these industrialists were advocates of social Darwinism, believing that competition rewarded people according to their abilities and that huge wealth disparities were justified.

The Gilded Age, the Great Depression of the 1930s, and the two world wars brought strong incentives for changes in capitalism and governance. Following World War II, an organized form of capitalism evolved globally that was compatible with the democracies in Western Europe, America, and Japan (Merkel, 2014). Organized capitalism was characterized by a strict regulatory framework and a Keynesian doctrine, in which governments intervened to stabilize economies.

British economist John Maynard Keynes introduced theories of economics that set a new standard for economic policy makers in Europe, America, and much of the world following World War II (Crain, 2018). Keynesian economics held that optimum economic performance could be achieved through government intervention in monetary and fiscal policy. In the United States the Federal Reserve could temper inflation and slow the economy by raising interest rates or could stimulate the economy in down times through the reduction of interest rates. The federal government through its fiscal policy could stimulate the economy by reducing taxes and increasing spending or slow it by raising taxes and reducing spending.

Nations exerted increasing regulation over the economy by enacting laws to protect labor and labor unions, granting selective subsidies, and instituting financial and labor market regulations. Labor unions were at the height of their economic and political power. Nations also expanded social policy and created many welfare state provisions to provide for the basic needs of their citizens. In the United States of the 1930s and 1940s, President Franklin Roosevelt enacted the New Deal, and similar welfare programs took place in European and Scandinavian countries.

Spurred by new democracies and the newly organized capitalism, there was an unprecedented period of prosperity over the three decades following World War II. Output per capita and real income achieved unparalleled growth in Western Europe and America, and unemployment reached new lows (Crain, 2018). Workers and owners alike shared the new wealth, and income inequality fell throughout the developed world. Democracy and capitalism were flourishing as synergistic partners.

But things began to change. In 1973, a new economic monster appeared—stagflation, a chimera of inflation, recession, and unemployment. Keynesian economists were at a loss how to handle this demon and became vulnerable to criticism. American economist and Nobel Prize winner Milton Friedman and other critics discredited Keynesian economics and advocated that the government should greatly reduce its role in tampering with the economy.

British prime minister Margaret Thatcher and President Ronald Reagan initiated the deregulation of capital and labor markets in the early 1980s. They triggered a strong global movement emphasizing self-regulating market forces, and they deprecated regulation and intervention by nation-states. Globalization and global trade facilitated this movement. Organized capitalism had been confined to national borders and could be regulated by nation-states, but with globalization, capitalism and free markets had no boundaries and could no longer be effectively regulated by individual nations. The decades of organized capitalism came to an end, and a new era of laissez-faire capitalism ensued. This was "the end of the postwar social contract" (Kuttner, 2018).

From the 1970s to the present, the economy continued to grow, but the rewards were not shared equally. Most of the economic gains were obtained by those at the top, resulting in huge social and economic gaps between the rich and the poor. By 2018, the top 1% of earners in the United States had a median income 39 times the median income of the bottom 90% of earners (Inequality.org, 2019). With such inequality, it is not surprising that workers lost faith in the capitalistic system and their democratic governments.

Globalization, Free Trade, and the Workers Left Behind

Global trade has been heralded as a boon to the world economy, offering economic growth, lower prices, higher variety of consumer goods, a faster rate of product innovation, more jobs, and higher wages. However, as global trade was gaining steam in the 1990s, most economists underestimated its effect on workers in developed countries directly exposed to competition.

Nobel Prize–winning economist Paul Krugman has been a strong advocate of global trade but now admits he underestimated the effect it would have on low-skilled workers in manufacturing plants in the United States and other developed countries (Ozimek, 2019). Krugman attributes the unanticipated downside of global trade to what he calls hyperglobalization, with its dramatic increase in imports of manufactured goods from 1995 to 2010 from China, Mexico, and other developing countries that had huge labor-cost advantages. Along with hyperglobalization, there was a lack of policies to help people cope with massive displacement as entire industries were lost and whole communities devastated.

MIT professor of economics David Autor and collaborators (2016) introduced the term "China shock" to describe China's disruptive integration into Western trade. China joined the World Trade Organization in 2001, catalyzing a surge in Chinese exports. Between the late 1990s and the financial crisis of 2008, importation of Chinese manufactured goods increased dramatically and displaced millions of jobs in the United States, mostly in the labor-intensive industries that produced shoes, textiles, and other goods. Manufacturing jobs in the United States as a percentage of the workforce fell from 39% early after World War II to 8.6% in 2015. Initially, the great majority of economists attributed the loss in manufacturing jobs and the fall in wages to technological innovations and automation, but it soon became clear that the trends were related primarily to globalization and outsourcing. Unfortunately, gains in employment in non-outsourced industries have been disappointing.

Robert Kuttner (2018), American journalist and professor of social policy at Brandeis University, provides an empathetic description of the plight of the working class in his insightful book *Can Democracy Survive Global Capitalism?* For most working people, this is not a great time to be alive. Over the past four decades, the economy has turned against them. Strong unions and economic regulations that provided good wages, benefits, and job security in the decades following World War II have been dismantled. In 1993, President Bill Clinton signed the North American Free Trade Agreement (NAFTA) and in 2000 normalized trade with China. Jobs began to move overseas. Factory workers across the country felt betrayed. Those who made parts for GM cars in Michigan, stitched shirts in textile mills in Pennsylvania, and assembled wooden chairs in North Carolina all lost their jobs to outsourcing to China and Mexico. When local factories shut down due to globalization, free trade, and outsourcing, the surrounding suppliers and supporting businesses closed. These included retailers, bars, social clubs, churches, schools—an entire way of life. Communities declined and fell into poverty. Many of the areas that lost factories due to outsourcing also had an influx of immigrants who competed with the displaced factory workers for the remaining low-paying jobs. The social status and self-esteem of these working-class people, who struggled to provide for their families, were loyal members of their churches, and were patriotic supporters of their country, were being destroyed by corporate elites who sent their factories and jobs overseas. Patriotism was for suckers. The message to workers—that their skills were no longer competitive and that they would require more education and training to qualify for modern jobs—was clear: *It is your fault.*

Meanwhile the Democrats were advocating for the rights of gay, lesbian, and transgender people; immigrants, many of who entered the country illegally; and African Americans, who often benefited from affirmative action. There was little attention to the lost White working class. This was like rubbing salt in the wound. For these displaced workers, NAFTA has become a symbol of betrayal. The treaty gave up blue-collar factory jobs so that corporate elites could invest in Mexico's banking and insurance sectors. Small wonder that the displaced workers have come to despise these elites. It is not surprising that those who have been left behind, both here in the United States and abroad, have formed the basis for right-wing populist rebellions against globalization, free trade, and the establishment.

The Assault on Labor

In the first few decades after World War II, strong unions and a well-regulated economy allowed labor markets in which workers could count on a regular paycheck, with a middle-class salary and fringe benefits. Labor unions were responsible for many worker benefits, including the 40-hour workweek, higher wages, overtime pay, workplace safety, and workers' compensation for work-related injuries. Workers in auto assembly plants and other industries could afford a house in the suburbs and were able to send their kids to college.

In the 1970s and 1980s, this began to change. Trade unions, which historically had been the most important advocate for working-class people, came under relentless attack by business elites. Capitalists began to argue that strong unions, minimum wage laws, and protections against arbitrary dismissals gave labor too much power to keep union members employed at high wages while other workers were idle. They began a movement to deregulate labor. Management suppressed union enrollment and activity by firing union organizers and outsourcing unionized plants. Republican administrations under Presidents Reagan and George H. W. Bush supported regulations that favored corporations over unions. This became abundantly clear in 1981 with Reagan's notorious firing of the nation's air traffic controllers for going on strike. National union membership dropped from 20% of workers in 1983 to 12% in 2012 (Levs, 2012). The decline in union membership has been due partly to the outsourcing of unionized manufacturing jobs to China, Mexico, and other developing countries and partly to business pressure and government laws designed to hinder union membership. Michigan and Wisconsin passed right-to-work laws, which allow workers to get or keep jobs without having to join an existing union. Currently, 27 states have passed similar laws. In 2011, Governor Scott Walker of Wisconsin was instrumental in passing an anti-union law that took away collective bargaining rights from the state's public employees. All these measures have greatly reduced the influence and enrollment in labor unions.

In recent decades corporations have discovered new ways to save money on their employees. They have reclassified many regular workers into what are called "casual" workers, which include part-time, temporary, and contract workers (Kuttner, 2018). By transitioning regular salaried workers to casual workers, corporations can eliminate full-time employment and no longer have to offer regular raises, health insurance, or pensions. This has also allowed employers to avoid minimum wages, overtime, and anti-discrimination laws by insisting that such workers are not their employees in any legal sense. Such arrangements are characteristic of the gig economy (a labor market in which short-term contracts or freelance work, as opposed to permanent jobs, are most prevalent), which has the attraction of flexibility and freedom for the worker but also has many downsides, including lower salaries and no benefits. The gig economy eliminates unions and creates a process in which workers compete with one another, driving down wages.

FedEx is a good example of a corporation that uses contract workers. It classifies its drivers as independent contractors, denying them benefits and basic workers' rights. Federal lawsuits and IRS audits challenging this approach have so far been unsuccessful (Kuttner, 2018). In contrast, United Parcel Service (UPS) drivers are unionized employees with benefits and workers' rights. In another example, Walmart warehouse workers are employees of an intermediate staffing firm whose only client is Walmart. Walmart avoids any obligations for workers' rights and benefits. Today about one worker in three is hired not by the corporation whose product they produce but by some intermediate firm, fracturing the connection between employer and employee.

Unions used to provide workers with a strong voice for lobbying Congress and the government. But lobbying requires money, and unions have lost their wealth and their clout. Rich corporations and special interests now have the ear of Congress and are able to lobby successfully for their positions. Without organizations to represent and advocate for them, workers feel alienated from society and the government.

The Rules of Capitalism

Capitalists hold that when government intrudes into the market to reduce inequality, it runs the risk of making the market less efficient. Economist Robert Reich (2016) in his thought-provoking book *Saving Capitalism: For the Many, Not the Few* argues that we have been living under a false narrative that we have to choose between free-market capitalism and big government. Free market capitalism is a human creation, and it requires the government to make and enforce the rules of the game. In a democracy, the people should control the government and by extension shape those rules.

The question is, who really shapes the market's rules, and to what purpose? Over the last several decades, large corporations, Wall Street, and wealthy individuals have twisted the rules to their benefit thanks to lobbying and contributions to the legislature and administrative agencies. This has resulted in the concentration of income and wealth at the top.

Reich provides numerous examples of how the laws governing the markets have benefited corporations and the elite at the expense of the worker and consumer, creating a huge economic divide. For instance, what is the proper balance between granting pharmaceutical companies enough ownership that they are incented to discover new drugs and giving the public opportunities to benefit from those drugs at reasonable prices? Patent law currently protects newly approved drugs for 20 years. But it also allows pharmaceutical companies to make minor changes to drugs and restart the patent clock. These companies are also allowed to pay makers of generic drugs to delay their cheaper versions—what are called pay-for-delay agreements. These laws and loopholes allow pharmaceutical companies to market their brand-name drugs for decades at the expense of the consumer, who must pay their high prices. The pharmaceutical industry has huge advantages over consumers because it has the resources to lobby Congress to pass laws to its benefit. The results are huge profits for the pharmaceutical industry while American consumers pay the highest drug prices in the world.

Employee contracts are usually biased to protect the corporation. When employees sign a contract to work for a corporation, they must often agree to take any grievances to an arbitrator chosen by the corporation rather than taking the company to court. The arbitrator often has biases favoring the corporation, and most decisions go against employees.

Bankruptcy laws frequently discriminate against the poor. In the financial crisis of 2008, homeowners whose mortgages outstripped the falling value of their homes were not allowed to declare bankruptcy. People with large student debt cannot use bankruptcy to renegotiate their loans. When airlines declare bankruptcy, contracts with unions stipulating workers' pay are generally given low priority.

Over the last several decades, health insurers and hospital systems have undergone growth and mergers, and they have been able to ratchet up healthcare costs because they have had local monopolies. In order to get congressional support for the Affordable Care Act, the Obama administration had to bend the rules to benefit insurers, hospital systems, and the pharmaceutical and device industries. Our healthcare is so expensive because so many players are making huge profits off the system.

Reich (2016) believes reshaping capitalism for the benefit of the people requires reinventing the corporation. He believes corporations have no fiduciary duty to maximize profits for their shareholders and believes that their mission should change to taking responsibility for all stakeholders—employees, customers, their community, and the environment, in addition to their shareholders. There has been some movement toward this concept with what are called benefit corporations. Patagonia, a large apparel manufacturer based in Ventura, California, has organized itself as one of these corporations. Its articles of incorporation require it to consider the interests of its workers, the community, and the environment, as well as its shareholders. Investors could drive a movement toward benefit corporations by selectively investing in these corporations, but it would likely require incentives and government regulation to prevent hostile takeovers.

Politics Shapes the Rules of Capitalism

We are in a vicious cycle. Economic dominance creates wealth and political power, and political power shapes market rules that further economic dominance. This is not corruption in the legal sense, but politicians are influenced by campaign contributions and by expert and legal opinions provided by wealthy corporations, banks, and individuals. Inequality is currently baked into the rules of the free market, which direct the majority of income and profits to corporations, executives, and owners of capital and a much smaller proportion to workers. French economist Thomas Piketty (2014) explains it well in his insightful book *Capital in the Twenty-First Century*:

> When the rate of return on capital exceeds the rate of growth of output and income, as it did in the nineteenth-century and seems quite likely to do again in the twenty-first, capitalism automatically generates arbitrary and unsustainable inequalities that radically undermine the meritocratic values on which democratic societies are based.

Current trends are not sustainable. If they continue, income and wealth inequality will grow to such an extent that both capitalism and democracy will no longer be able to function. This is a disastrous outcome that no one wants—neither the wealthy elite nor the general population—and this dire possibility should provide strong incentives for change.

Redirecting capitalism is a political challenge. Inequality cannot be rectified through redistributive taxes alone. The objective is how to change the rules to provide a fair distribution of income and wealth for all. This is possible, but it will require a majority of workers to understand what is needed and come together to make change.

Since the time of Franklin Roosevelt, the Democratic Party has been regarded as the party of working-class people, but over the past two to three decades the Democratic Party has often supported the interests of big corporations and Wall Street at the expense of workers. As we have seen, President Bill Clinton pushed for passage of NAFTA, and he also supported the establishment of the WTO, both of which promoted global trade and business opportunities abroad but led to the loss of manufacturing jobs here at home. Clinton and the Democrats also eliminated many restraints on large banks. In 1994, they supported the Interstate Banking and Branching Efficiency Act, which eliminated restrictions in interstate banking, and in 1999, Clinton pushed for repeal of the 1933 Glass-Steagall Act, which separated commercial from investment banking. In 2015, the Obama administration negotiated the Trans-Pacific Partnership, designed to open trade and commerce between the U.S. and the nations of the Pacific region. Such global trade agreements provide new business opportunities abroad but generally hurt workers in manufacturing plants here at home. The Trump administration terminated the Trans-Pacific Partnership before it was implemented, but the agreement illustrates how the Democratic Party has supported business and banking interests at the expense of the working class.

The Republican Party has traditionally been the party of big business, Wall Street, and wealthy individuals. It has been a strong advocate of limited government, fiscal austerity, and a limited social net for the disadvantaged and poor. Republican administrations under George W. Bush and Donald Trump passed tax laws that benefited the wealthy. In 2016, when Donald

Trump won the presidency, he captured the support of the White working class and Evangelical Christians based on social issues and resentment against corporate and professional elites and the establishment. But he and the Republican Party did little to help the working class during his administration, and the Party has no platform to help workers going forward. Neither party has fully advocated the cause of the working class, and as a consequence its members' incomes and wealth have suffered.

How Capitalism Undermines Democracy

Unregulated capitalism has produced socioeconomic inequality that has transformed directly into political inequality. As we discussed, citizens at the top of the socioeconomic ladder have influence with legislatures and regulators and can shape the rules of capitalism in their favor. Citizens in low socioeconomic groups, including those mired in poverty, are less likely to participate in democratic institutions. A single mother living from paycheck to paycheck, working two jobs, and raising two kids likely has little time for civic involvement and low interest in politics or voting. Those who have lost their jobs due to outsourcing and those who are poor have little faith in government institutions and little interest in participating in governance. The lack of participation in democratic institutions by the disenfranchised can be most easily measured by voter turnout. The turnout in U.S. presidential elections over the last three decades has averaged only 56% of eligible voters and in non-presidential congressional elections only 45% (Merkel, 2014). Most of those staying away were in low-income groups. The 2020 presidential election was an exception, with a record turnout of 66% of eligible voters. Voter turnout in European democracies is also low, ranging from 57% to 75%. Like in the United States, most of those who do not participate are in lower socioeconomic groups. As the wealth gap continues to increase, voter turnout has trended downward. Those at the lower end of the socioeconomic scale feel alienated from a society and a government that don't respond to their needs. As those in the lower classes drop out of democratic processes, plutocrats seize control of democracy. Unfortunately, the United States is drifting toward this fate.

Capitalism with deregulated and globalized markets, which have no national boundaries, have seriously limited the ability of democratic governments to govern and regulate them. If no democratic and economic reforms deal with this problem, democracy could slowly transform into oligarchy (Merkel, 2014).

Finally, a major consequence of capitalism-induced socioeconomic inequities is the potential rise of right-wing populism. As we have discussed, when right-wing populist leaders come to power through democratic elections, there is a great risk of erosion of democratic institutions and transition to autocratic rule.

Capitalism and Human Nature

Conservatives argue that humans are basically selfish and competitive, and our economic system needs to accommodate these traits. Conservatives value entrepreneurs who take risks and drive the economy by creating businesses and providing jobs, and they believe their wealth and power are justified. They believe in a hierarchical society, with owners of capital and corporate executives at the top and workers at the bottom. They cite the impressive growth in our economies as evidence that the system is working.

But we have seen that the rewards of capitalism have not been shared by all and have created a great economic divide. If we are to mitigate the growing inequities in income and wealth, we must change the rules of the capitalistic system to provide a level playing field and greater opportunities for all. Without closing this great divide, we will not be able to achieve an egalitarian society, and our democracy may not survive. We will remain a divided and polarized country, and our selfish, hierarchical, and tribal instincts will prevail over the cooperative, altruistic side of our human nature.

CHAPTER 13
OUR FRAGILE DEMOCRACY

Given the right conditions, any society can turn against democracy. Indeed, if history is anything to go by, all societies eventually will.

—Anne Applebaum, ***Twilight of Democracy: The Seductive Lure of Authoritarianism***

Our American democracy, as imperfect as it is, provides the best hope for bringing a better life to our people. Democracies are fragile institutions and have been in life-or-death struggles with authoritarian governments for as long as they have existed. In recent times, democracies across the globe have been sliding further and further toward authoritarian rule (Shapiro & Diamond, 2017). Democracies have retreated in Russia under Vladimir Putin, in Turkey under Recep Tayyip Erdoğan, in Venezuela under Nicolas Maduro, in the Philippines under Rodrigo Duterte, in Poland under Jarosław Kaczyński's Law and Justice Party, in Hungary under Viktor Orbán's Fidesz party, and in the United States under Donald Trump. Our fragile democracy is fighting for its survival.

The Great American Experiment

On July 4, 1776, Thomas Jefferson and the Second Continental Congress in Philadelphia produced and approved the Declaration of Independence. This was an act of courage—a treasonous act against the British empire, the world's greatest power, punishable by death (Reed, 2018). The ideas expressed in the document were revolutionary and had a profound impact upon the world that still resonates today:

> We hold these truths to be self-evident, that all men are created equal, that they are endowed by their Creator with certain unalienable rights, that among these are life, liberty and the pursuit of happiness. That to secure these rights, governments are instituted among men, deriving their just powers from the consent of the governed. That whenever any form of government becomes destructive to these ends, it is the right of the people to alter or to abolish it, and to institute new government, laying its foundation on such principles and organizing its powers in such form, as to them shall seem most likely to affect their safety and happiness. (Jefferson et al., 1776)

The ideas of the declaration reflected the principals of the eighteenth-century Enlightenment. All men are created equal and are entitled to basic rights, which include life, liberty, and the pursuit of happiness. Government must be limited to preserving these rights and protecting the peace, and governance must be done with the consent of the governed.

After seven years of arduous conflict, the Americans gained their independence with Britain's recognition of their new nation in 1783. In 1787, after four years of negotiations and uncertainty under the Articles of Confederation, the Philadelphia Constitutional Convention brought together a council of great talent for the purpose of creating the Constitution of the United States and forming a government to secure liberty for its people (Image 13.1). The Founding Fathers included George Washington, James Madison (who was the major architect of the Constitution), John Adams, Benjamin Franklin, Alexander Hamilton, John Jay, Thomas Jefferson, and many more. Never before had a greater assembly of genius and wisdom been convened for the purpose of creating a government.

Image 13.1 The Constitution of the United States. Written by the founders in 1787, this document persists as one of the greatest gifts given by one generation to subsequent generations. But after more than 200 years, many question its current relevance and ask, is our Constitution still working?

The founders' vision was broad. They were creating a system of governance not just for themselves and their generation but for generations to come. George Washington, who presided over the convention, reflected the broad vision and wisdom of the founders when he said, "If, to please the people, we offer what we ourselves disapprove, how can we later defend our work? Let us raise a standard to which the wise and honest can repair; the rest is in the hands of God" (Reed, 2018).

Here are the key elements of the United States Constitution (Reed, 2018):

1. The nation is a republic, not a majoritarian democracy. Representatives of the people vote for laws. The Constitution protects basic human rights, which are not subject to popular vote. (Of course, women and people of color did not initially have the right to vote.)

2. The government has limited powers, deferring most powers to the states.

3. There is a separation of powers that disperses many powers to the states and creates three distinct branches of government (the executive, legislative, and judicial branches), each with its own prescribed powers and limitations.

4. There is a network of checks and balances that limit the power of any single branch of government. The president can veto laws passed by Congress. Congress can withhold funds from executive agendas. The Supreme Court has the power by precedent to declare laws unconstitutional. The president appoints federal judges, but they must be approved by the Senate. The president can also grant pardons to individuals found guilty of crimes by the judiciary.

5. The Bill of Rights, the first 10 amendments to the Constitution, guarantees basic freedoms, including freedom of religion, speech, press, and assembly and the freedom to keep and bear arms.

Washington described the establishment of the new government as **The Great American Experiment**. The framers realized that the Constitution and its principles would require diligent work and modification over time to fulfill their purpose. When a woman asked Benjamin Franklin, "Mr. Franklin, what form of government have you given us?" he replied, "A republic, madam, if you can keep it" (Reed, 2018). In the more than two centuries since the Constitution was implemented, it was amended to abolish slavery in 1865, to establish the right of all male citizens to vote regardless of race or previous servitude in 1870, and to declare women's right to vote in 1920. The size of the government has grown far beyond what our forefathers intended or imagined. While the Constitution persists as one of the greatest gifts given by one generation to subsequent generations, many question its current relevance. Is our Constitution still working?

The Decline of Democracies

Democracies have been on the decline over the past two to three decades. The Varieties of Democracy (V-Dem) Institute, an independent research institute headquartered at Sweden's University of Gothenburg, collaborates with a number of international experts to evaluate the state of democracy in the world (V-Dem Institute, 2021). Nations are rated on their democracy or autocracy based on their adherence to principles of democracy, including free and fair elections, rule of law, civil liberties, citizen participation in government, and citizens' equal access to resources, opportunities, and freedoms. The institute found a steep decline in liberal democracies over the past decade that continued through 2020, such that the degree of democracy enjoyed by the average global citizen was reduced to levels last seen in 1990. Over two-thirds (68%) of the world's population live in nations governed by autocracies, while about one-third (32%) live in democracies. The United States, once the vanguard for liberal democracy, became less democratic and more autocratic over the past decade, according to V-Dem's liberal democracy index (LDI). This decline was due in part to President Trump's attacks on opposition politicians and the media and the weakening of the legislature's checks and balances on executive power. The institute's evaluation preceded Trump's challenge to the 2020 presidential election results and the January 6, 2021, insurrection.

Why Democracies Fail

International affairs professor Ethan Kapstein and economist Nathan Converse (2008) systematically studied 120 democracies that have originated in 90 countries since the 1960s, examining potential reasons why these democracies may fail. Two conditions top the list. Democracies with great income and wealth inequalities are at great risk of failure, as are those with high ethnic diversity. We discussed these two conditions in Chapters 9 and 10 and will revisit them briefly below.

Effective constraints on executive power appear to be especially important in maintaining democracies. Such constraints should include checks and balances between the executive, legislative, and judicial branches, a vibrant free press, and an educational system open to diverse ideas (Kapstein & Converse, 2008). Leaders that face only weak constraints tend to gather political power. One of the first things that authoritarian elected leaders do as they move to consolidate power is roll back existing constitutional constraints.

Young democracies are more prone to failure. Democratic institutions take time to build and mature. Central banks need time to maintain stable monetary policies. Judicial systems need to establish political independence. The executive and legislative branches of government need to develop power-sharing relationships. Political parties need time to mature. So, it is not surprising that democracies tend to fail early on. The longer a democratic regime endures and the more stable its institutions, the less likely it is to regress to authoritarian rule.

Failure rates of democracies vary by geographic region. Kapstein and Converse (2008) found sub-Saharan Africa was the origin of more democracies than any other region, but 63% of these democracies failed. Democracies in Asia and Latin America, with failure rates of 57% and 35% respectively, were more likely to fail than those in Europe.

Income and Wealth Inequalities Weaken Democracies

Nineteenth-century French diplomat and political scientist Alexis de Tocqueville (1805–1859) believed that democracies with severe economic inequality tended to be unstable and dysfunctional. He understood that poor citizens do not enjoy the same access to political and policy influence as the wealthy, and he maintained that without some measure of economic equality, there cannot be political equality.

Income inequality is significantly greater in democracies that fail compared to those that succeed, and many experts believe this may be the most important cause of failed democracies (Kapstein & Converse, 2008). As we discussed in Chapter 10, inequities in income and wealth adversely affect the democratic process in many ways (Chowdhury & Sundaram, 2018; Levin-Waldman, 2016). Elites and corporations with great wealth have ready access to political and policy officials, while those at the low end of the income scale have little or no influence with government officials. Many of those at the bottom levels of society have lost trust in the government and have dropped out of the democratic process altogether (Levin-Waldman, 2016).

As we have discussed in Chapter 10, the alienation of the poor and disenfranchised has opened the way for right-wing populist movements. Once in power, right-wing populist leaders all too often transition from democracy to authoritarian rule.

Ethnic Diversity and Structural Racism Threaten Our Democracy

Structural racism, which denies Black people and other ethnic minorities equal rights, opportunities, and justice, is the antithesis of democracy, which is built on the foundation of equality. Discrimination makes Black people feel disenfranchised and erodes their trust in the establishment and the government. Many drop out of participation in the democratic process. This creates an imperfect and weakened democracy. As we have discussed in Chapter 9, throughout history, democracies with high ethnic diversity have been more fragile and are more likely to fail than those with more homogeneous ethnicity.

Unfortunately, the advancement of civil rights has been accompanied by intense political polarization. Following passage of the Civil Rights Act in 1964, southern White people fled the Democratic Party and joined the Republicans, while Black people aligned with the Democrats in appreciation for their support. The fundamental issue of race has divided the parties, and the intense political polarization has been toxic to our democracy.

Political Polarization Undermines Democracies

Political polarization in the United States has crippled our democracy. The extreme political positions of both parties have stifled legislative compromise and have almost eliminated the passage of new laws needed to deal with pressing issues. Our court system, especially the Supreme Court, has been politicized and is no longer viewed as a fair judge to settle our differences. The party out of power opposes almost any position of the existing administration and has as its major objective replacing the party in power. This may have been best illustrated when Senate Majority Leader Mitch McConnel, announced in 2010 that the single most important thing he wanted to achieve is for President Obama to be a one-term president.

Political polarization has contributed to a dramatic rise in political violence. Over the past five years we have seen death threats to public health officials, a plot to kidnap Michigan's governor, and the January 6th insurrection to cite a few examples (Kleinfeld, 2021). White supremacist ideas and conspiracy theories that blur the lines between posturing and provoking violence have become mainstream. The new reality is that millions of Americans are willing to support or excuse political violence. White supremacists and far-right-wing extremists have become the most significant domestic terrorism threat facing the United States.

Political partisanship has reached a level in this country where it permeates our social interactions and friendships. Most Republicans and Democrats would object if their children married someone from the opposite party. And most Republicans and Democrats regard the other party as an existential threat. Many have become willing to sacrifice democratic principles to keep the other party out of power.

A study by political scientists at Yale University highlights how tribal loyalty trumps democratic principles in the current environment of political polarization (Cummings, 2020; Graham & Svolik, 2020). The investigators performed a survey in which respondents were presented with a choice between two hypothetical candidates for a state legislature, one from each party, each supporting conventional positions of their respective parties. In the first scenario, neither candidate violated democratic norms, and the respondents voted their party allegiance with very little crossover. In the second scenario, one of the candidates violated democratic norms by supporting voter suppression and ignoring unfavorable court decisions. Despite these transgressions, only 3.5% of respondents crossed over and voted against their candidate and against their party's interests to protect democratic principles. This small crossover in response to violation of democratic norms reflects the strength of our political polarization and the tribal nature of our politics. Our human nature makes us very reluctant to go against loyalty to our tribe. With most voting districts heavily weighted to one party or the other because of gerrymandering and the urban-rural divide, the margin of victory in most elections is much more than 3.5%, so there is little incentive for candidates to refrain from undemocratic behavior. This puts our democracy at great peril.

The Carnegie Endowment for International Peace, using data from the Variety of Democracies (V-Dem) database, assessed the levels of political polarization in 202 countries and found that political polarization has been increasing globally over the past two decades (McCoy and Press, 2022; Mounk, 2022). The study found that perniciouspolarization —polarization that divides society into mutually distrustful political camps in which political identity becomes a social identity—is linked to the erosion of democracies. Since 1950, 52 democracies reached levels of pernicious polarization: 26, including the United States, experienced a downgrade of their democracies assessed by the V-Dem point system, and 23 of these descended into some form of autocracy. The United States' pernicious polarization stands out because it is among the most severe of all democracies and because it has been present for an extended period of time.

The Carnegie study found that about half the time since 1900, countries with serious polarization never recovered. In the other half, some had only moderate improvement and some had improvement but then relapsed. Those that did improve in a lasting way required a major political disaster —a civil war or cruel dictatorship—to make the change (Mounk, 2022).

The outlook sounds alarming, but our polarization may not be quite as dire as the Carnegie study suggests. Our democratic institutions have a long history and are more durable than institutions of other democracies, and this may give us a better chance to withstand our political polarity. In addition, in contrast to many other polarized democracies, our polarization is more tied to ideology and less tied to demographics. While Black people are more often aligned with Democrats and Evangelical Christians are more often aligned with Republicans, we Americans cannot judge each other's political persuasion by how we look or talk. When we interact at work or at Little League softball games, we don't discuss political differences and are often not aware of another person's political preferences. This may allow us to overcome our differences more easily. It is not too difficult to imagine how our country might look if we are able to depolarize our politics. But this will require urgent new leadership and institutional reforms—and some willingness for compromise from our political partisans.

The Constitution Is Not Enough

As valuable as the Constitution was, the Founders realized that it was not enough to preserve our democracy. Our nation's wealth, our strong middle class, and an involved vibrant civil society were all important for the survival of our democracy. But we have come to realize that perhaps the most important safeguard of democracy is the development and protection of strong democratic norms. These norms are customs or guardrails that prevent political competition from degenerating into no-holds-barred conflict.

Harvard professors Steven Levitsky and Daniel Ziblatt (2019) explain how political hyperpolarization can lead to the degradation of the basic democratic norms that are so essential to a functioning democracy. They describe two basic categories of norms that have preserved the checks and balances of American democracy over many years. One is mutual toleration. Politicians must have tolerance and respect for their political opponents, as long as they abide by the rules. They must accept that their opponents should have equal rights to compete for power and governance. The other category of norms is forbearance. Politicians should exhibit restraint and abide by the precedents of previous administrations. They must avoid actions that, while respecting the letter of the law, violate the spirit of the law.

The president of the United States has great potential for unilateral action through executive orders, as granted by the Constitution. Given the potential for abuse, the importance of executive restraint is hard to overstate. George Washington set an exemplary standard in establishing democratic norms of forbearance. He vetoed only two bills passed by Congress and issued only eight executive orders during his eight years in office. And not wanting to set a precedent that could lead to autocratic rule, he declined to run for a third term.

Democratic norms have been violated to varying degrees throughout our nation's history. In 1934, President Franklin D. Roosevelt's New Deal was having trouble making it through the courts. So, FDR attempted to expand the Supreme Court to 15 judges, with plans to fill the vacancies with pro-administration judges. Article III of the Constitution does not specify the number of Supreme Court judges, but court-packing was certainly viewed as a violation of norms. Fortunately, cooler heads prevailed. Both parties opposed FDR's court-packing, and it failed to pass through Congress (Levitsky & Ziblatt, 2019). But FDR broke other norms. He issued over 3,000 executive orders and sought and won unprecedented third and fourth presidential terms in 1940 and 1944. Congress subsequently passed the 22nd Amendment to the Constitution, limiting presidents from serving more than two four-year terms.

When Georgia congressman Newt Gingrich arrived in Washington in 1979, he brought with him a new vitriol to American politics. He instructed Republican candidates to vilify their Democratic opponents with words such as "pathetic," "sick," "anti-family," and "traitors." The traditional norm of mutual tolerance was coming to an end. Gingrich later became Speaker of the House and expanded his toxic rhetoric.

In 2003, Republican House Majority Leader Tom DeLay drew up a redistricting plan in his home state of Texas that crowded Black and Latino voters into a small number of congressional districts and added Republican voters to districts of White incumbent Democrats, ensuring their defeat. The changes increased Texas' Republican representation in Congress from 15 to 21 seats, out of a total of 32 seats. This was an early example of the gerrymandering that was subsequently adopted in many states by both parties, and which represents a stark departure from democratic norms and values.

Barack Obama's 2008 presidential campaign and his administration marked a watershed in partisan intolerance. Right-wing media, including Fox News, portrayed Obama as a Marxist and an anti-American Muslim and questioned his birthplace and citizenship—a conspiracy theory known as birtherism. This hateful rhetoric was picked up by leading Republican politicians.

After the Democrats lost control of the House in the 2010 elections, President Obama was unable to get legislation passed through the Republican Congress. As a result, he bypassed Congress and issued 276 executive orders during his two terms in office. This approach was not new. George W. Bush had issued 291 executive orders during his eight years as president, and Donald Trump issued 195 during his four years in office (Federal Register, 2020). Unable to get the Iran nuclear treaty ratified by the Republican Senate, Obama bypassed the chamber and negotiated an "executive agreement" to seal the treaty. A group of Republican Senators led by Arkansas' Tom Cotton wrote a letter to the leaders of Iran insisting Obama had no authority to make such a deal. One of the final events of the Obama administration that was particularly illustrative of the violation of democratic norms was Senate Majority Leader Mitch McConnell's refusal to hold a vote on Obama's nomination of Merrick Garland to the Supreme Court. Never before had a Presidential nominee been refused a vote by the

Senate. We'll visit Donald Trump's disregard for democratic norms in the next chapter.

Conclusion

A democracy dies when a nation loses its common identity and vision and when its citizens lose faith in government, feel there is no justice or equal opportunity, and lose hope for a better future. Many of our country's citizens feel a deep alienation from our society and our government due to the growing racial and socioeconomic inequities that divide our country. These inequities have bred an intense political polarization that has fostered a disregard for democratic norms and threatens our democracy. If we are to save and strengthen our democracy, we will need to address and reduce the twin inequities that so divide our society and have led to our intense political polarization.

CHAPTER 14

AMERICA'S DRIFT TOWARD AUTHORITARIANISM

Trump was precisely the kind of figure that had haunted Hamilton and other founders when they created the American presidency.

—Steven Levitsky and Daniel Ziblatt, ***How Democracies Die***

The V-Dem Institute reached the following chilling conclusions about the United States' drift toward autocracy in its 2020 report, published just before the United States' 2020 presidential election:

> Three years into the Trump administration, American democracy has eroded to a point that more often than not leads to full-blown autocracy. Only 1 in 5 democracies that start down this path are able to reverse the damage before succumbing to full-blown autocracy. (Ingraham, 2020)

Political scientist Staffan Lindberg, a founding director of the Institute, says the United States in not unique (Ingraham, 2020). The decline in democratic indicators in the United States follows a pattern seen in the formerly democratic countries of Poland, Hungary, and Turkey.

The United States historically has been a champion of democracy. We have supported democratic regimes across the globe and have fought against autocratic rule. We did not expect autocratic rule to come to our shores, but we have just come close to losing our democracy in our recent presidential election, and we are not yet out of danger. We are in a battle for survival, and the outcome is not certain.

The Rise of American Populism

Populist movements have arisen across the globe over the past two decades, and by 2018, as many as 20 populist leaders have come to power (Serhan, 2020). Populism is a political movement that appeals to ordinary people who feel their concerns are disregarded by the elite establishment. Populism is not intrinsically bad, but there is a rising tide of exclusionary and authoritarian populism—right-wing populism—that pits the populist group against outside groups—the establishment, business elites, immigrants, ethnic minorities, and all others who disagree with the populist agenda (Rohac et al., 2018). Understood in this way, right-wing populism is divisive and is the antithesis of egalitarian democracy, which promotes the equality of all peoples. There is a rising tide of right-wing populist movements on both sides of the Atlantic that are eroding established democracies and transforming them into authoritarian rule.

In the United States, the growth of right-wing populism has paralleled a decline in trust of government and institutions and a rise in political polarization. Voters see Washington's growing political dysfunction and inability to get things done, and they feel government is unresponsive and unable to address their concerns. As we have seen, the growing socioeconomic divide over the past three decades may be the most important contributor to the rise of right-wing populism. Working-class and middle-class Americans resent exploding CEO compensation. They rage at the $700 billion bailout of Wall Street banks at taxpayer expense during the financial crises of 2008, while millions of Americans had foreclosure on their homes. Workers see the economic system as unfair and rigged against them, with no one on their side to help. The alienation of working-class and middle-class Americans makes them vulnerable to autocratic demagogues who feed off their resentment and pit them against the establishment and privileged elites.

America's growing right-wing populism also has racial undertones. White working-class Americans assail liberal elites for advocating for immigrants, Muslims, Black people, and other people of color. White people see their influence waning and feel threatened by the demographic changes that are occurring in our society. By midcentury, non-Hispanic White people will become an ethnic minority (Craig et al., 2018). These people are part of the right-wing populist base.

Racial tensions have contributed to the rise of right-wing populism. Since the Democrats passed the Civil Rights and Voting Rights Acts, most Black people have gravitated to the Democratic Party. The Democratic Party's championing of Black people's civil rights and affirmative action has put them at odds with populist working-class White people, who are aligned with the Republicans. The White working class have become part of the right-wing populist movement.

Successful populist leaders are masters at exacerbating cultural divisions and conflict in societies (Naím, 2017). They exaggerate their nation's problems and criminalize their political opposition. They inflate external threats and glorify the military. They discredit the experts and delegitimize the media. In every way, they feed into the dark side of our human nature—our anger, resentment, and our tribal instincts. This is right-wing populism—it's us against them.

Christian Fundamentalism

Christian fundamentalism has been an integral part of the forces that have propelled America's drift toward authoritarianism. Evangelical Christians became politically active and aligned with the Republican Party after the Supreme Court established women's right to abortion in 1973 with its decision in *Roe v. Wade*. Presidents Ronald Reagan and George H. W. Bush embraced the Christian right by adopting pro-Evangelical positions— opposition to abortion, support for school prayer, and, later, opposition to gay marriage. Both sides have benefited from the alliance. Evangelicals comprise a healthy proportion of the electorate and overwhelmingly support Republicans. Exit polls from the 2016 presidential election found 26% of voters self-identified as White Evangelical Christians, and 79% of these people voted for Donald Trump over Hillary Clinton (Husser, 2020). Trump repaid the favor with his nomination and confirmation of three socially conservative Supreme Court justices.

Evangelicals have had a major influence in politics not only because they comprise a large proportion of the electorate and solidly support Republican candidates but also because they are passionate, motivated, and very politically active. They serve on many local and state committees and drive local policy.

A solid majority of Evangelicals score very high on the right-wing authoritarianism (RWA) scale, meaning they often have authoritarian personalities and tend to follow authoritarian figures (Altemeyer, 2006). They submit to established authority, have prejudicial and aggressive behavior toward outside groups, and conform to old traditions and values. Evangelicals are very tribal—they support their own kind but are often intolerant to those outside their group. Because of their authoritarian personalities, their passionate involvement in American politics, and their large numbers, it is easy to see how these religious fundamentalists may play an important role in transitioning our country to authoritarian rule.

The Republican Coalition

In less than a year, elections involving Brexit in Great Britain, Marine Le Pen in France, and Donald Trump in the United States showed the strength of right-wing populism in three of the world's oldest democracies. Right-wing populists in Britain, France, the United States, and much of Europe share common values—opposition to globalization, opposition to immigration, and hostility toward the establishment and technocrats. The populist movements also have a common base of support—older White working-class voters without higher education, mostly in rural areas, who feel they have been left behind by globalization and automation.

The Republican coalition that emerged before the presidential primaries in 2016 was a strange mixture of the populist base, Evangelical Christians, establishment Republicans, and plutocrats (Pierson, 2017; Zakaria, 2017). Donald Trump, an outsider who had never held public office, was able to gain the support and allegiance of the populist base by touting familiar themes, which energized that base but riled establishment Republicans. The establishment Republicans opposed Trump's nomination, but once he won the primaries and the nomination, they supported him—partly out of loyalty to the party, partly because Trump had the support of the populist base, and partly because of their strong opposition to the Democrats and Hillary Clinton at a time of intense political polarization. This mixture of support from diverse constituencies would propel Trump to the Republican nomination and the presidency.

Culture Wars

The populist base played a crucial role in electing Donald Trump president, but once he and the Republicans gained power, the populists had little influence on policy. While Trump continued to tout populist themes, railing against global trade and immigration, his administration enacted economic policies that benefited the plutocratic elite (Pierson, 2017). He filled his cabinet with reactionary billionaires. The signature achievement of his administration was his tax bill, which benefited those elites at the expense of the populists. The Joint Committee on Taxation and the Congressional Budget Office calculates that in 10 years, people making the median income in America ($50,000 to $75,000) would effectively pay a whopping $4 billion more in taxes, while people making $1 million or more would pay $5.8 billion less (Zakaria, 2017). Trump loosened regulations on businesses and banks, including rules that protect consumers, workers, and the environment. His attempts to abolish Obamacare would also have hurt his populist base. Trump and the Republican Party have successfully deceived their supporters, promising them populism while enacting plutocratic capitalism. They have been able to work this magic by dangling social issues in front of their populist base.

Political battles over contentious social issues comprise what we call culture wars. American sociologist James Davison Hunter popularized the term "culture wars" in his 1991 landmark book *Culture Wars: The Struggle to Define America*. Culture wars had their origins in the early 1960s with the civil rights movement, the sexual revolution, the gay rights movement, the women's liberation movement, and the backlashes that followed (Stanton, 2021). Abortion became the primary issue of the culture wars of the 1970s, '80s, and '90s. Race has now joined abortion as a primary issue. Sexuality, family values, church-state issues, and education are also part of the battle.

The Republican base appears to be motivated more deeply by social issues than by traditional policy issues. Trump has exploited this deeply embedded bias. He brags at the annual March for Life rally in Washington, DC, that "unborn children have never had a stronger defender in the White House." He poses for a photo op with a Bible in hand at St. John's Episcopal Church in Washington, DC. He fights with Black athletes who fail to stand for the national anthem. He sends racial signals to White working-class and middle-class voters, demonstrating that he is part of their tribe and against the establishment (Edsell, 2020). He ridicules a judge of Mexican descent, describes Haiti as a "shithole," and says that there are good people on both sides of a violent neo-Nazi rally. He issues a Muslim ban—an executive order banning travel from several mostly Muslim countries—and he promises to build the wall and not yield on immigration. He clearly excommunicates himself from the liberal elite and the establishment, and he solidifies his membership in the populist tribe. It is like having a tattoo that irreversibly binds him to his gang. He surely understands his base better than outsiders do (Zakaria, 2017).

The Republicans have elevated the culture war rhetoric leading into the 2022 midterm elections (Smith, 2022). Republican-controlled states are passing sweeping laws targeting abortion, LGBTQ rights, and the teaching of some controversial social issues in public schools. In anticipation of the Supreme Court overturning *Roe v. Wade*, which guarantees a woman's right to abortion through the second trimester, seven Republican-controlled states have imposed new restrictions on abortion, and many more are expected. Texas and Idaho have passed laws banning abortion after six weeks, with enforcement through "sue thy neighbor" laws. Numerous Republican-controlled state legislatures have introduced anti-LGBTQ bills, many targeting transgender people. Florida has passed the "Don't Say Gay" law, censoring discussion of sexual orientation in Florida schools from kindergarten through the third grade. Nine Republican-led states have banned the teaching of critical race theory (CRT), and several Republican legislatures have introduced bills to ban the teaching of books dealing with controversial cultural issues.

Our culture, values, and way of life are what animate our passions. Culture wars are a struggle over how we want America to be. Those who oppose our side and our way of life represent an existential threat, so it is not surprising that a working-class electorate that values cultural issues over economic issues would so often vote against its economic interests.

Cultural wars have become a big part of politics. With most political issues, such as federal taxes and social spending, there is room for compromise, but with cultural issues there is little such room. How can you have a stable democracy without compromise? Culture wars have become a major threat to our democracy.

The Electoral College and the Senate

One of the great challenges our Founding Fathers faced at the Constitutional Convention in 1787 was how to pick a president (Roos, 2020). One option was for Congress to select the president, but it was opposed by delegates who felt it provided too much opportunity for corruption within the executive and legislative branches. Another option was letting the people elect the president by straight popular vote, but many delegates thought voters lacked the resources to be fully informed about the candidates and feared that a populist leader appealing directly to an uninformed electorate could accrue dangerous amounts of power.

The delegates finally came up with the Electoral College as a compromise. The legislatures of each state would determine electors who would then cast the actual ballots for the presidency. The number of electors assigned to each state was based on the state's population. A compromise was reached with the South in which each enslaved Black person would be counted as three-fifths of a person, even though they were not permitted a vote. The Constitution says nothing about how the state legislatures should allot their electoral votes, but over time, all but two states (Maine and later Nebraska) passed laws giving all the electoral votes to the candidate who wins a plurality of the state's popular votes (Roos, 2020).

Today, states are allotted electoral votes based on the number of representatives they have in Congress, plus one for each of their two senators. To win the presidency, a candidate needs to capture 270 of 538 total electoral votes. Since most states award all their electoral votes to the candidate who wins the popular vote in that state, it is quite possible to win the national popular vote but lose the electoral vote. In 2000, Gore won the popular vote by a narrow margin, while George W. Bush won the disputed electoral vote, and in 2016, Hillary Clinton won the popular vote by almost 2.9 million votes but lost the electoral vote to Donald Trump.

The Electoral College is at odds with the basic principle of democracy that every vote should count equally. The Electoral College also provides an electoral vote advantage to low-population states. Every state gets one electoral vote for each member of Congress and two bonus electors for its two senators. Wyoming, with a population of 578,000, and California, with a population of 39 million, both get two bonus electors (Black, 2012). There are other limitations. The Electoral College system provides little or no incentive for candidates to campaign in solid blue or red states where the outcomes are predetermined. The three most populous states—California, Texas, and New York—are in this category. Similarly, voters in solid red and blue states have little incentive to vote, since their votes will not likely affect the outcome. They feel their vote doesn't really count. This is especially true for many African Americans who support Democratic candidates in southern states, which are strongly Republican.

Unfortunately, the prospects for changes to the Electoral College in the near future are small. A constitutional amendment requires approval by two-thirds of the House and Senate and must be ratified by three-fourths of the states. If one party feels the Electoral College offers them an advantage, it is not likely to vote for change. Alternatively, a number of states have supported a pact that commits all of its state electors to vote for the candidate who wins the national popular vote. If enough states comply to reach 270 votes for an Electoral College victory, this will assure the presidency to the popular vote winner. Currently, fifteen states totaling 196 electoral votes have agreed to comply, but there is little chance in our current political climate of recruiting enough states to reach 270 electoral votes. And if this goal is somehow reached, the system may face constitutional challenges.

The rules and structure of the Senate pose an even greater threat to the principles of democratic representation (Ladd, 2019). The Founding Fathers, amid much controversy, reached a compromise with the smaller states and created a Senate in which each state had equal representation—two senators—regardless of population. This has given big advantages to voters in small states. California with 39 million people gets two senators, and Wyoming with a population of 578,000 also gets two senators. In our current environment, many of the small states are inland, rural, predominantly White, and mostly Republican (Wyoming, North Dakota, South Dakota, and Montana, for example). Many of the large states are coastal, largely urban, ethnically diverse, and predominantly Democratic (California, New York, Pennsylvania, and Illinois, for example). This gives an advantage in Senate votes to the rural, White, Republican electorate and a disadvantage to the urban, diverse, Democratic electorate. In the vote to confirm Justice Brett Kavanaugh to the Supreme Court in 2018, for example, the 50 senators voting for confirmation represented just 44% of the U.S. population (143 million), while those voting against confirmation represented 56% of the population (181 million) (Tauberer, 2018). In the 2016 general election, the Democrats won only a minority of Senate seats despite capturing a majority of votes for the Senate.

The rules of the Senate can also impede majority rule. The filibuster, which has a long history in the chamber, allows a single senator to block the vote on a bill by endless debate, which can only be stopped if 60 senators agree to end it—a procedure called cloture (Reynolds, 2020). This has allowed the minority party to block bills and appointments supported by the majority party. (Today, senators only must indicate their intention to filibuster rather than actually begin the debate.) The Senate has recently created exceptions to the filibuster rules through a parliamentary procedure labeled the nuclear option. The Democrats invoked the nuclear option in 2013 to eliminate the filibuster and permit approval of executive branch nominations and federal judicial appointments by President Obama. Once the precedent was set, the Republicans used the nuclear option to allow approval of President Trump's Supreme Court nominees—Neil Gorsuch, Brett Kavanaugh, and Amy Coney Barrett—with a simple majority. There may be more exceptions to the filibuster in the future, but there is some reluctance to change it because the party in power realizes any modifications could be used against it when it is no longer in power.

The rules of the Senate also dictate that the leader of the majority party has the authority to decide which bills the Senate should consider. This usually means that only bills that are supported by a majority of the majority party are brought to the floor of the Senate for consideration. Many bills supported by a bipartisan majority of senators do not get a vote. This clearly thwarts the rule of the majority. In just one of many examples, former Senate Majority Leader Mitch McConnell refused to bring gun control legislation to votes in the Senate, despite a majority of senators supporting the bill, because there was not a majority of Republican senators who supported it.

Voter Suppression and Gerrymandering

The United States has a long history of voter suppression. The Voting Rights Act in 1965 greatly enhanced African American suffrage, but in 2013, the U.S. Supreme Court struck down part of the law requiring specified states with a history of discrimination against people of color to get advanced approval from the Department of Justice before revising their election laws. The Supreme Court's decision led to renewed voter suppression, primarily in the South. Many southern states implemented restrictions on early voting, elimination of same-day registration, and strict voter ID requirements (Tausanovitch & Root, 2020).

Every 10 years, each state in the U.S. redraws its electoral districts. These districts define the regions that will vote for each congressional representative. In a majority of states, the state legislature carries out the redistricting process, while in several states independent commissions are responsible (Dews, 2017). When state legislatures redraw districts, they often create boundaries that favor the party in power—a process called political gerrymandering.

In the 2018 congressional elections, there were four states (North Carolina, Michigan, Pennsylvania, and Wisconsin) in which the Democratic Party won the majority of votes but captured only a minority of state legislative seats due to political gerrymandering. In North Carolina, for example, Democrats received 50.5% of the vote but only won 42% of the seats in the state senate and 46% of the seats in the state House (Tausanovitch & Root, 2020). The results in North Carolina were even more skewed in the election for representatives to the U.S. House of Representatives. Democrats received 48% of the votes but captured only 3 of 13 seats. Following a state court order to redraw the districts because of racial gerrymandering, the results were only slightly better in 2020. Both the Democrats and the Republicans received 49% of the votes, but the Democrats captured only 5 of 13 seats (Corriher, 2020).

Gerrymandering greatly influences which party controls the local, state, and federal legislatures. It devalues the vote in solidly red and solidly blue districts, undermining the democratic process. It also contributes to political polarization. Districts that are heavily weighted to one party, be it Republican or Democratic, will attract candidates on the extreme right or left, and moderates have little chance of winning.

Progress has been made in reforming gerrymandering, but it has been slow. The Supreme Court has labeled racial gerrymandering unconstitutional but so far has not done the same for partisan gerrymandering (Amy, 2020). Reformers have had some success in transferring the redistricting process to bipartisan commissions and, in rare cases, to civil servants. In most states, state legislatures with secure majorities unwilling to give up their power have resisted this process (Amy, 2020). In a few states (Michigan, for example) citizens have created and passed ballot initiatives to create independent commissions for districting. In 2019, the U.S. House of Representatives passed a bill requiring all states to use independent commissions to draw districts for federal elections, but the bill died in the Senate (Tausanovitch & Root, 2020). Fixing gerrymandering would be one big part of reversing the downward spiral of democracy and voter suppression in the United States.

Ranked-choice voting is a promising voting method that advocates believe will help reduce political polarization (Montanaro, 2021). It can be used in local, district, state, and national elections. In this system, primaries are eliminated, and all candidates run in one nonpartisan election. Voters rank the candidates from first to last. If one candidate gets 50% of the first-place votes plus one, that candidate wins. If no one wins 50% plus one on the first count, it's on to round two. The candidate with the lowest number of first-place votes is eliminated and that candidate's second-place votes are redistributed. The process continues until one candidate has 50% of the votes plus one. This can potentially reduce political polarization because candidates need to appeal to all the electorate to win, and candidates with more moderate views are likely to prevail. Maine and Alaska use ranked choice voting for statewide and presidential elections, and a few states use it for presidential primaries. But the method is complicated, and some voters don't fill in all their choices, so it has not yet been adopted very widely.

Donald Trump's Rise to Power

When Donald Trump announced his candidacy for presidency on June 16, 2015, with the slogan "Make America Great Again," he was a big underdog, an outsider shunned by the Republican establishment. But Trump knew how to appeal to a disenfranchised group who were to become his populist base. This group consisted largely of White blue-collar workers, who felt left behind by globalization and automation, felt alienated from government technocrats, the business elite, and the Republican establishment, and felt ignored by the Democrats, who seemed more interested in advocating for ethnic minority groups.

Trump knew the right issues to fire up his populist base (Cassidy, 2016). He promised to be tough on immigration—to deport millions of undocumented workers and build a wall on the southern border. Responding to fears of terrorism, he called for a ban on Muslims entering the country. He ignored Republican economic dogma, which advocated globalization, free trade, and fiscal responsibility, and he instead railed against NAFTA and the expanded trade with China, which had cost American jobs. He promised to keep jobs at home and advocated nationalism and America First.

Trump's victory in the primary elections was helped by current primary rules, which in many states give all delegates to the candidate with a plurality of votes. The Republican field consisted of 17 candidates, none of whom were particularly strong. Trump's populist, anti-establishment base was usually large enough to give him a plurality of votes in most states, as the other candidates split the establishment vote. Through mid-March, he captured 43% of the delegates while getting 35% of the votes, which generated enough momentum to carry him to the nomination at the Republican National Convention in July 2016 (Uhrmacher et al., 2016).

Trump's Drift Toward Autocracy

Trump revealed basic autocratic traits early in his campaign (Levitsky & Ziblatt, 2018). He questioned the electoral process from the beginning. He denied the legitimacy of his opponents, beginning by discrediting Obama with the birther conspiracy and then launching caustic rhetoric against Hillary Clinton with chants of "Lock her up." He encouraged violence by encouraging his supporters to assault protesters at his rallies and by asking police to not treat protesters too gently. And he was eager to curtail civil liberties, as he promised to investigate and imprison Clinton after the election and pass new libel laws to hush his critics in the media.

Donald Trump violated democratic norms almost daily once he assumed the presidency. He asked the director of the National Park Service to find photos documenting that his audience at the inauguration was greater than that of President Obama (Havercroft et al., 2018). He appointed a commission to investigate voter fraud and refute the claim that Clinton won the popular vote by 2.9 million votes. He pressured FBI director James Comey to stop the investigation of his national security advisor Michael Flynn, and he later fired Comey for disloyalty. He accused President Obama of wiretapping his offices in Trump Tower, threatened North Korea with "total destruction" at his inaugural speech to the United Nations, and endorsed a sexual predator, Roy Moore, in the Senate race in Alabama. He revived the use of torture in interrogation of enemy combatants and authorized the tragic separation of children and infants from their parents who were seeking immigration at the Mexican border. He pressured the FBI and the Justice Department to pursue cases against his political adversaries (Hillary Clinton, Barack Obama, and Hunter Biden) and to drop cases against his corrupt allies, whom he later pardoned (Michael Flynn, Paul Manafort, and Roger Stone). He treated Attorney General William Barr as his personal lawyer and often expressed frustration at not being able to control and direct the Justice Department. He ran an extortion campaign against Ukraine, withholding military aid until Ukrainian officials announced an investigation into false corruption charges against Joe Biden's son Hunter. This interference in our election process led to his impeachment in the House, although the Republican-controlled Senate failed to convict him.

The Big Lie and January 6

Following the presidential election in 2020, Trump refused to concede that Joe Biden had won, and he promulgated the Big Lie that the election was fraudulent despite mountains of evidence showing the election was fair and not corrupt. He and his Republican enablers repeated the Big Lie and encouraged his right-wing nationalist supporters to storm the Capitol in attempts to overturn the election. The mob's insurrection at the Capitol on January 6, 2021, resulted in five deaths and a lasting stain on our democracy (Image 14.1). These acts of sedition led to Trump's second impeachment by the House of Representatives, although the Senate fell short of the two-thirds supermajority needed for conviction. Fully a year after the 2020 presidential election, 71% of Republicans still viewed Joe Biden's victory as illegitimate despite overwhelming evidence to the contrary (Nteta, 2021). The Big Lie poses a major threat to the integrity of elections, a cornerstone of democracy.

Image 14.1. Trump Loyalists Storm the Capitol. On January 6, 2021, Trump followers attempted to overturn the Presidential election. The mob's insurrection resulted in five deaths and a lasting stain on our democracy

Do Republicans actually believe the Big Lie, or is it a ploy to get back into power?

Surprisingly, many Republicans really do believe the Big Lie, in part due to its unrelenting repetition since the 2020 election. "Repeat a lie often enough and it becomes the truth," affirmed Joseph Goebbels, chief propagandist of the Nazi Party (Stafford, 2016). Psychology experiments have shown the truth of this principle. Investigators have found that, after repeated exposure, participants tend to rate statements they've seen many times before as more likely to be true than statements repeated less often, whether they are true or not. If you repeat a lie often enough, it is likely to be believed as the truth.

There is another reason why so many of Trump's followers may believe the Big Lie. Recall that the deception of others provides selfish advantages, and that self-deception has evolved to enhance the deception of others (von Hippel & Trivers, 2011). Many Trump followers may believe the Big Lie through self-deception.

Donald Trump's Incompetence

Donald Trump is one of a number of populist autocrats who have recently risen to power across the world. Others include Narendra Modi in India, Jair Bolsonaro in Brazil, Viktor Orbán in Hungary, Vladimir Putin in Russia, Jarosław Kaczyński in Poland, and Recep Tayyip Erdoğan in Turkey. They have much in common (Tufekci, 2020). They all campaigned against globalization, immigration, and the establishment and liberal elite. They all won democratic elections and then subverted democratic norms by suppressing dissent, demonizing the media, stacking the courts, and placing loyalists in positions of influence.

But there is one important difference between Trump and these other populist leaders. Sociologist Zeynep Tufekci (2020) argues that the other autocrats are competent, talented politicians who are able to win election after election and retain their power. In contrast, Trump is largely an incompetent reality-TV star who came to power through a series of unlikely events. His opponent, Hillary Clinton, while experienced and qualified, was a polarizing, unpopular nominee who had been around too long and had too many vulnerabilities. In the election, Trump was aided by Russian influence and miscues from FBI director James Comey, who reopened Clinton's email controversy just days before the election. And the electoral college gave Trump a majority of electoral college votes, with narrow victories in swing states, despite losing the popular vote by 2.9 million votes.

We may be fortunate that Trump and not someone more capable was our first right-wing populist leader. Our democracy survived his administration because he was corrupt, incompetent, abrasive, and personally flawed. He used his office to promote his own personal economic gain and surrounded himself with corrupt advisors. He cost us hundreds of thousands of lives and worsened a deep economic recession by his gross incompetence and mismanagement of the COVID-19 pandemic. He lashed out against generals, senators, Gold Star families, and anybody who failed to show him complete loyalty. He boasted on tape about assaulting women and spewed a continuous litany of lies in tweets and at political rallies. Without these flaws and without the COVID-19 pandemic, it is quite possible he would have won a second term, derailed our democracy, and led our country into full-scale autocratic rule.

But make no mistake—we are not out of danger. Smarter political talent, without all the baggage and character flaws of Donald Trump, is coming and will be ready to take advantage of the disenfranchised Trump base. Given our electoral system, a populist leader can capture the presidency with a plurality of votes and once elected, can conceivably, through voter suppression and manipulation of the voting process, capture a second term. This would provide plenty of time to further erode our democratic norms and establish autocratic rule. We have shown our vulnerability to autocracy during the four years of the Trump administration, and we almost lost our democracy in the contested 2020 election and the January 6 insurrection. Saving our fragile democracy from future autocrats will require vigilance and hard work.

Trump's Next Coup

During the 2020 presidential campaign, Donald Trump claimed he could only lose the election if it was fraudulent. After Biden was declared the winner, Trump and his Republican enablers tried to intimidate legislators and election officials in multiple swing states to overturn the election, but their attempts were unsuccessful because those officials bravely stood up for election integrity. Brad Raffensperger, Georgia's Republican secretary of state, famously refused to "find votes" for Trump to win the state. Trump pressured Republican election officials in Michigan to refuse to certify the election results for Biden, but the officials did not cave. There were many more failed attempts to overturn the election results at the state level. Finally, Vice President Mike Pence resisted intense pressure from Trump to reject certification of the Electoral College results for Biden, and as the infamous January 6 insurrection was finally tamed, Pence certified those results.

Most Americans, including many Republicans, thought the January 6 insurrection crossed a red line and marked the death of Trump and the populist MAGA movement. But these thoughts were short lived. Republican enablers, reversing their positions and bowing to Trump's control of the party through his populist and Evangelical base, downplayed the insurrection and continued to propagate the Big Lie. Trump became politically active again, holding rallies and advocating for Trump candidates in primary elections at the state level. Trump and his enablers were preparing for the next big battle.

Pulitzer Prize–winning author Barton Gellman (2021) in his chilling *Atlantic* article "Trump's Next Coup Has Already Begun" warns that January 6 was just practice and that the next attempt to overthrow the government could be for real. In every dominion of the battle to control the next election—state legislatures, state election officials, courthouses, Congress, and the Republican Party—Trump has learned from his experiences in the 2020 election, and his position has improved. Republicans have identified the vulnerabilities of the election apparatus and are working to exploit them.

Article II of the Constitution gives the state legislatures the authority to determine the electors from their respective states. But for more than 150 years, states have decided to select their electors according to the popular vote of the citizens of the state, which is not required by the Constitution. The strategy of the Trump team is to have state legislators take back their constitutional authority to directly choose electors, claiming the voters' choices have been tainted by fraud. In the 2024 election, the Trump team would target swing states with Republican legislatures and ask those legislatures to override the choice of the voters.

What Trump and the Republicans need are election officials and judges who have bought into the Big Lie to declare the election fraudulent and give cover for the legislature to appoint its own electors. Republicans are intervening at the state level to remove election officials who were not compliant with the Trump team's request to decertify elections in states that Biden won (Gellman, 2021; Gross, 2021). In Georgia, for example, the Republican state legislature has removed Secretary of State Brad Raffensperger as a voting member of the state election board so that he will not be able to vote in certifying the next election. In Arizona, Katie Hobbs, the Democratic secretary of state who certified that Biden won the state's 2020 election, has been pushed out. The Republican state legislature passed a law stating that she has no powers in legal matters related to presidential elections. Meanwhile, county and precinct election officials are resigning in large numbers. Their voicemails and emails are filled with hatred and violent threats against them and their families. They are saying, I didn't sign up for this. I was just trying to do my patriotic duty. And they are being replaced by true believers in the Big Lie.

If Trump's strategy is successful, many swing states would send competing electors—those chosen by the popular vote and those chosen by Republican legislatures—to the House of Representatives and Senate for certification (Gellman, 2021). The Constitution gives the House and Senate the authority to certify electors. In the 2020 election, 139 House Republicans and 8 Republican senators voted not to certify Biden's electors in Arizona or Pennsylvania. They were outvoted, but this attempt demonstrates what could possibly happen. Whoever wins control of the House and Senate in the 2022 elections could be in a position to certify the winner of a contested presidential election in 2024. The Supreme Court would likely be brought in to resolve such a disputed election, and unfortunately the Supreme Court has become politicized.

HUMAN NATURE AND THE STRUGGLE FOR OUR DEMOCRACY

IS HUMAN NATURE COMPATIBLE WITH EGALITARIAN DEMOCRACY?

The most important reason for the rarity of democracy is that evolution has endowed our species, as it has other primates, with a predisposition for hierarchically structured social and political systems.

Albert Somit and Steven Peterson, *Darwinism, Dominance, and Democracy: The Biological Basis of Authoritarianism*

As we have discussed, human nature is a hybrid of conflicting psychological traits. We are all partly selfish and partly cooperative, partly hierarchical/ authoritarian and partly egalitarian—and we are all tribal. Parts of our human nature seem more compatible with an authoritarian form of governance, while other parts seem more compatible with an egalitarian democracy. In this chapter, we will discuss how our behavioral traits support either autocratic or democratic governance, and we will examine the challenges this creates as we try to preserve and strengthen our democracy.

Tribal Instincts Threaten Democracy

Tribal instincts are part of human nature and play a major role in shaping our lives. We are social animals. We all want to belong to tribes, and we prefer to associate with people who are like us—people of the same race, religion, political party, and nationality.

Tribal instincts are the antithesis of a diverse democracy. They require loyalty toward those within the tribe and hostility and xenophobia toward those outside the tribe, who are often viewed as inferior and less competent. This is diametrically opposed to the values of an egalitarian democracy, in which all individuals are regarded as morally equal, with equal rights and equal justice. Tribal instincts are a major obstacle to the trust and cooperation between diverse groups that are so essential for a functioning democracy. Large democracies with great ethnic diversity have an increased potential for tribal conflict, and throughout human history, they have been fragile and often fail (Fish & Brooks, 2004).

America is a nation of diverse groups that has transcended tribal conflicts and has united its citizens with a common purpose of shared values. We have shared the values outlined in our Declaration of Independence and our Constitution, that all men are created equal and are endowed with the rights of life, liberty, and the pursuit of happiness and equal justice under the law. We have shared the vision of the American Dream—that any of us can climb the ladder of economic and social success through hard work and perseverance. These common values have transcended religious, ethnic, and other tribal loyalties. Admittedly, Black people had few chances to share this vision prior to the civil rights movement of the 1960s, and even afterward, they have not had equal opportunities to pursue it.

Unfortunately, today, we have lost much of our national identity. Growing inequities in income, wealth, and social status have led to socioeconomic immobility, and the American Dream seldom becomes a reality. We have digressed into identity politics, in which groups—Blacks, working-class White people, Evangelical Christians, the LGBTQ community, plutocrats and more—advocate their own causes often at the expense of others. Affirmative action, implemented to make up for past inequities, provides a good example how political tribes compete in a zero-sum game. Liberals advocate for affirmative action to help Black people gain admission to college and other institutions at the exclusion of White people.

As we have degenerated into identity politics, our tribal instincts have been unleashed, and there has been growing hostility and sometimes hatred between groups. As we have seen, the tribes defined by identity politics have coalesced into our two major political parties today. Black people and other ethnic minorities, the LGBTQ community, secular America, feminists, college educated professionals, and liberal elites have come together in the Democratic Party, while the White working class, Evangelical Christians, small business owners, and the wealthy elite (plutocrats) have coalesced in the Republican Party. The two parties are now separated by issues of race, religion, and social status, rather than policy issues such as taxes and government spending. These differences are more impassioned than policy issues and have created an intense polarization between the two parties. Each party views the other as an existential threat to its own vision of who and what our country should be. The intense political polarization has caused gridlock in our governance, as each party is intent on preventing the other party from achieving its goals to solve the people's problems. When the electorate believes the government is not solving their problems and meeting their needs, it looks for alternatives. As we have seen, this provides an opportunity for right-wing populist movements, which create a great threat to our democracy.

As utopian as it sounds, if we are to mitigate our tribal instincts, we must change our behavior from the ground up. We must recognize that tribal instincts are part of our DNA, and that they shape our behavior. We should identify and nurture the ways in which we differ from our own tribe, and we should value and relate to human beings independent of their membership to any group. We must be able to forgive transgressions from the other side. No tribal conflict has been resolved without forgiveness and reconciliation.

The history of our country shows that we have been able to transcend our tribal instincts and support our democracy by finding a common vision and identity that unites us all. Let's hope we can recapture that shared identity and come together to save and strengthen our democracy.

Hierarchical and Authoritarian Traits Predispose People to Authoritarian Rule

Recall political scientists Albert Somit and Steven Peterson's (1997) hypothesis that authoritarian regimes have dominated human history because evolution has embedded humans with a predisposition for hierarchically structured social and political systems. Humans have a genetic bias toward hierarchy and authoritarian rule (Corning, 2000).

As we discussed in Chapter 11, psychologist Bob Altemeyer (2006) used an extensive questionnaire to identify an authoritarian personality type. Those with very high scores on the questionnaire have strong authoritarian and racist beliefs and right-wing politics and make up 26% of American society—a far greater percentage than that of other Western countries (Venaglia & Maxwell, 2021). As we discussed in Chapter 5, twin studies have shown that the predisposition to an authoritarian personality appears to have a strong genetic basis (Funk et al., 2012; Ludeke & Krueger, 2013).

Egalitarian traits, which we inherited from our hunter-gatherer ancestors, are also part of our human nature. Individuals with egalitarian personality traits hold that all humans are equal in fundamental worth and moral status. They believe all individuals should have equal social, economic, political, and civil rights. The egalitarian personality, like the authoritarian personality, has a strong genetic basis (Funk et al., 2012; Morin, 2013).

We all harbor a mixture of hierarchical/authoritarian traits and egalitarian traits, but many of us are weighted toward one side or the other. These traits are predispositions that can be modified by our cultural environment. Our early years are dominated by hierarchical relationships with our parents, our teachers, our coaches, and others. As teenagers and young adults, we devote a substantial portion of our lives perceiving status, seeking dominance, and offering submission when necessary. We learn to internalize hierarchy early in life, an experience that may strengthen a genetic bias in support of hierarchy and extend it into adulthood (Van Berkel et al., 2015). In contrast, egalitarian behavior does not usually emerge until late childhood and correlates with cognitive development (Fehr et al., 2008). Psychologists believe that only through cognitive effort can egalitarian traits suppress hierarchical/authoritarian traits (Van Berkel et al., 2015).

Human history has seen many conflicts between our attraction to power and hierarchy and our desire for social parity—conflicts between authoritarian rule and egalitarian democracy. Given the predominantly hierarchical and authoritarian tendencies of our human nature, we can better understand why authoritarian regimes have dominated liberal democracies over the years. We can better understand why 74 million Americans voted for Donald Trump. And we can better understand the great challenges we face in overcoming our innate authoritarian traits as we struggle to save and strengthen our egalitarian democracy.

Herd Mentality, Obedience to Authority, and Peer Pressure

Authoritarian leaders and dictators have exploited human traits to command the obedience of their followers. Adolf Hitler spawned a revolution that devastated the world. How did he do it? How did he convince 70 million rational people to engage in horrible atrocities and wage a brutal war against the world? Scholars have debated this question for decades. Here is part of the answer. Hitler was a master at the science of coercion. Some of his success hinged on his ability to bend the will of ordinary people through speeches and propaganda (Surve, 2008). His inspiration came from French social psychologist Gustave Le Bon, who was an authority on the psychology of crowds (Castello, 2020). Le Bon observed that individuals experience their emotions more intensely and are more suggestible when they are part of a group. A crowd of people can share emotions and become bonded by a common belief, idea, or ideology. The crowd exerts a hypnotic influence over the individual as the individual surrenders their usual self-restraints, sense of personal responsibility, and critical judgment. In other words, the group identity becomes more important than the individual identity. This is herd behavior or mentality, and Hitler was able to steer it toward his ends.

Why does this happen? How does this work? Recall from Chapter 2 that humans have an innate ability to synchronize emotions with other individuals, whether consciously or unconsciously, in a process known as emotional contagion. This happens when we empathize with others and share their emotions. At these times, we have mirror neurons in our brains that activate as if we were performing the same actions or feeling the same emotions ourselves (Wicker et al., 2003).

Emotional contagion can not only synchronize emotions between individuals but also within groups, contributing to herd behavior (Castello, 2020). Behavioral scientists have learned that we humans are equipped with neural and psychological mechanisms that make us receptive to social norms (Kameda & Hastie, 2015). We have an innate tendency to depend on and adopt the suggestions, recommendations, and information obtained from others through social channels. This trait is fundamental to our ability to learn from our culture and has been essential to the advancement of our civilization. It has survived natural selection and the long journey of evolution because it has facilitated learning and cooperation within our societies. Herd mentality is a consequence of this fundamental characteristic of our minds.

Herd behavior is frequently associated with images of mass hysteria, mobs, and panics, and is usually regarded as problematic. It is well-known from its association with malevolent dictators, such as Hitler and Mussolini, who ignited crowds with their passion for nationalistic goals. But herd behavior can also be channeled for good. Franklin D. Roosevelt's 1933 inaugural address ("The only thing we have to fear is fear itself") and Martin Luther King's 1963 "I Have a Dream" speech united their followers with a common purpose, a call to action, and hope for the future. Because leaders have such power to influence a crowd or a nation to adopt their values and purpose through herd behavior, the importance of our choice of leadership cannot be overestimated.

Humans have a natural predisposition to be obedient to authority that is part of the innate hierarchical/authoritarian traits discussed above. As we discussed in Chapter 11, American psychologist Stanley Milgram (1963) performed studies with student volunteers showing that they were inclined to follow orders given by authority figures, even when it violated their conscience. When they saw other student volunteers following orders, peer pressure augmented this inclination. Milgram's experiments show us how difficult it may be to resist orders from a malevolent authority and how difficult it may be to go against the behavior of one's peers. Individuals with authoritarian personalities succumb more easily to these pressures than those with egalitarian personalities, but with enough pressure, most of us will cave (Altemeyer, 2006). It is not too difficult to see the analogy with Nazi Germany.

Herd mentality and obedience to authority and peer pressure—all part of our human nature—have survived the long journey of evolution and are with us today because they have adaptive advantages in helping us work together toward common goals. But they also have a dark side. They can be exploited by malicious leaders to lead us toward a dystopian future and threaten our democracy.

Power Corrupts

Nineteenth-century British historian Lord Acton famously said, "Power tends to corrupt. Absolute power corrupts absolutely" (Shea, 2012). Power and corruption have been partners throughout world history and are with us today, little abated. Corruption divides societies and is toxic to democracy.

There has been increasing attention to governmental corruption on a global scale the past several decades, and there is a broad consensus that corruption is escalating. In 2020, the United States' score on the Corruption Perception Index (CPI) dropped to its lowest level in a decade, and our international ranking dropped to 25th place—meaning there were 24 countries less corrupt than our own (Transparency International, 2020). Not surprisingly, Americans' trust in government hit a historic low of 17% (Pew Research Center, 2019). The social implications of governmental corruption are profound, and it has caused a loss of trust in the institutions essential to our democracy.

Corruption is universal in autocracies and less common, but not absent, in democracies (Pei, 2009). Corruption can be decreased in democracies by seeking institutional reforms that grant heads of state less discretionary power while making them more accountable to the people.

Image 15.1. Power Corrupts. Power tends to amplify underlying personality traits. Those who are selfish and dishonest at baseline will tend to become more corrupt when they attain power than those who are honest and prosocial at baseline. Leaders with more discretionary power are more likely to become corrupt

While there is little argument that power is associated with corruption, does power make an individual corrupt, or do corrupt individuals seek and obtain power?

Investigators at the University of Lausanne in Switzerland attempted to answer this question. They divided participants into a number of groups to play what they called a dictator game (Antonakis, 2014; Bendahan et al., 2014). They selected a leader or dictator for each group who had a pot of real money to distribute to the team. The default distribution gave the leader slightly more money than the followers. The leader could also choose the prosocial option, in which the leader received less and the followers more, or the selfish option, in which the leader took much more and gave the followers much less. Some leaders were given more power (more options for money distribution and three loyal followers) and other leaders less (fewer options for money distribution and only one loyal follower). The study found that leaders who were given more power acted in the most selfish ways—allotting more money for themselves. The study also found that individuals who exhibited predominantly selfish and antisocial traits prior to the experiment (as assessed by questionnaires) were more likely to become corrupt, and in a sub-study, young males with high testosterone levels were also much more likely to become corrupt (Bendahan et al., 2014).

This and other studies show that power tends to unleash corrupt behavior that is hidden in all of us, but not everyone becomes equally corrupt. Power tends to amplify the underlying personality traits of the individual. People who are more selfish and dishonest will tend to become more corrupt, while those who are honest and prosocial will be less likely to become corrupt (Image 15.1).

The innate desire for power in many humans and the ability of that power to corrupt put democracies at great risk. If a leader with a genetic predisposition to having an authoritarian personality and being a social dominator comes to power through democratic means, that leader will be more likely to drift into authoritarian rule and corruption (Altemeyer, 2006).

How We Think and Make Decisions

Israeli psychologist and economist Daniel Kahneman (2011), recipient of the Nobel Prize for economics, in his transformative book *Thinking, Fast and*

Slow introduced a novel paradigm about how our brain makes decisions. He maintains that most of our decisions and behavior in response to events are intuitive or instinctive, with little conscious reasoning. These reactions are like algorithms operating subconsciously in response to specific stimuli.

Kahneman explains our brains evolved this intuitive thinking—"thinking fast"—because it provides a survival benefit. There was an evolutionary advantage for our ancient ancestors to act quickly and intuitively to avoid predators and other environmental dangers. If we hear rustling in the grass, we don't go through a slow process of reasoning to determine if it is the wind or a dangerous predator. Rather, we hear the rustling in the grass, and we react quickly with fear and flee. Intuitive reactions are often associated with emotions that motivate animals and humans to focus attention on a stimulus and to respond quickly. Intuitive responses are a product of evolution and are hardwired in our genes.

Kahneman describes a second thought process, which he calls "thinking slow," as a conscious, deliberate process of rational thinking leading to a decision or action. Our rational thought seeks to acquire new knowledge and understandings of our world through cognitive analysis of experience and data, and it uses this knowledge and understanding to make decisions. Unfortunately, this slow process does not make most of our decisions. Most of our rational thinking is used to justify positions and decisions formed through subconscious intuitive thinking, despite the fact that these intuitive decisions are often wrong. Scottish philosopher David Hume notoriously said, "Reason is and ought to be only the slave of the passions" (Nuyun, 1984). We react intuitively and emotionally and then justify our actions rationally.

Kahneman calls the processes by which decisions are made quickly and subconsciously without rational input "heuristics." We often refer to the heuristic approach as relying on our gut feeling, common sense, or intuition. Heuristics solve problems and make decisions based on previous experiences with similar problems, rather than theory. They are an approach to learning and problem solving that is not guaranteed to be optimal or correct, but they do speed up the process of finding satisfactory solutions, and they do ease the cognitive load of making decisions.

Kahneman's ideas provide a new paradigm. We are far less rational and far less correct in our decisions and beliefs than we think we are. The heuristic process by which we make unconscious decisions is subject to cognitive bias and often leads to wrong choices. When we interview a candidate for a position in our organization, studies have shown that we usually make a decision about whether to hire them within the first 10 minutes (Groenewegen, 2021). What happens here? We make quick, mostly unconscious judgments, based on our mental heuristics. If the person's demeanor, character, and background are similar to our own, we instantly like them. If the person is well groomed and appropriately dressed, we feel that they are responsible and will fit in. If the person wears glasses, we suspect they may be smart. We form an initial impression based primarily on these subconscious intuitive reactions and then reaffirm these initial impressions with rational support and justification.

Kahneman helps us understand that human decision-making, for the most part, is not rational. This explains why it is so difficult to resolve our differences through rational discussions—especially during these times of immense political polarity. If we are liberals discussing an issue with conservative counterparts, and we realize that we all make decisions that, for the most part, are based on genetic predispositions and intuitive reactions, rather than rational thinking, we can understand how difficult it is to find common ground.

Psychologist Jonathan Haidt (2012) in his book *The Righteous Mind* also argues that our decisions and actions are fundamentally made through intuitive processes and not through rational thinking. His basic thesis of moral psychology is that "Intuitions come first, strategic reasoning second." We are emotional actors who act first from intuition, and *after* the fact, we work overtime to provide rational justification for our actions. Our minds are more like lawyers defending a client's position than like scientists trying to find the truth.

In this age of intense political polarization, we retreat into our tribes and are fixed in our beliefs. We cannot appreciate why our adversaries feel as they do. We have difficulty understanding why our rational arguments have little or no success in swaying their views. To provide an example from politics, a conservative may have the intuitive position that unregulated capitalism and competition provide the best opportunity for economic growth that will benefit all. A liberal may argue that unfettered capitalism has created great socioeconomic inequities that degrade the poor and pose a great threat to our democracy. The conservative will weigh in with arguments that there has never been a period of prosperity in the world greater than today and those at the bottom have the opportunity to rise to the middle class and beyond. It becomes clear that rational arguments will not be able to penetrate the intuitive values of either side.

Once we recognize that our opponent's views are based on innate predispositions and intuition, rather than rational thinking (just like our own), we can understand why rational arguments have little chance of changing their minds. Democracies function through rational discussions, debate, and compromise. Unfortunately, the way we make decisions through intuition is not conducive to the democratic process. We need to begin thinking slow. We need to use a conscious, deliberate process of rational thought to lead us to decisions and actions that make our democracy work.

Haidt (2012) believes we can make progress. When we understand how each of us arrived at our beliefs, we can better empathize with one another and may be able to have a rational exchange. We certainly won't agree on everything, but maybe we can find areas of common ground and achieve greater tolerance. As Haidt suggests, "We're all stuck here for a while, so let's try to work it out."

Human Nature and Autocracy Versus Democracy

We have seen that much of our human nature predisposes us to autocratic rule. Many of us have authoritarian personalities that incline us to be obedient to authority figures and to embrace hierarchical societies, in which some groups are dominant over other groups. We all have some genetic predisposition to succumb to conspiracy theories, participate in herd mentality, and be influenced by peer pressure, and these traits make us vulnerable to authoritarian leaders. We all have selfish traits and tribal instincts that make it difficult for us to cooperate with one another, especially with those who differ from us in religion, race, socioeconomic status, and politics.

While the dark side of our human nature predisposes us to support an autocratic society, we have a brighter side that gives us great hope in our struggle to save and strengthen our egalitarian democracy. Many of us have genetic predispositions to support a society that upholds the equality of all human beings and fosters the common good. We are highly social animals, and our human nature has evolved to enable us to cooperate with one another far better than any other species on the planet. This has allowed us to build the great civilizations we have today. Deep within us, we have an innate morality that values love and respect for human life, honesty, fairness, empathy, compassion, and altruism, while condemning murder, theft, dishonesty, deception, corruption, and hypocrisy. Our moral code guides us toward good (cooperative) behavior and away from bad (selfish) behavior. Our morality evolved to help us cooperate with one another in our large societies, and this has provided us a major adaptive advantage.

To help protect society against selfish behavior, we have evolved social emotions that reward cooperative behavior and discourage selfish behavior. If I resuscitate a fallen stranger from cardiac arrest and save a life, I feel a sense of great pride. If a stranger gives me water when I am thirsty, I feel gratitude. If a biochemist invents a drug that saves many lives, we all feel great admiration. Alternatively, if I shoplift two apples from the grocery store, I feel guilt. If my co-workers repeatedly leave extra work for me to do, I feel contempt for them. These social emotions steer us toward cooperative, prosocial behavior.

We should also be encouraged by knowing that human nature, through the coevolution of culture and biology, is slowly becoming more cooperative, a trend that should continue into the future. While the evolution of human nature may be too slow to help us in the short term, we may be able to bring out more of our cooperative instincts and the better side of our human nature in the near term by creating the proper cultural environment. We will address this in the next chapter.

CULTURE SHAPES HUMAN BEHAVIOR

It is impossible to overlook the extent to which civilization is built upon a renunciation of instinct.

—Sigmund Freud, ***Civilization and Its Discontents***

As we have discussed, humans have evolved innate behavioral traits that guide our behavior—this is our human nature. But our material and cultural environment also shape our behavior. If we have no food, and our family is starving, we may steal from our neighbor, but if we have an abundance of food, we may share with our neighbor. In this chapter we will discuss how cultural evolution has transcended biological evolution, how cultural and biological evolution have coevolved, and how this coevolution has created a more cooperative human nature. We will examine how the current cultural environment in America is shaping our behavior—for both good and bad.

Cultural Evolution Transcends Biological Evolution

About 70,000 years ago, our hunter-gatherer ancestors began a transformation that would distinguish our species from all other animals— the evolution of human culture. Humans began to communicate through language and build and use complex and intricate tools—arrows for hunting, needles for sewing, boats for navigating. They began to create art, practice religion, and engage in trade with other tribes. They coalesced into groups and formed larger societies. They shared and accumulated information, skills, and technology, and over time, each society evolved its own distinctive culture. Each culture consists of the collective sum of its language, religion, values, customs, politics, technology, skills, government, institutions, and characteristics shared by its members. Society's culture is its way of life. The many disparities that we see among the diverse human societies on our planet today are due to differences in culture, not genetics. We are all *Homo sapiens*, and the genetic and biological differences between any of us, regardless of differences in our ethnicities or our societies, are actually quite small. We are, to a large extent, defined by our culture.

A number of forces came together to drive the evolution of human culture. Our linguistic capacity gave us an unparalleled ability to communicate with one another and to pass and store information and knowledge. We learned how to cooperate with one another through indirect reciprocity that far surpassed the abilities of other species. Our cultural evolution evolved rapidly through the Agricultural Revolution, the Industrial Revolution, and the current Technological and Digital Revolution. Cultural evolution and technological evolution have transcended the slow pace of biological evolution and are now the driving forces of change.

Since Darwin's time, social scientists have explored analogies between cultural and biological evolution in attempts to better understand how culture evolves. Richard Dawkins (1976) in *The Selfish Gene* proposed a model for cultural evolution in which the transmittable units of culture, analogous to genes, are called memes. Memes are discrete ideas, beliefs, and behaviors that spread throughout society, from brain to brain. Examples of memes are songs, fashions, scientific theories, religious beliefs, economic systems, and types of government. But while memes are similar to genes in some ways, they are transmitted quite differently. Genes are transmitted vertically from parents to offspring through the union of sperm and egg, while memes, being abstractions, can in theory be transmitted linguistically to anyone. They can be passed vertically, like genes, from parent to child, but a child can also receive memes laterally, from siblings, friends, and teachers or from radio, TV, books, video games, newspapers, and social media. Genes are transferred as precisely defined information, albeit sometimes with mutations. Memes, on the other hand, are more often altered or modified by transmission.

There is an important caveat in the analogy between biological and cultural evolution. In biological evolution, random mutations provide a variety of characteristics in offspring, and those best adapted to the environment survive, reproduce, and pass their genes to the next generation. Variations in offspring are due to random chance mutations and are not self-directed. In contrast, the generation of new memes is not random. The human brain is capable of inventing new ideas, methods, and products, and in doing so we create new memes that shape the evolution of our culture. The search for new sources of renewable energy to decrease the carbon imprint on our planet, for example, is self-directed and has begun to move our culture toward solar and wind energy. The ideas and initiatives of individuals and groups drive much if not most of our cultural evolution. And as culture has become the main force of change, we have hope that we may have some control over the future direction of life on our planet.

The Coevolution of Culture and Biology

As human societies create and evolve their own unique cultures, they transform their environment. As their environment changes and evolves, human biology must then also adapt. Cultural and biological evolution are intertwined and deeply affect one another—they coevolve.

A classic example of cultural evolution triggering a change in biological evolution occurred about 11,000 years ago, during the Agricultural Revolution (Richerson & Boyd, 2005). For the first time, domesticated animals introduced milk into the diet of adult humans. We were not initially equipped to handle this. When we are born, most of us have an intestinal enzyme called lactase, which helps us digest the sugar lactose that is abundant in our mother's milk. But because breast milk is a temporary food source for us all, this enzyme typically disappears from our guts after weaning—which means that many adults simply cannot digest lactose-rich milk. However, many of us today digest milk just fine because our forebearers, at the time of the Agricultural Revolution, adapted and evolved a lactase enzyme in their guts that persisted into adulthood. The Agricultural Revolution and the domestication of animals, which altered our diet, changed the biology of our guts.

The coevolution of biology and culture has introduced a new paradigm in evolution (Richerson & Boyd, 2005). We have some control over the evolution of our culture, which shapes our environment, and we and the rest of life on our planet must adapt to this new environment in order to survive and reproduce. By shaping our culture and environment, we have some influence over how our biology evolves.

Human Nature Is Becoming More Cooperative—But Slowly

Biologist Peter Richerson and anthropologist Robert Boyd in their paradigm-changing book *Not by Genes Alone: How Culture Transformed Human Evolution* have described how the coevolution of culture and biology has been responsible for the high level of cooperation in our societies (Boyd & Richerson, 2009; Richerson & Boyd, 2005). As humans came together in social groups, they established cultures with moral standards and norms that rewarded individuals with cooperative, prosocial behavior and punished individuals with selfish, antisocial behavior. This gave cooperative individuals a survival and reproductive advantage over antisocial individuals, and these cooperative individuals were more likely to pass their prosocial cooperative traits to the next generation. Cooperative individuals in the next generation could then create a culture with a stronger moral code that encouraged more cooperative behavior. Culture and human nature coevolved, a process that continues today.

As we have seen, cooperative behavior also evolves through group selection. Groups with a strong moral code that encourages prosocial behavior and cooperation among members will have an advantage over groups with less internal cooperation. When these groups compete against one another, the group with more internal cooperation prevails and passes the cooperative genes of its members to subsequent generations. Many nation-states have failed in the course of human history because of internal divisions and poor cooperation among its citizens (Acemoglu & Robinson, 2012).

While many believe biological evolution, including human nature, has slowed over recent millennia, the opposite is actually true. Human biological evolution has accelerated over the last 5,000 years. About 7% of our gene pool are new genes that have evolved over this time period, a rate about 100 times the previous rate of evolutionary change (Hawks et. al, 2007). The acceleration of biological evolution is certainly related to the need to adapt to the rapid changes in our environment due to the explosion of cultural evolution. Despite this acceleration, the pace of biological evolution pales against the rapid pace of cultural evolution (Perreault, 2012). It may take many generations and many millennia for meaningful biological changes in the cooperative side of our human nature to occur. If we are to shape our behavior in the shorter term to become more cooperative individuals, we will need to do so through changes to our cultural environment.

Nation-States and the Rule of Law Have Shaped Our Behavior

Most of us have the perception that the world is becoming a more violent and cruel place. We are bombarded with 24/7 cable news and social media coverage that highlights violence and conflict. We are shown repeated episodes of gun violence and mass shootings in the United States, genocide against ethnic Rohingya Muslims in Myanmar, the horrific civil war in Syria, the Russian invasion of Ukraine and the accompanying indiscriminate killing of civilians, and so much more. This gives us the impression that things are getting worse, and it is easy to become pessimistic about our future. But the news selectively covers violence, suffering, and world conflict and may give us a biased picture.

Psychologist Steven Pinker (2011) in his extensively researched book *The Better Angels of Our Nature: Why Violence Has Declined* describes how changes in our cultural and material environment have changed human behavior for the better. He describes, surprisingly to many, how our world has become less violent, less cruel, and more humane over the past millennia. Archaeological studies of gravesites have found that the proportion of people dying violent deaths from murder or tribal conflict was much greater among hunter-gatherers than in agricultural and industrial societies. This trend has continued, and the frequency of death from violent causes since World War II has reached an all-time low. Pinker attributes this decline to changes in our culture. Paramount is the rise of nation-states and their monopoly on the legitimate use of power to control violence and maintain the rule of law (Image 16.1). Pinker calls this the "pacification process," which has improved the well-being of everyone living under nation-states.

Seventeenth-century English philosopher Thomas Hobbes (2011) makes similar arguments in his classic book *Leviathan*, in which he professes that without the control of a state, life would be nasty, brutish, and short and would decline into anarchy. There are many examples of failed states that have met this fate. When a government can no longer provide basic security for its people due to a rise in violence or extreme poverty, or when it loses control over part of its territory to domestic or foreign terrorist groups, the state has failed. Recent examples include Somalia, Yemen, Syria, Libya, and Afghanistan. Failed states not only impoverish their citizens but, by providing natural breeding grounds for international terrorists, are a great threat to global security and stability.

Image 16.1. Law and Order. Surprisingly to many, our world has become less violent over the past millennia. Psychologist Steven Pinker attributes this to the rise of nation-states and the legitimate use of power to maintain rule of law to control violence (Pinker, 2011). Cultural environment can greatly influence our behavior

Commerce and Trade and the Empowerment of Women Shape Our Behavior

While the rule of law provided by nation-states may be the biggest reason for changes in behavior and the decline in violence, Pinker cites several other factors (2011). He believes the rise in commerce, both domestic and international, has contributed to pacification. We realize that we can gain more by cooperation with other nations than by conflict. As we become more connected and dependent upon one another, violence against one another becomes more counterproductive.

Pinker (2011, pp. 684–689) argues that the empowerment of women has also had a pacifying influence. Violence is mainly committed by men. From the time they are boys, males play more violent games, consume more violent entertainment, and as they grow older, commit the great majority of violent crimes and are the major initiators and participants in war. As women assume a greater role in society, violence has declined. Nations with greater gender equality—as measured by such metrics as the percentage of women in the labor force, the percentage of women in government, the duration of woman suffrage, and fertility rates—have less domestic and international violence than nations with less gender equality (Caprioli, 2000; Crespo-Sancho, 2018). The low levels of violence in the democracies of Western Europe, which champion women's rights, contrasts with higher levels of violence in the Sharia states of Islamic Africa and Asia.

A Japanese draftsman for Mitsubishi Heavy Industries, Tsutomu Yamaguchi, provided a unique perspective on gender and violence. He survived the 1945 nuclear bombing of Hiroshima, fled to Nagasaki, and survived that city's bombing as well three days later. He passed away in 2010 at the age of 93. Before he died, he offered a prescription for peace in the nuclear age: "The only people who should be allowed to govern countries with nuclear weapons are mothers, those who are still breast-feeding their babies" (Pinker, 2011, p. 684). We are a long way from that, but the empowerment of women should make peace more prevalent.

The Enlightenment Fueled Progress

Pinker provides convincing evidence about the great progress we have made in human rights and the human condition over the past two centuries (Pinker, 2011). Global extreme poverty has been reduced from 90% to 10%, global primary school enrollment has increased from 17% to 80%, and global literacy rates have risen from 12% to 83%. The United States abolished slavery in 1865, gave women the right to vote in 1920, passed the Civil Rights Act in 1964, and passed the Voting Rights Act in 1965. Average longevity in the United States has increased from 49 to 79 years over the last century. These are just a few of the metrics of progress. While there is so much more to be done, these improvements are impressive.

Pinker gives much credit for this progress to changes in our culture that occurred during the Enlightenment. This intellectual and philosophical movement in seventeenth- and eighteenth-century England and Europe brought an awakening of reason, science, and humanism. Killings such as human sacrifices, witch hunts, and inquisitions were mostly eliminated as advancing knowledge and science overturned superstitions supporting their practice. People began to look disdainfully at forms of violence that had previously been taken for granted, such as slavery and extreme forms of cruel punishment. Pinker and others have referred to this as the "humanitarian revolution." This also brought more tolerance for those in outside groups, fostering revulsion against violence inflicted on ethnic minorities, gay people, women, children, and animals. While anti-violence movements have not achieved all their goals, we have come a long way from the days when the lynching of Black people was commonplace in America's South and domestic violence was tolerated to such a degree that a 1950s magazine ad could show a husband with his wife over his knee, spanking her for failing to bring home his preferred brand of coffee (Singer, 2011).

As our powers of rational and abstract thinking continued to improve following the Enlightenment, we became able to detach ourselves from our immediate experiences and our own parochial perspectives and think in more universal terms. The expansion of global commerce, travel, and communication has further expanded our views. With this increased exposure, we can more easily identify and empathize with others who are different from us, broadening our moral perspective. It is easier for us to treat others as we would like to be treated, even if they are different. This wider perspective and tighter connection to others has expanded our tribal boundaries.

Political and Economic Institutions Shape Behavior

Economists Daron Acemoglu and James Robinson (2012) make the case in *Why Nations Fail* that nations decline and break down when political and economic institutions benefit the elite and no longer support the common good. The authors distinguish between inclusive and extractive political and economic institutions. Inclusive political institutions are democracies with broad public participation in governance; inclusive economic institutions provide rule of law, protection of property rights, incentives for innovation and production, and a level playing field. Extractive political institutions are authoritarian regimes controlled by an individual or a small group of elites; extractive economic institutions are structured such that wealth and resources are corruptly taken from the public for the benefit of the elite.

A nation's institutions and the social environments that they create greatly influence the behavior of a nation's populace. Inclusive political institutions represented by egalitarian democracies provide the populace with a sense of control and the ability to make changes, and inclusive economic institutions provide incentives for innovation, hard work, and cooperation and offer hope for a better life. On the other hand, extractive political institutions represented by authoritarian regimes provide the populace with little control and little chance to make change, and extractive economic institutions set the rules to benefit the elite, who draw wealth and resources from the populace. Without property rights and rule of law, there are few incentives for innovation, hard work, and investment in the future, without which sustained economic growth is not possible. Extractive institutions bring out our selfish and tribal instincts and create great resentment and polarity in society.

Unfortunately, our country's political and economic institutions are becoming more extractive.

Racial and Socioeconomic Inequities Unleash Our Inner Demons

Steven Pinker highlights how changes in our culture can shape our behavior in a positive way, but the U.S. and other Western democracies are facing cultural changes that negatively influence the behavior of their citizens. The twin demons of racial and socioeconomic inequities divide our society, polarize our politics, and undermine our egalitarian democracy. These cultural afflictions bring out our tribal instincts and provide major obstacles to intergroup cooperation.

While we have made much progress in civil rights and racial equity, America is still largely segregated. Black people and other ethnic minorities face a litany of discriminatory policies in labor, housing, education, healthcare, voting, justice, and more. Structural racism persists today to some degree in every institution in America. It has infiltrated and polarized our politics and continues to threaten our democracy.

The White supremacy movement has surfaced in our country over the last decade or more and has become our greatest domestic terrorist threat. A minority of our White citizens regard Black people and other ethnic minorities as inferior and treat them with contempt. This is the worst of our tribal instincts.

As we have discussed in Chapter 9, large democracies with great racial diversity have been more fragile and less successful throughout history than smaller democracies with more homogeneous ethnic populations (Fish & Brooks, 2004). If our democracy is to survive and flourish, we must address this cancer which divides our nation. We must mitigate structural racism and make progress in overcoming our prejudice toward ethnic minority groups.

As we discussed in Chapter 10, growing social and economic inequities resulting from globalization, technological change, unfettered capitalism, and the selfish greed of Wall Street and corporate elites have created great divisions in our society. Such great income and wealth inequities are morally wrong and are the antithesis of egalitarian democracy. They have stoked social discontent and political polarization, and they have given rise to divisive right-wing populist nationalism that threatens our democracy. Without some resolution of the great wealth and income inequities in our country, cooperation across diverse groups and national solidarity may be out of reach. Cultural changes to mitigate the twin scourges of systemic racism and socioeconomic inequities appear to be prerequisites to salvaging our democracy.

Social Media Polarizes Our Politics and Threatens Our Democracy

When Facebook was introduced in 2006, its mission was to make the world more connected. This connectivity was believed to be good for personal relationships and for democracy. As Facebook grew, it made design changes attempting to improve user experience, altering the way news and posts were distributed throughout the platform. It added a Like button, providing a metric for popularity of content, and created algorithms that determined which posts a user would see based on the user's profile and previous likes. Facebook added a Share button and Twitter included a Retweet button to allow the wide distribution of information or disinformation to followers of followers of followers.

Facebook and other social media outlets have provided great benefits in connecting friends and family, but unfortunately, bad actors have used these platforms in unforeseen ways with negative societal repercussions. Facebook has long faced criticism for failing to restrict the flow of disinformation and conspiracy theories, which grab the most attention on its platform. The platform's algorithms propagate such content widely because it generates greater engagement and has larger potential to make money through advertising revenue (Porter, 2021). Facebook has made attempts to screen for toxic content, but these have been inconsistent and not very effective.

Authoritarian regimes have used social media to incite hatred, violence, and genocide abroad. Myanmar's military used Facebook posts to foment hate against the country's Muslim Rohingya minority group, leading to displacement and genocide. Autocratic leaders in Honduras and Azerbaijan have used fake social media accounts to attack opponents and the independent news media. Facebook has been used during Ethiopia's civil war to stoke violence. Multiple foreign political leaders have misled their citizenry and attacked their opponents with social media (Bouie, 2020). And there is much more.

Facebook has facilitated a number of activities that undermine our democracy. Prior to the 2016 presidential election, Russia's Internet Research Agency set up fake accounts on all social media platforms and posted disinformation and material that inflamed partisan divisions (Haidt & Rose-Stockwell, 2019). Also leading up to the 2016 presidential election, Cambridge Analytica, a political consulting firm, harvested data of about 87 million Facebook users without their consent. These data were used to provide analytical assistance to the presidential campaigns of Ted Cruz and Donald Trump. This breach of privacy was revealed and prosecuted; Facebook was heavily fined, and Cambridge Analytica went bankrupt.

Humans thrive when they have strong, positive face-to-face relationships with other humans. Online social relationships may not be so positive. Investigators at the University of California, San Diego, and Yale studied the relationship between Facebook use and well-being (Shakya & Christakis, 2017). They found that high Facebook use was associated with a reduction in self-reported physical health, mental health, and life satisfaction. The reasons for this are not entirely clear but may be related to negative comparisons with other users and to time spent away from more meaningful real-life social relationships. It is clear that online social relationships are no substitute for face-to-face interaction.

Instagram has similar problems. Facebook whistleblower Frances Haugen testified before Congress in October 2021 that Facebook was putting Instagram users in danger in pursuit of profits. Leaking internal communications and research performed by Facebook, she provided evidence that Instagram use by teenage girls posed risks to mental health, including suicidal thoughts and eating disorders. The most common themes were loss of self-esteem and body image issues related to comparisons with other users (Romo, 2021).

Haugen also described in her testimony before Congress and in an interview on *60 Minutes* how Facebook promotes divisive and extremist content to users who do not search for it. Experimental researchers created new accounts with no friends and no activity except for becoming a follower of Donald Trump, and in a short time their page was inundated with right-wing content, hate speech, and disinformation, including content related to QAnon and White supremacy. Facebook algorithms search out and disseminate extreme posts to right-wing and conservative users because they generate great engagement and high advertising revenues. These algorithms and the content they propagate contribute to the radicalization of users (Porter, 2021).

There is a widespread belief that social media has fueled political polarization in this country. While we can all agree that it doesn't bear sole responsibility—polarization began long before Facebook—political polarization has certainly gotten worse in recent years (Barrett et al., 2021). Facebook's content-ranking algorithms limit users' exposure to material contrary to their political viewpoints and enhance users' exposure to subject matter that aligns with their political profile. When individuals on the right share their perspectives with one another, their opinions are strengthened, and they move further to the right. The same process happens on the left. Members of each group feel loyalty to the group and hostility toward members of the opposing group. The groups become highly polarized and tribal. Siva Vaidhyanathan (2018) in her book *Antisocial Media: How Facebook Disconnects Us and Undermines Democracy* warns that "Facebook is the worst possible forum through which we should conduct our politics." The messages that grab the most attention on social media are those that are highly charged with emotion and highly polarizing—not rational arguments. In this era of social messaging, political partisanship trumps statesmanship, and divisive rhetoric trumps policymaking (Carr, 2018).

The political polarization enhanced by social media unleashes our tribal instincts and poses a great threat to our democracy. It paralyzes progress on social and economic issues because there is little or no compromise and the party out of power is intent on obstruction. When there is no progress on issues important to the public, the electorate will look for alternatives, and authoritarian leaders will be ready to fill the void.

Conclusion

We began this chapter with the premise that our behavior is guided by our human nature but is shaped by our cultural environment. We examined how our current cultural environment is shaping our behavior. Many aspects of our culture—the rise of nation-states and the rule of law, the empowerment of women, advancements in commerce and trade, new cultural perspectives from the Enlightenment, and the development of inclusive institutions—have brought out the better side of our human nature and have reduced violence and enhanced communication and cooperation. Other aspects of our culture—systemic racism, social and economic inequities, extractive institutions, and some parts of social media—have unleashed our tribal instincts and have created great divisions and polarity within our society. In the next chapter, we will discuss how we might modify and change our cultural environment to allow us to tame our tribal instincts, heal our divisions, and come together with a common purpose and a national identity that will allow us to restore and strengthen our democracy.

CHAPTER 17
WHERE ARE WE GOING?

At the higher level of biological organization, groups compete with groups, favoring cooperative social traits among members of the same group. At the lower level, members of the same group compete with one another in a manner that leads to self-serving behavior. This opposition between the two levels of natural selection has resulted in a chimeric genotype in each person. It renders each of us part saint and part sinner.

—E. O. Wilson, The Social Conquest of Earth (2012)

Where are we going? What is the future of our democracy? In this chapter we will examine what we can do to overcome our tribal and selfish instincts and what major cultural changes are needed to overcome our divisions and to facilitate cooperative behavior. We will discuss how addressing our racial and economic inequities and initiating a change in attitudes will be required to preserve and strengthen our democracy and to prevail over the forces of autocracy.

Addressing Socioeconomic Inequities

Darren Walker, president of the Ford Foundation, has a unique perspective on inequality in America. He began life as the son of a single Black mother mired in poverty in Louisiana, but he found his way to the top. In an editorial in *The New York Times* entitled "Are You Willing to Give Up Your Privilege?" he explains that inequality in America was neither born of the market's invisible hand nor an unavoidable destiny (Walker, 2020). It was created by the sustained effort of capitalists who engineered benefits for themselves at the expense of everyone else, one expensive lobbyist and policy change at a time. He argues it will take a concerted effort to reverse this.

Walker believes the boardroom elite are beginning to realize that unfairly structured incentives have distorted our economy and that our income and wealth inequities are existential threats that have stretched our republic to a breaking point. Those of us who are the beneficiaries of a system that perpetuates inequality will need to be ready to give something up. Change will not come easily. We will need to surrender the tax policies that bolster our wealth, the system of legacy admissions at American colleges, the expectation that we are entitled to a place at the front of the line, and much more. We will need to change the rules of capitalism to provide a level playing field for all. Corporations must no longer view profits as their primary objective but rather work for the benefit of all stakeholders—customers, employees, suppliers, communities, and shareholders. We must provide a broader social safety net that provides affordable medical care for all, free education, including preschool and community college or college, retirement benefits, and equal opportunities for all.

Those of us at the top must be willing to give up our privilege. If we believe as Walker does that our great income and wealth inequities are an existential threat to our democracy and our way of life, this may give us great incentive for change.

Addressing Structural Racism

We have made much progress in addressing racial inequities since the onset of the civil rights movement, but we still have much work to do. The American Civil Liberties Union (ACLU) has taken the position that systemic racism requires systemic solutions (Moore & Brooks, 2021). From this perspective, the solutions for systemic racism overlap those for income and wealth inequality and should provide equal rights and opportunities for all. These changes should include free education, including preschool and college for those who qualify academically, affordable healthcare, and a higher minimum wage. Minority ethnic groups' voting rights should be protected through legal challenges to voter suppression and through legislation, including passage of the John R. Lewis Voting Rights Advancement Act, which would restore the Justice Department's authority to block discriminatory voting changes by the states. New legislation should dismantle barriers to fair housing. Broadband internet should be made available and affordable for all households, especially in rural regions. The child tax credit should be extended and enhanced to lift millions of Black children out of poverty. Public and private programs should be initiated to provide support for Black-owned businesses, including removing institutional barriers, enabling better access to capital, and providing support through knowledge and mentorship (Baboolall et al., 2021). These actions may seem radical to conservatives, but we have a moral responsibility to live up to our country's mantra that all people should have equal rights and opportunities, and we should realize the preservation of our democracy may depend on healing our racial divide.

This may be a delicate balancing act as we try to address racial inequities without alienating the White working class. Solutions to racial and socioeconomic inequities must be done in a fair and balanced way.

What can we do individually to combat systemic racism? We must first admit there is a problem (Wright, 2019). We each need to learn about the history of slavery and the Jim Crow South and develop an understanding that racism is systemic in all our institutions. With this perspective, we can better see the world through the eyes of Black people and empathize with their feelings and perspective.

We all have tribal instincts, which means we all have some racism within us. Examine yourself and understand your own prejudices. Adopt a zero tolerance attitude toward racism. Challenge cruel jokes or offhand comments degrading people of color. Silence condones such behavior. Step out of your comfort zone and involve yourself in activities that put you in an environment with people of diverse ethnic backgrounds. Finally, vote in every election and support candidates that promote the inclusion of all peoples.

As a large nation with great ethnic diversity, our democracy is at risk. Ethnic conflict can erode the sense of solidarity and common purpose so essential for successful democracies. Racial divisions are the antithesis of egalitarian societies and have been a stain on our democracy since its beginning. Addressing the problem of systemic racism in America is not only our moral responsibility: it may be a prerequisite for the preservation of our democracy.

Overcoming Tribal Instincts

Harvard psychology professor Daniel Shapiro (2017) advocates that the best way to overcome tribal instincts and loyalties is to establish a common identity with a larger group—a larger tribe—for a greater cause. The need to connect with something greater than ourselves is part of our human nature and gives us a sense of grand purpose. It is part of who we are as social animals. Events and movements can sometimes bring together diverse peoples with a common identity and purpose, forming new larger groups that are able to transcend smaller tribes and their parochial instincts (Institute for InterGroup Understanding, 2021). People come together when they perceive a common enemy or feel a sense of danger. We saw this after the attack on Pearl Harbor, when America unified to fight the aggression of Imperial Japan and Nazi Germany in World War II. We also saw this briefly after the 9/11 attacks. Unfortunately, this unity did not last. There has been hope that the threat of damage and disruption from climate change would bring together nations and the diverse groups within them to meet the challenge. So far, little has changed.

America is unique. We once had a common identity through shared values that transcended racial, religious, and socioeconomic groups. We all held the common values affirmed in our Declaration of Independence and Constitution that all men are created equal. America was the land of opportunity. We all shared the American Dream that anyone can achieve success with hard work and perseverance. But today, the American Dream has faded, and many at the bottom of our society have lost hope.

America's best hope of achieving a common identity and overcoming our tribal behavior may be through the restoration of the American Dream. The two biggest obstacles to accomplishing this are our widening income and wealth inequities and systemic racism. If we can address these inequities and restore the American Dream, we can bring hope to the poor and bring our nation together with a common identity and purpose. When people no longer feel alienated from the establishment, when they feel they have opportunities and hope for a better future, and when they feel they are contributing members of society, they will become part of a larger identity that includes all Americans. Their tribal instincts based on race, religion, socioeconomic status, and politics will fade. Maybe once again we can cooperate with one another across the political aisle and address the existential problems that threaten our nation and the world.

We should be encouraged by the expansion of tribal boundaries over the long journey of human history. Our hunter-gatherer ancestors lived in small tribes that included only about 100 individuals, while today, our nation-states include millions of people who work together on so many issues. Admittedly, nation-states have multiple tribes within their borders based on race, religion, socioeconomic class, politics, and more, but having these tribes under one roof provides opportunities for the creation of a common identity and purpose.

What can we do individually to mitigate our tribal instincts? Tribal instincts are part of us all, and we must understand how destructive they are to us as individuals and to society. Much of our tribal behavior today is related to the rivalry between our two political parties. When we discuss an issue with an acquaintance from the other party, we are frustrated that our rational arguments have little success in changing their minds. We must understand that their positions on issues are made through intuition and not rational thinking, and these positions are reinforced by party loyalty. Once we have a greater awareness of why those in the other party believe and behave as they do, we can better empathize with them. We can bridge the gap with members of the opposite party by finding shared values and common interests and using these to develop and enhance personal relationships. We need to make an effort to eliminate the vitriol and personal attacks against one another. We cannot directly control the behavior of those in opposing tribes, but we can lead by example. We must agree on core values of behavior—good will, inclusion, and honesty—that should govern our behavior inside and outside our party. If we demonstrate this positive behavior toward those in the other party, with time they may react in kind. We need to develop a mentality in which we want each other to succeed and collectively achieve the American Dream.

Empowerment of Women

As we learned in Chapter 5, our two closest relatives, chimpanzees and bonobos, have different social structures that may give us some insights about the empowerment of women in our own society. Chimpanzees have a male-dominated, hierarchical society led by an alpha male. They have violent behavior against members of their own troop and against members of neighboring troops. Bonobos are a gentler, kinder brand of ape with a female-dominated, egalitarian society (Angier, 1997; de Waal & Lanting, 1997). They are less aggressive, less violent, and less obsessed with power.

Perhaps women should play a larger role in our societies. They are more empathetic, less hierarchical, less tribal, and less violent than men. They are much less likely to have authoritarian personality traits and more likely to support an egalitarian society (Lee et al., 2011).

Would the world be more peaceful if women were in charge? The evidence suggests so. As we discussed in the last chapter, studies have shown that countries with greater gender equality have less internal violence, less international violence, and increased internal stability and security (Caprioli, 2000; Crespo-Sancho, 2018). The continuing effort to empower women should be a major priority as we struggle to save and strengthen our democracy (Image 17.1).

Image 17.1. Empowerment of Women. Countries with greater gender equality have less internal violence, less international violence, and more security within the country (Caprioli, 2000; Crespo-Sancho, 2018). Empowerment of women should be a priority as we struggle to save our democracy

Overcoming the Dark Side of Meritocracy

Most of us believe that basing success on merit can provide the ultimate answer to injustice. If everyone is provided with equal opportunities and has a chance to rise as far as their talent and hard work will take them, what could be fairer? Meritocracy provides everyone with the hope of climbing the ladder of success. Presidents from Bill Clinton to George W. Bush to Barack Obama have preached the importance of equal opportunity and personal responsibility as the answer to growing inequality. They have made access to higher education the centerpiece in the struggle to overcome inequality.

Harvard political philosopher Michael Sandel (2020) in his insightful book *The Tyranny of Merit: What's Become of the Common Good?* advocates that even a perfect meritocracy with equal opportunities for all has a dark side. Meritocracy is not a remedy for inequality—it is a justification for it. Inequalities persist, but they are based on talent and skill rather than privilege and greater opportunities. Meritocracy creates a polarizing divide in our country. Those who rise to the top feel that they deserve their success, and they frequently look down at those who remain on the bottom. Those who have not been able to climb the ladder of success feel humiliation and lose self-esteem because they feel it is their fault that they are not successful. They feel a deep resentment toward the successful elites who look down on them, resulting in a huge polarizing divide that erodes our society and threatens our democracy.

Michael Young (2001), author of *The Rise of the Meritocracy*, puts it this way: "In a society that makes so much of merit, it is hard to be judged as having none. No underclass has ever been left as morally naked as that." Liberal elites often feel a righteous disgust for racism in working-class White people and in polite society will often belittle the working class with epithets such as "poor white trash" and "redneck." And we all remember Hillary Clinton's comment about the "deplorables" and Barack Obama's remark about people who "cling to guns or religion." Who can be surprised that there has been a populist backlash? The backlash is as much a rebellion against the system of meritocracy as it is against the great divide in income and wealth. This helps us understand the anti-science, anti-tech, anti-expert, and anti-elite sentiment of the right-wing populist movement.

Michael Sandel argues that society needs to enable those who are not able to climb the ladder of success in a meritocratic society to see themselves as a meaningful part of society, contributing to the common good. Individuals should be able to lead a life of dignity and solidarity with society whether they rise or not. This is what Sandel (2020) refers to as equality of condition.

A change of attitudes must begin at the top, with those who have achieved success in the meritocratic society. The winners need to adjust their attitude from hubris and self-righteousness to humility. Humility is a necessary antidote to the meritocratic arrogance that has so divided us. The winners need to appreciate the contingency of success—the many advantages and opportunities they have had along the way and the help from friends and relatives that has made their success possible. They need to appreciate the adage "there but for the grace of God or for an accident of fortune, go I." With genuine humility, the winners will no longer look down on those who have not been able to climb the meritocratic ladder to success. They will no longer scorn the two-thirds of Americans without a college degree.

Those at the top need to appreciate the contributions that less skilled, low-paid workers provide to society. We need to begin a debate about the dignity of workers, including compensation and esteem. The COVID-19 pandemic gave us a new appreciation for frontline workers. We saw how deeply dependent we are on nurses, teachers, policemen, firemen, delivery workers, grocery store clerks, warehouse workers, auto repair workers, home healthcare providers, childcare workers, and so many more. We should work to maintain that perspective as we come out of COVID-19. There needs to be a reevaluation of esteem as well as money, and more of it needs to go to the millions of Americans whose work does not require a college degree. We need to bridge the social status gap, which has so divided our country. Robert F. Kennedy, in a speech during his 1968 presidential campaign, stressed the importance of the dignity of work:

> Fellowship, community, shared patriotism—these essential values of our civilization do not come from just buying and consuming goods together. They come instead from dignified employment at decent pay, the kind of employment that lets a man say to his community, to his family, to his country, and most importantly, to himself, 'I helped build this country. I am a participant in its great public ventures.' (Sandel, 2020)

If we can make progress in addressing our country's income and wealth inequities and if we can change attitudes of those at the top and those at the bottom of our meritocratic society, we may be able to come together and find solidarity in our search for the common good. We need to overcome the false sense of freedom—that we are self-made, self-sufficient, and independent. We need to appreciate that we are all dependent upon one another. With this, we will gain mutual respect and appreciation for one another and a new sense of solidarity. This understanding will help rid the feelings of resentment from those at the bottom and the feelings of self-righteousness from those at the top. If we can gain a renewed perspective of our dependence on one another and our value to one another, we can overcome our divisions and become one nation with solidarity of purpose.

The Political Challenge

America is currently engaged in a struggle for our democracy against Donald Trump and his enablers, who have captured the Republican Party and morphed into agents for authoritarian rule. We are fighting against global trends in which authoritarian regimes are on the rise and democratic governments are on the decline. The V-Dem Institute (2021) suggested even before the Big Lie and the January 6 insurrection that our American democracy had eroded to the point that more often than not leads to full-blown autocracy. We may be losing the battle.

We have made the case that many traits of our human nature are counterproductive to our struggle to create an egalitarian society and save and enhance our democracy. These counterproductive traits include our selfish and tribal instincts, which pit us against one another; our hierarchical and authoritarian traits, which predispose many of us to authoritarian rule; and our predispositions to herd mentality, peer pressure, and obedience to authority, which make us more vulnerable to authoritarian leadership. Our innate behavioral traits also include the inclination in some of us to be social dominators who seek power and often engage in corruption. Our way of thinking provides another obstacle. We humans think and react primarily intuitively rather than through cognitive analysis, rational thinking, and compromise, which is so essential to functioning democracies.

Our challenge to preserve and strengthen our egalitarian democracy is a political one. If we are to heal the great divisions in our country, we must enact policies and laws that will address the inequities in our society. Because of the intense political polarization in our society, and because our government is so dysfunctional, the challenge is daunting.

Our electoral system is flawed in many ways and does not always provide equal representation. As we discussed in Chapter 14, the Electoral College can award the Presidency to candidates who have lost the popular vote. The Senate does not provide equitable representation. Each state is entitled to representation by two senators, regardless of the state's population. This gives an advantage to citizens in small population states. The filibuster rules in the Senate allow the minority party to obstruct passage of legislation supported by a majority of senators. For these reasons, many bills supported by a majority of Americans are often blocked in the Senate. Because of these policies and because of the intense political polarization between our two parties, our congress has been almost powerless to pass needed legislation. The lack of action by our congress to enact common sense gun laws supported by a majority of Americans after multiple mass shootings is a frustrating recent example.

Gerrymandering of voting districts is a major contributor to our toxic polarization (Bennett, 2018). State legislatures have the power to determine voting districts, and the majority party almost always draws these districts to favor their candidates. Ninety percent of congressional voting districts are gerrymandered to the extent that one party is almost guaranteed to win elections. This means that whichever candidate wins the primary will win the general election, and the candidate who appeals mostly to highly partisan voters will usually win the primary. Only about fifteen percent of voters usually participate in primaries, and these voters are generally highly motivated and reside on either the far right or the far left. This means that in about 90% of congressional voting districts the outcome is decided by 15% of the electorate, and the winning candidates generally have extreme political views, contributing to our politically polarized environment. Solving the problem of gerrymandering would be a major step in reducing political polarization, but it will not be easy. In each state, the party with the legislative majority will likely be unwilling to agree to nonpartisan districting, so changes will likely need to be made in the courts or by federal statutes. Geographic gerrymandering also makes solutions difficult. Democratic voters are concentrated in cities while Republican voters dominate rural districts, complicating the drawing of competitive districts.

Cooperation Is the Driving Force of Evolution

Psychologists and philosophers throughout history have emphasized the dark side of human nature. Deeply embedded in Western thought is the belief that humans are selfish, tribal, and governed primarily by self-interest, and that competition and conflict are the driving forces of evolution (Dawkins, 1976).

Today, most evolutionary biologists have a different perspective (Sober & Wilson, 1998; Wilson, 2012). As humans have come together in societies, cooperation has become the driving force of evolution. Individuals working with one another have gained great adaptive advantages for themselves and their group. Natural selection, acting both at the level of the individual and the group, has selected cooperative individuals and cooperative groups for survival, resulting in the passing of cooperative traits to subsequent generations (Sober & Wilson, 1998). As Darwin (1871) advocated, groups whose members really care about one another have a distinct survival advantage over less caring groups.

Over our long natural history, humans have become a more cooperative species (Richerson & Boyd, 2005). Our human nature has evolved more cooperative and prosocial traits, and our cultures have evolved and created environments that promote more cooperative and prosocial behavior. These trends should provide hope that biological and cultural evolution will lead us toward more cooperative societies, which should favor egalitarian democracies. And democracies that have the greatest internal cooperation should prevail.

Where Are We Going?

French sociologist Alexis de Tocqueville (1851) traveled to American in 1831 and published his observations about our democracy in *Democracy in America* (1835). He strongly believed that equality was the strength of our democracy. He argued that without some degree of economic equality, there cannot be political equality, and without political equality, democracy cannot survive. Economists Daron Acemoglu and James Robinson (2012) carry this precept further by making the case that nations fall apart when institutions serve the elite and not the common good.

Our country is deeply divided, and our politics are highly polarized. The Republican Party under the leadership of Donald Trump has embraced the right-wing populist movement, shattered democratic norms, undermined election results, and is steering our country toward autocratic rule. The Democratic Party has embraced diversity but has alienated the White working class and is struggling to remain in power. The Democrats are committed to addressing the inequities in our society, restoring the American Dream, and preserving our democracy, yet any progress will be incremental, and it is uncertain whether the Democrats will be able to achieve large enough majorities in the short term to accomplish these goals. Both sides view the other as existential threats to their vision of how America should be.

If we look back at human history, we see a world dominated by authoritarian rule and filled with conflict, pain, and suffering. Democracies have been a bright, but flickering, light within this dark history. If we view human history from an historical perspective, we may become pessimistic. Democracies are fragile and are currently in decline. But if we look at human history through an evolutionary lens, there is much reason for hope. Our human nature is hardwired for cooperation, engagement, and collective action. Both through our culture and the evolution of our human nature, we are becoming a more cooperative species. Our ancient hominin ancestors were able to cooperate only within small tribes, but today we have been able to cooperate across large diverse nation-states with people we don't even know. We are social animals and have traits that bind us together–altruism, love, empathy, kindness. We have inherited an innate moral compass that helps us choose cooperative, prosocial behavior over selfish, antisocial behavior. Over the long term, our better traits should prevail and allow us to work together to build a more egalitarian society and preserve our democracy. But in the short term our democracy is in danger.

America has been the champion of democracy and the leader of the free world since World War II. The future of global democracy depends to a great extent on our success in preserving and strengthening our own democracy. If we are to sustain our democracy, we must create a cultural environment that will mitigate our selfish and tribal instincts and bring out the positive side of our human nature. We must create a cultural environment that will bring our diverse groups together. This will require that we reduce our great income and wealth inequalities and make progress in diminishing the structural racism that so divides and polarizes our country. And this will require that we change our attitudes and perspectives. Human behavior is greatly driven by the need to be respected and appreciated. Those at the bottom of society, who feel they have been treated unfairly and disrespectfully, harbor great resentment and anger. They deserve dignified employment with decent pay and an appreciation for what they do so that they can feel they are contributing members of society. Those at the top need to cultivate humility and an appreciation of the contingency of their success. We all need to understand how we are all connected with one another and how we must all contribute to making our country a better place to live.

American Democracy is a Great Experiment. Few societies in history with great economic inequalities and great racial diversity have been able to preserve a democratic form of government. This is our challenge. If we can reduce the inequities in our society and change our attitudes, if we can recover our nation's solidarity, restore the American Dream, and preserve and strengthen our democracy, we will truly be extraordinary. If we can accomplish these things, we can once again be the land of opportunity and a beacon of hope for the world.

REFERENCES

249

Introduction

Ikenberry, G. J. (2018). The end of liberal international order? *International Affairs*, *94*(1), 7–23.

Chapter 1: Human Nature: The Nature-Nurture Debate

Books

Darwin, C. (2004). *On the origin of species by natural selection*. Barnes and Noble Books. (Original work published 1859)

Darwin, C. (1872). *The expression of the emotions in man and animals*. John Murray. http://darwin-online.org.uk/content/frameset?itemID=F1142&viewtype=side&pageseq=1

Loehlin, J. C. (2009). History of behavior genetics. In Y.-K. Kim (Ed.), *Handbook of behavior genetics*. Springer. https://doi.org/10.1007/978-0-387-76727-7_1

Pinker, S. (2003). *The blank slate: The modern denial of human nature*. Penguin.

Wilson, E. O. (1975). *Sociobiology: The new synthesis*. Harvard University Press.

Other References

MacNeill, A. (2009, March 22). Darwin on instincts and the expression of emotions. *Evolutionary Psychology*. http://evolpsychology.blogspot.com/2009/03/summary-in-chapter-vii-of-origin-of.html

McGue, M., Bouchard, T. J., Iacono, W. G., & Lykken, D. T. (1993). Behavioral genetics of cognitive ability: A life-span perspective. In R. Plomin & G. E. McClearn (Eds.), *Nature, nurture, and psychology*. American Psychological Association.

Origins Editors (2020). Nature vs nurture. http://experimental-origins.weebly.com/nature-vs-nurture.html

Plomin, R., & Spinath, F. M. (2004). Intelligence: Genetics, genes, and genomics. *Journal of Personality and Social Psychology, 86*(1), 112–129.

Whitam, F. L., Diamond, M., & Martin, J. (1993). Homosexual orientation in twins: A report on 61 pairs and three triplet sets. *Arch Sexual Behavior, 22*(3), 187–206.

Chapter 2: Empathy: Evolution's Precious Gift

Books

de Waal, F. (2009). *The age of empathy: Nature's lessons for a kinder society*. Random House.

Whitman, W. (2009). *Leaves of Grass*. American Renaissance Books. (Original work published 1855)

Other References

Allott, R. (2019). Evolutionary aspects of love and empathy. http://cogprints.org/3392/1/lovempat.htm

Barraza, J. A., & Zak, P. J. (2009). Empathy toward strangers triggers oxytocin release and subsequent generosity. *Annals of the New York Academy of Sciences, 1167*, 182–189.

Bartal, I. B., Decety, J., & Mason, P. (2011). Empathy and pro-social behavior in rats. *Science, 334*(6061), 1427–1430.

Bartal, I. B., Rodgers, D. A., Sarria, M. S. B., Decety, J. & Mason, P. (2014). Pro-social behavior in rats is modulated by social experience. *eLife, 3*, e01385.

Brethel-Haurwitz, K., & Marsh, A. (2016, October 18). Animal altruism? *Psychology Today*. https://www.psychologytoday.com/us/blog/goodness-sake/201610/animal-altruism

Daughters, K., Manstead, A. S. R., & Rees, D. A. (2017). Hypopituitarism is associated with lower oxytocin concentrations and reduced empathic ability. *Endocrine, 57*(1), 166–174.

Derntl, B., Finkelmeyer, A., Eickhoff, S., Kellermann, T., Falkenberg, D. I., Schneider, F., and Habel, U. (2010). Multidimensional assessment of empathic abilities: Neural correlates and gender differences. *Psychoneuroendocrinology, 35*(1), 67–82.

de Waal, F. (2005, September 1). The evolution of empathy. *Greater Good Magazine*. https://greatergood.berkeley.edu/article/item/the_evolution_of_empathy

de Waal, F. (2008). Putting altruism back into altruism: The evolution of empathy. *Annual Review of Psychology, 59*, 279–300.

di Pellegrino, G., Fadiga, L., Fogassi, L., Gallese, V., & Rizzolatti, G. (1992). Understanding motor events: A neurophysiological study. *Experimental Brain Research, 91*(1), 176–180.

Doherty, C. (2013, August 27). Remembering Katrina: Wide racial divide over government's response. Pew Research Center. https://www.pewresearch.org/fact-tank/2015/08/27/remembering-katrina-wide-racial-divide-over-governments-response/ft_13-08-28_katrinaanniv_640x300/

Dvash, J., & Shamay-Tsoory, S. G. (2014). Theory of mind and empathy as multidimensional constructs. *Topics in Language Disorders, 34*(4), 282–295.

Feldman, R., Weller, A., Zagoory-Sharon, O., & Levine, A. (2007). Evidence for a neuroendocrinological foundation of human affiliation: Plasma oxytocin levels across pregnancy and the postpartum period predict mother-infant bonding. *Psychological Science, 18*(11), 965–970.

REFERENCES

Fletcher, G. J. O., Simpson, J. A., Campbell, L., & Overall, N. C. (2014). Pair-bonding, romantic love, and evolution: The curious case of *Homo sapiens*. *Perspectives on Psychological Science, 10*(1), 20–36.

Gallese, V., Fadiga, L., Fogassi, L., & Rizzolatti, G. (1996). Action recognition in the premotor cortex. *Brain, 119*(2), 593–609.

Hurlemann, R., Patin, A., Onur, O. A., Cohen, M. X., Baumgartner, T., Mezler, S., Dziobek, I., Gallinat, J., Wagner, M., Maler, W., & Kendrick, K. M. (2010). Oxytocin enhances amygdala-dependent, socially reinforced learning and emotional empathy in humans. *Journal of Neuroscience, 30*(14), 4999–5007.

Konrath, S., O'Brien, E. H., & Hsing, C. (2011). Changes in dispositional empathy in American college students over time: A meta-analysis. *Personality and Social Psychology Review, 15*(2), 180–198.

Loehr, A. (2017, December 6). 7 practical tips for increasing empathy. *HuffPost.* https://www.huffpost.com/entry/seven-practical-tips-for-_b_9854350

Marazziti, D., Baroni, S., Mucci, F., Piccini, A., Moroni, I., Giannaccini, G., Carmassi, C., Massimetti, E., & Dell'Osso, L. (2019). Sex-related differences in plasma oxytocin levels in humans. *Clinical Practice and Epidemiology in Mental Health, 15*, 58–63.

Masserman, J. H., Wechkin, S., & Terris, W. (1964). "Altruistic" behavior in rhesus monkeys. *Am Journal of Psychiatry, 121*, 584–585.

Miller, S. C., Kennedy, C. C., De Voe, D. C., Hickey, M., Nelson, T., & Kogan, L. (2015). An examination of changes in oxytocin levels in men and women before and after interaction with a bonded dog. *Anthrozoos, 22*(1), 31–42.

Moore, K. B. (2016, May 16). Does oxytocin give women an edge? It's not quite that simple. *Verily.* https://verilymag.com/2016/05/oxytocin-sex-differences-women-hormones-bonding-sex-trust

Nagasawa, M., Mitsui, S., En, S., Ohtani, N., Ohta, M., Sakuma, Y., Onaka, T., Mogi, K., & Kikusui, T. (2015). Oxytocin-gaze positive loop and the coevolution of human-dog bonds. *Science, 348*(6232), 333–336.

Olmos, D. (2019, February 27). When watching others in pain, women's brains show more empathy. UCLA Newsroom. http://newsroom.ucla.edu/stories/womens-brains-show-more-empathy

Pappas, S., & Harvey, A. (2015, October 27). Oxytocin: Facts about the "cuddle hormone." *Live Science.* https://www.livescience.com/42198-what-is-oxytocin.html

Radzvilavicius, A. L. (2019, April 10). Empathy is the secret ingredient that makes cooperation—and civilization—possible. *The Conversation.* http://theconversation.com/empathy-is-the-secret-ingredient-that-makes-cooperation-and-civilization-possible-115105

Radzvilavicius, A. L., Stewart, A. J., & Plotkin, J. B. (2019, April 9). Evolution of empathetic moral evaluation. *eLife, 8*, e44269. https://doi.org/10.7554/eLife.44269

Rueckert, L., Branch, B., & Doan, T. (2011). Are gender differences in empathy due to differences in emotional reactivity? *Psychology, 2*, 574–578.

Schneiderman, I., Zagoory-Sharon, O., Leckman, J. F., & Feldman, R. (2012). Oxytocin during the initial stages of romantic attachment: Relations to couples' interactive reciprocity. *Psychoneuroendocrinology, 37*(8), 1277–1285.

Schulz, A. (2019). The evolution of empathy. http://people.ku.edu/~a382s825/The%20Evolution%20 of%20Empathy%20RD.pdf

Smith, A. (2006). Cognitive empathy and emotional empathy in human behavior and evolution. *Psychological Record, 56*(1), 3–21.

Uribe, C., Puig-Davi, A., Abos, A., Baggio, H. C., Junque, C., & Segura, B. (2019). Neuroanatomical and functional correlates of cognitive and affective empathy in young adults. *Frontiers in Behavioral Neuroscience, 13*(85), 1–8.

Wicker, B., Keysers, C., Plailly, J., Royet, J.-P., Gallese, V., & Rizzolatti, G. (2003). Both of us disgusted in my insula: The common neural basis of seeing and feeling disgust. *Neuron, 40*(3), 655–664.

Winerman, L. (2005). The mind's mirror. American Psychological Association. https://www.apa.org/ monitor/oct05/mirror

Chapter 3: Emotions: The Essence of Humanity

Books

Darwin, C. (2004). *On the origin of species by natural selection.* Barnes and Noble Books. (Original work published 1859)

Darwin, C. (1872). *The expression of the emotions in man and animals.* John Murray. http://darwin-online.org.uk/content/frameset?itemID=F1142&viewtype=side&pageseq=1

Kisak, P. F. (Ed.). (2016). *The evolution of emotion: The study and origins of human emotion.* CreateSpace.

Other References

Algoe, S. B., & Haidt, J. (2009). Witnessing excellence in action: The "other-praising:" emotions of elevation, gratitude, and admiration. *Journal of Positive Psychology, 4*(2), 105–127.

Allott, R. (2019). Evolutionary aspects of love and empathy. http://cogprints.org/3392/1/lovempat.htm

Al-Shawaf, L., Conroy-Beam, D., Asao, K. & Buss, D. M. (2015). Human emotions: An evolutionary psychological perspective. *Emotion Review, 8*(2), 173–186. https://labs.la.utexas.edu/buss/ files/2013/02/Al-ShawafEmotion-Review-2015.pdf

Bekoff, M. (2000). Animal emotions: Exploring passionate natures. *BioScience, 50*(10), 861–870.

Cabanac, M. (1999). Emotion and phylogeny. *The Japanese Journal of Physiology, 49*(1), 1–10.

Collins, J. (2011, August 17). Envy has its benefits. *Jason Collins Blog.* https://jasoncollins. blog/2011/08/17/envy-has-its-benefits/

REFERENCES

Cosmides, L., & Tooby, J. (2008). The evolutionary psychology of the emotions and their relationship to internal regulatory variables. In M. Lewis, J. M. Haviland-Jones, & L. F. Barrett (Eds.), *Handbook of emotions* (pp. 114–137). Guilford Press.

Curtis, V., de Barra, M., & Aunger, R. (2011). Disgust as an adaptive system for disease avoidance behavior. *Philosophical Transactions of the Royal Society B, 366*(1563), 389–401.

Devlin, H. (2019, May 12). Science of anger: How gender, age and personality shape this emotion. *The Guardian.* https://www.theguardian.com/lifeandstyle/2019/may/12/science-of-anger-gender-age-personality

de Waal, F. (2005, September 1). The evolution of empathy. *Greater Good Magazine.* https://greatergood.berkeley.edu/article/item/the_evolution_of_empathy

Ekman, P. (1992). An argument for basic emotions. *Cognition and Emotion, 6*(3–4), 169–200.

Estrada, A. (2017, February 13). Pride may actually be key to our social lives. *Futurity.* https://www.futurity.org/pride-evolution-emotions-1357352-2/

Fels, A. (2017, April 14). The point of hate. *The New York Times.* https://www.nytimes.com/2017/04/14/opinion/the-point-of-hate.html

Fisher, M. (2019). *Feelings: The essential essence of who we are.* Trans4mind. https://trans4mind.com/counterpoint/index-happiness-wellbeing/fisher2.html

Fletcher, G. J. O., Simpson, J. A., Campbell, L., & Overall, N. C. (2014). Pair-bonding, romantic love, and evolution: The curious case of *Homo sapiens. Perspectives on Psychological Science, 10*(1), 20–36.

Haidt, J. (2003). The moral emotions. In R. J. Davidson, K. R. Sherer, & H. H. Goldsmith (Eds.), *Handbook of affective sciences* (pp. 852–870). Oxford University Press.

Hareli, S., & Parkinson, B. (2008). What's social about social emotions? *Journal for the Theory of Social Behavior, 38*(2), 131–156.

Jarrett, C. (2011). The deadly sins. *The Psychologist, 24,* 89–104.

Lambert, H., Carder, G., & D'Cruze, N. (2019). Given the cold shoulder: A review of the scientific literature for evidence of reptile sentience. *Animals, 9*(10), 821.

LeDoux, J. E., & Brown, R. 2017. A higher-order theory of emotional consciousness. *Proceedings of the National Academy of Sciences, 114*(10), E2016–E2025.

Ramachandran, V.S., & Jalal, B. (2017). The evolutionary psychology of envy and jealousy. *Front Psychology, 8,* 1619.

Rodgers, J. E. (2014, March 11). Go forth in anger. *Psychology Today.* https://www.psychologytoday.com/us/articles/201403/go-forth-in-anger

Roxo, M. R., Franceschini, P. R., Zubaran, C., Kleber, F. D., & Sander, J. W. (2011). The limbic system conception and its historical evolution. *Scientific World Journal, 11,* 2428–2441.

Sell, A., Tooby, J., & Cosmides, L. (2009). Formidability and the logic of human anger. *Proceedings of the National Academy of Sciences, 106*(35), 15073–15078.

Shapiro, E. (2017). Key moments in Charleston church shooting case as Dylan Roof pleads guilty to state charges. ABC News. https://abcnews.go.com/U.S./key-moments-charleston-church-shooting-case-dylann-roof/story?id=46701033

Simons, I. (2009, November 15). The four moral emotions. *Psychology Today*. https://www.psychologytoday.com/us/blog/the-literary-mind/200911/the-four-moral-emotions

Sznycer, D., Al-Shawaf, L., Bereby-Meyer, Y., Curry, O. S., De Smet, D., Ermer, E., Kim, S., Kim, S., Li, N. P., Lopez Seal, M. F., McClung, J., O, J., Ohtsubo, Y., Quillien, T., Schaub, M., Sell, A., van Leeuwen, F., Cosmides, L., & Tooby, J. (2017). Cross-cultural regularities in the cognitive architecture of pride. *Proceedings of the National Academy of Sciences, 114*(8), 1874–1879.

Tangney, J. P., Stuewig, J., & Mashek, D. J. (2007). Moral emotions and moral behavior. *Annual Review of Psychology, 58*, 345–372.

Texas A&M University Veterinary Medicine and Biomedical Sciences. (2011). Reptile Emotions. https://vetmed.tamu.edu/news/pet-talk/reptile-emotions/

Tyng, C. M., Amin, H. U., Saad, M. N. M., & Malik, A. S. (2017). The influences of emotion on learning and memory. *Frontiers in Psychology, 8*, 1454.

van Kleef, G. A., Cheshin, A., Fischer, A. H., & Schneider, I. K. (2016). Editorial: The social nature of emotions. *Frontiers in Psychology, 7*, 896.

Chapter 4: Cooperation: The Driving Force of Evolution

Books

Alexander, R. D. (1987). *The biology of moral systems*. De Gruyter.

Boehm, C. (2012). *Moral origins: The evolution of virtue, altruism, and shame*. Basic Books.

Corning, P. (2018). *Synergistic selection: How cooperation has shaped evolution and the rise of humankind*. World Scientific.

Darwin, C. (1871). *The descent of man, and selection in relation to sex*. John Murray. http://darwin-online.org.uk/content/frameset?itemID=F937.1&viewtype=text&pageseq=1

Dawkins, R. (1976). *The selfish gene*. Oxford University Press.

Dunbar, R. (1998). *Grooming, gossip, and the evolution of language*. Harvard University Press.

Harari, Y. N. (2015). *Sapiens: A brief history of humankind*. HarperCollins.

Hölldobler, B., & Wilson, E. O. (2008). *The superorganism: The beauty, elegance and strangeness of insect societies*. Norton.

Smith, J. M., & Szathmary, E. (1999). *The origins of life: From the birth of life to the origins of language*. Oxford University Press.

Sober, E., & Wilson, D. S. (1998. *Unto Others: The Evolution and Psychology of Unselfish Behavior*. Cambridge, MA: Harvard University Press.

Wilson, E. O. (2012). *The social conquest of earth.* Norton.

Other References

Bassler, B. (2009, February). *How bacteria "talk"* [Video]. TED Conferences. https://www.ted.com/talks/bonnie_bassler_on_how_bacteria_communicate

Campbell, A. (2010). Oxytocin and human social behavior. *Personality and social psychological review, 14*(3), 281–295.

Constable, G.W.A., Rogers, T., McKane, A. J., & Tarnita, C. E. (2016). Strength in numbers: Demographic noise can reverse the direction of selection. *Proceedings of the National Academy of Sciences, 113*(32), E4745–E4754.

Hamilton, W. D. (1964). The genetic evolution of social behavior I, II. *Journal of Theoretical Biology, 7,* 1–52.

Maynard Smith, J. (1964). Group selection and kin selection. *Nature, 201,* 1145–1147.

Nowak, M.A., Tarnita, C. E., & Wilson, E. O. (2010). The evolution of eusociality. *Nature, 466,* 1057–1062.

Okasha, S. (2013). Biological altruism. *Stanford encyclopedia of philosophy.* https://plato.stanford.edu/archives/fall2013/entries/altruism-biological/

Ortiz, C., & Swinderman, J. (2012). Eusocial and colony behavior in ants. https://www.reed.edu/biology/courses/BIO342/2012_syllabus/2012_WEBSITES/COJS_animalBehavior/index2.html

Poulin, M. (2012, November 27). Our genes want us to be altruists. Association for Psychological Science. https://www.psychologicalscience.org/observer/our-genes-want-us-to-be-altruists

Poulin, M., Holman, A., & Buffone, A. (2012). The neurogenetics of nice: Receptor genes for oxytocin and vasopressin interact with threat to predict prosocial behavior. *Psychological Science, 23*(5), 446–452.

Rubenstein, D., & Kealey, J. (2010). Cooperation, conflict, and the evolution of complex animal societies. *Nature Education Knowledge, 3*(10), 78.

Taylor, K. (2010, June 11). Psychological vs. biological altruism. *Philosophy Talk.* https://www.philosophytalk.org/blog/psychological-vs-biological-altruism

Trivers, R. L. (1971). The evolution of reciprocal altruism. *The Quarterly Review of Biology, 46*(1), 35–57.

Wilson, D. S., Van Gugt, M., & O'Gorman, R. (2008). Multilevel selection theory and major evolutionary transitions. *Current directions in psychological science, 17*(1), 6–9.

Wilson, D. S., & Wilson, E. O. (2007). Rethinking the theoretical foundation of sociobiology. *The Quarterly Review of Biology, 82*(4), 327–348.

Chapter 5: Hierarchical and Egalitarian Instincts
Books

Boehm, C. (1999). *Hierarchy in the forest: The evolution of egalitarian behavior.* Harvard University Press.

de Waal, F. (1998). *Chimpanzee politics: Power and sex among apes.* Johns Hopkins University Press.

de Waal, F., & Lanting, F. (1997). *Bonobo: The forgotten ape.* University of California Press.

Sidanius, J., & Pratto, F. (2001). *Social dominance: An intergroup theory of social hierarchy and oppression.* Cambridge University Press.

Wrangham, R., & Peterson, D. (1996). *Demonic males: Apes and the origins of human violence.* Houghton Mifflin.

Other References

Angier, N. (1997, April 22). Bonobo society: Amicable, amorous and run by females. *The New York Times.* https://www.nytimes.com/1997/04/22/science/bonobo-society-amicable-amorous-and-run-by-females.html

Angle, S. C., Appiah, K. A., Baggini, J., Bell, D., Berggruen, N., Bevir, M., Chan, J., Fraenkel, C., Macedo, S., Puett, M., Qian, J., Risse, M., Romano, C., Tiwald, J., & Wang, R. (2017, March 22). In defense of hierarchy. *Aeon.* https://aeon.co/essays/hierarchies-have-a-place-even-in-societies-built-on-equality

Cohen-Brown, B. (2018, July 10). From top to bottom, chimpanzee social hierarchy is amazing! *Jane Goodall's Good for All News.* https://news.janegoodall.org/2018/07/10/top-bottom-chimpanzee-social-hierarchy-amazing/

Fehr, E., Bernhard, H., & Rockenbach, B. (2008). Egalitarianism in young children. *Nature, 454,* 1079–1083.

Funk, C. L., Smith, K. B., Alford, J. R., Hibbing, M. V., Eaton, N. R., Krueger, R. F., Eaves, L. J., & Hibbing, J. R. (2012). Genetic and environmental transmission of political orientations. *Political Psychology, 34*(6), 805–819.

Goldhill, O. (2018, March 28). The shape of your brain influences your political opinions. *Quartz.* https://qz.com/1238929/your-political-views-are-influenced-by-the-size-of-your-brains-amygdala/

Kanai, R., Feilden, T., Firth, C., & Rees, G. (2011). Political orientations are correlated with brain structure in young adults. *Current Biology, 21*(8), 677–680.

Khan, S. (2016, June 5). When does equality flourish? *The New Yorker.* https://www.newyorker.com/tech/annals-of-technology/when-does-equality-flourish

Kleppestø, T. H., Czajkowski, N. O., Vassend, O., Røysamb, E., Eftedal, N. H., Sheehy-Skeffington, J., Kunst, J. R., & Thomsen, L. (2019). Correlations between social dominance orientation and political attitudes reflect common genetic underpinnings. *Proceedings of the National Academy of Sciences, 116*(36), 17741–17746.

Lee I.-C., Pratto, F., & Johnson, B. T. (2011). Intergroup consensus/disagreement in support of group-based hierarchy: An examination of socio-structural and psycho-cultural factors. *Psychological Bulletin, 137*, 1029–1064.

Morin, R. (2013, December 9). Study on twins suggests our political beliefs may be hard-wired. Pew Research Center. https://www.pewresearch.org/fact-tank/2013/12/09/study-on-twins-suggests-our-political-beliefs-may-be-hard-wired/

Nam, H. H., Jost, J. T., Kaggen, L., Campbell-Meiklejohn, D., & Van Bavel, J. M. (2018). Amygdala structure and the tendency to regard the social system as legitimate and desirable. *Nature Human Behavior, 2*, 133–138.

Pinchbeck, D. (1996, November 17). Men, monkeys and mayhem. *The Washington Post.* https://www.washingtonpost.com/wp-srv/style/longterm/books/reviews/demonicmales.htm

Saini, A. (2017, July 20). Scientists assumed that patriarchy was only natural. Bonobos proved them wrong. *Quartz.* https://qz.com/1033621/scientists-assumed-that-patriarchy-was-only-natural-bonobos-proved-them-wrong/

Van Berkel, L., Crandall, C. S., Eidelman, S., & Blanchar, J. C. (2015). Hierarchy, dominance, and deliberation: Egalitarian values require mental effort. *Personality and Social Psychology Bulletin, 41*(9), 1207–1222.

Wayman, E. (2012, October 19). What is war good for? Ask a chimpanzee. *Slate.* https://slate.com/technology/2012/10/chimpanzee-wars-can-primate-aggression-teach-us-about-human-aggression.html

Chapter 6: Tribal Instincts

Books

Chua, A. (2018). *Political tribes: Group instinct and the fate of nations.* Penguin.

Darwin, C. (1871). *The descent of man, and selection in relation to sex.* John Murray. http://darwin-online.org.uk/content/frameset?itemID=F937.1&viewtype=text&pageseq=1

Pinker, S. (2011). *The better angels of our nature: Why violence has declined.* Penguin.

Smith, D. L. (2007). *The most dangerous animal: Human nature and the origins of war.* St. Martin's.

Wilson, E. O. (2012). *The social conquest of earth.* Norton.

Wrangham, R., & Peterson, D. (1996). *Demonic males: Apes and the origins of human violence.* Houghton Mifflin.

Other References

Barraza, J. A., & Zak, P. J. (2009). Empathy toward strangers triggers oxytocin release and subsequent generosity. *Annals of the New York Academy of Sciences, 1167*, 182–189.

Bartal, I. B., Rodgers, D. A., Sarria, M. S. B., Decety, J. & Mason, P. (2014). Pro-social behavior in rats is modulated by social experience. *eLife, 3*, e01385.

Bowles, S. (2009). Did warfare among ancestral hunter-gatherers affect the evolution of human social behaviors? *Science, 324*(5932), 1293–1298.

Caprioli, M. (2000). Gendered conflict. *Journal of Peace Research, 37*(1), 51–68.

Crespo-Sancho, C. (2018, March 28). Can gender equality prevent violent conflict? *Development for Peace.* https://blogs.worldbank.org/dev4peace/can-gender-equality-prevent-violent-conflict

De Dreu, C. K. W., Greer, L. L., Van Kleef, G. A., Shalvi, S., & Handgraaf, M. J. J. (2011). Oxytocin promotes human ethnocentrism. *Proceedings of the National Academy of Sciences, 108*(4), 1262–1266.

Fixico, D. L. (2021). When Native Americans Were Slaughtered in the Name of 'Civilization.' https://www.history.com/news/native-americans-genocide-united-states

Hawks, J., Wang, E. T., Cochran, G. M., Harpending, H. C., & Moyzis, R. K. (2007). Recent acceleration of human adaptive evolution. *Proceedings of the National Academy of Sciences, 104*(52), 20753–20758.

King, M. L., Jr. (1963). I have a dream. NAACP. https://www.naacp.org/i-have-a-dream-speech-full-march-on-washington/

Kosfeld, M., Heinrichs, M., Zak, P. J., Fischbacher, U., & Fehr, E. (2005). Oxytocin increases trust in humans. *Nature, 435*, 673–676.

McDonald, M. M., Navaarete, C. D., & van Vugt, M. (2012). Evolution and the psychology of intergroup conflict: The male warrior hypothesis. *Philosophical Transactions of the Royal Society B, 367*(1589), 670–679.

Obama, B. (2004). Barack Obama's keynote address at the 2004 Democratic National Convention. PBS NewsHour. https://www.pbs.org/newshour/show/barack-obamas-keynote-address-at-the-2004-democratic-national-convention

Pritchard, J. K. (2012, November 1). How we are evolving. *Scientific American.* https://www.scientificamerican.com/article/how-we-are-evolving-2012-12-07/

The Century Foundation. (2019). The Benefits of socioeconomically and racially integrated Schools and classrooms. https://tcf.org/content/facts/the-benefits-of-socioeconomically-and-racially-integrated-schools-and-classrooms/?session=

Tropp, L. and Saxena, S. (2018). Re-weaving the social fabric through integrated schools: How intergroup contact prepares youth to thrive in a multicultural society. http://school-diversity.org/wp-content/uploads/2018/05/NCSD_Brief13.pdf

van Vugt, M. (2009). Sex differences in intergroup competition, aggression, and warfare. *Annals of the New York Academy of Sciences, 1167*, 124–134.

von Hippel, W., & Trivers, R. (2011). The evolution and psychology of self-deception. *Behavioral and Brain Sciences, 34*(1), 1–16.

Wade, N. (2011, January 10). Depth of the kindness hormone appears to know some bounds. *The New York Times*. https://www.nytimes.com/2011/01/11/science/11hormone.html

Wayman, E. (2012, October 19). What is war good for? Ask a chimpanzee. Slate. https://slate.com/technology/2012/10/chimpanzee-wars-can-primate-aggression-teach-us-about-human-aggression.html

Chapter 7: The Moral Animal

Books

Boehm, C. (2012). *Moral origins: The evolution of virtue, altruism and shame*. Basic Books.

Darwin, C. (1871). *The descent of man, and selection in relation to sex*. John Murray. http://darwin-online.org.uk/content/frameset?itemID=F937.1&viewtype=text&pageseq=1

de Waal, F. (2006). *Primates and philosophers*. Princeton University Press.

Dostoevsky, F. (1990). *The brothers karamazov*. Farrar, Straus and Giroux.

Joyce, R. (2007). *The evolution of morality*. MIT Press.

Pinker, S. (2003). *The blank slate: The modern denial of human nature*. Penguin.

Richerson, P., & Boyd, R. (2005). *Not by genes alone: How culture transformed human evolution*. University of Chicago Press.

Tomasello, M. (2016). *A natural history of human morality*. Harvard University Press.

Wilson, E. O. (1975). *Sociobiology: The new synthesis*. Harvard University Press.

Wright, R. (1994). *The moral animal: Why we are the way we are—the new science of evolutionary psychology*. Vintage.

Other References

Bloom, P. (2010, May 5). The moral life of babies. *The New York Times Magazine*. http://www.nytimes.com/2010/05/09/magazine/09babies-t.html

Burkart, J. M., Brugger, R. K., & van Carel, P. (2018). Evolutionary origins of morality: Insights from non-human primates. *Frontiers in Sociology, 3*(17), 1–12.

Byrnes, H. (2019, June 19). 13 countries where being gay is legally punishable by death." *U.S.A Today*. https://www.usatoday.com/story/money/2019/06/14/countries-where-being-gay-is-legally-punishable-by-death/39574685/

Curry, O. S. (2016). Morality as cooperation: A problem-centered approach. In T. K. Shackelford & R. D. Hansen (Eds.), *The evolution of morality*. Springer.

Curry, O. S., Mullins, D. A., & Whitehouse, H. (2019). Is it good to cooperate? Testing the theory of morality-as-cooperation in 60 societies. *Current Anthropology, 60*(1), 47–69.

Decety, J., & Cowell, J. M. (2016). Our brains are wired for morality: evolution, development, and neuroscience. *Frontiers for Young Minds.* https://kids.frontiersin.org/article/10.3389/frym.2016.00003

Hamlin, J. K., Wynn, K., & Bloom, P. (2007). Social evaluation by preverbal infants. *Nature, 540,* 557–559.

Jefferson, T., et al. (2020). Declaration of independence. National Archives. (Original work published 1776) https://www.archives.gov/founding-docs/declaration

Schmidt, M. F. H., Sommerville, J. A. (2011). Fairness expectations and altruistic sharing in 15-month-old human infants. *PLOS ONE, 6*(10), e23223.

Smith, E. E. 2015, (December 2). Is human morality a product of evolution? *The Atlantic.* https://www.theatlantic.com/health/archive/2015/12/evolution-of-morality-social-humans-and-apes/418371/

Van Wolkenten, M., Brosnan, S. F., & de Waal, Frans B. M. (2007). Inequity responses of monkeys modified by effort. *PNAS, 104*(47), 18854-18859.

Yardley, J. (2013, May 22). Report on deadly factory collapse in Bangladesh finds widespread blame. *The New York Times.* https://www.nytimes.com/2013/05/23/world/asia/report-on-bangladesh-building-collapse-finds-widespread-blame.html

Chapter 8: Social Darwinism

Books

Ruse, J. (2017). Social Darwinism. In M. Tibayrenc & F. J. Ayala (Eds.), *On human nature: Biology, psychology, ethics, politics and religion*. Academic Press.

Other References

Bergman, J. (2001). Darwin's influence on ruthless laissez faire capitalism. Institute for Creation Research. https://www.icr.org/article/darwins-influence-ruthless-laissez-faire-capitalis

Black, E. (2003). The horrifying American roots of Nazi eugenics. https://historynewsnetwork.org/article/1796

Bouche, T., & Rivard, L. (2014, September 18). America's hidden history: The eugenics movement. Scitable by Nature Generation. https://www.nature.com/scitable/forums/genetics-generation/america-s-hidden-history-the-eugenics-movement-123919444/

DeSantis, V. P. (1988). The gilded age in American history. Rutherford B. Hayes Presidential Library and Museums. https://www.rbhayes.org/research/hayes-historical-journal-the-gilded-age-in-american-history/

Gillham, N. W. (2001). Sir Francis Galton and the birth of eugenics. *Annual Review of Genetics, 35,* 83–101.

Hall, P. D. (2020). *Social Darwinism and the poor.* VCU Libraries Social Welfare History Project. https://socialwelfare.library.vcu.edu/issues/social-darwinism-poor/

Norrgard, K. (2008). Human testing, the eugenics movement, and IRBs. *Nature Education, 1*(1), 170.

Shermer, M. 2016. "Why Malthus Is Still Wrong." Retrieved April 2020 from https://www.scientificamerican.com/article/why-malthus-is-still-wrong/

Skagit Valley College. (2017). Herbert Spencer and social Darwinism. https://skagit.instructure.com/courses/5362/pages/herbert-spencer-and-social-darwinism?module_item_id=210436

Thomas, A. (2011). *American politics: Is social Darwinism once again present?* http://faculty.etsu.edu/odonnell/2011fall/engl3130/student_writing/social_darwinism.htm

Chapter 9: The Toxicity of Systemic Racism

Books

Foner, E. (2014). *Reconstruction: American's unfinished revolution* (1863–1877). HarperCollins.

Levitsky, S., & Ziblatt, D. (2019). *How democracies die.* Broadway Books.

Packard, J. (2002). *American nightmare: The history of Jim Crow.* St. Martin's.

Richerson, P., & Boyd, R. (2005). *Not by genes alone: How culture transformed human evolution.* University of Chicago Press.

Schermerhorn, C. (2018). *Unrequited toil: A history of united states slavery.* Cambridge University Press.

Other References

Allen D. (2017). Charlottesville is not the continuation of an old fight. It is something new. *The Washington Post.* https://www.washingtonpost.com/opinions/charlottesville-is-not-the-continuation-of-an-old-fight-it-is-something-new/2017/08/13/971812f6-8029-11e7-b359-15a3617c767b_story.html

Costigan, A., Garnett, K., & Troiano, E. (2020, September 30). The impact of structural racism on black Americans. Catalyst. https://www.catalyst.org/research/structural-racism-black-americans/

Dann, C. (2020, July 21). Poll: More voters acknowledge symptoms of racism but disagree about its causes. NBC News. https://www.nbcnews.com/politics/meet-the-press/poll-more-voters-acknowledge-symptoms-racism-disagree-about-its-causes-n1234363

Delgado, R., & Stefancic, J. (1998). Critical race theory: Past, present, and future. *Current Legal Problems, 51*(1) 467–491.

Fish, M. S., & Brooks, R. S. (2004). Does diversity hurt democracy? *Journal of Democracy, 15*(1), 154–166.

Fortin, J. (2021, November 8). Critical race theory: A brief history. *The New York Times.* https://www.nytimes.com/article/what-is-critical-race-theory.html

Ray, R., & Gibbons, A. (2021, November). Why are states banning critical race theory? Brookings. https://www.brookings.edu/blog/fixgov/2021/07/02/why-are-states-banning-critical-race-theory/

Ray, R., & Whitlock, M. (2019, September 12). Setting the record straight on black voter turnout. Brookings. https://www.brookings.edu/blog/how-we-rise/2019/09/12/setting-the-record-straight-on-black-voter-turnout/

Smith, D. (2021, November 3). How did Republicans turn critical race theory into a winning electoral issue? *The Guardian.* https://www.theguardian.com/us-news/2021/nov/03/republicans-critical-race-theory-winning-electoral-issue

Worland, J. (2020, June 11). America's long overdue awakening to systemic racism. *Time.* https://time.com/5851855/systemic-racism-america/

Chapter 10: The Growing Crisis of Socioeconomic Inequity

Books

Hochschild, A. R. (2017). *Strangers in their own land: Anger and mourning on the American right.* The New Press.

Kristof, N., & WuDunn, S. (2020). *Tightrope: Americans reaching for hope.* Knopf.

Piketty, T. (2014). *Capital in the twenty-first century.* Harvard University Press.

Scheidel, W. (2017). *The great leveler: Violence and the history of inequality from the Stone Age to the twenty-first century.* Princeton University Press.

Smith, H. (2013). *Who stole the American Dream?* Random House.

Other References

Bureau of Justice Statistics (2014). Persons at or below the federal poverty level have highest rates of violent victimization for the period 2008–12. Bureau of Justice Statistics. https://www.prnewswire.com/news-releases/persons-at-or-below-the-federal-poverty-level-had-highest-rates-of-violent-victimization-for-the-period-2008-12-283049301.html

Chowdhury, M. (2018). *The worst consequences of poverty.* The Borgen Project. https://borgenproject.org/worst-consequences-of-poverty/

REFERENCES

Congressional Budget Office. (2020). The distribution of household income, 2017. https://www.cbo.gov/publication/56575

Corak, M. (2016). How the Great Gatsby Curve got its name. *Economics for Public Policy.* https://milescorak.com/2016/12/04/how-the-great-gatsby-curve-got-its-name/

Edsall, T. B. (2020, December 9). The resentment that never sleeps. *The New York Times.* https://www.nytimes.com/2020/12/09/opinion/trump-social-status-resentment.html

Edsall, T. B. (2022, February 9). Status anxiety is blowing wind into Trump's sails. *The New York Times.* https://www.nytimes.com/2022/02/09/opinion/trump-status-anxiety.html

Giles, C. (2014, January 19). IMF warns on threat of income inequality. *Financial Times* https://www.ft.com/content/b3462520-805b-11e3-853f-00144feab7de

Hodgson, G. M. (2018, July 30). What the world can learn about equality from the Nordic model. *The Conversation.* http://theconversation.com/what-the-world-can-learn-about-equality-from-the-nordic-model-99797

Inequality.org. (2021). Covid-19 and inequality. https://inequality.org/facts/inequality-and-covid-19/

Kristof, N. (2021, February 13). Can Biden save Americans like my old pal Mike? *The New York Times.* https://www.nytimes.com/2021/02/13/opinion/sunday/working-class-dignity.html

Krueger, A. B. (2012, January 12). The rise and consequences of inequality in the United States. https://obamawhitehouse.archives.gov/sites/default/files/krueger_cap_speech_final_remarks.pdf

Mason, P. (2017, March 29). *The great leveler* by Walter Scheidel review—an end to inequality? *The Guardian.* https://www.theguardian.com/books/2017/mar/29/the-great-leveller-walter-scheidel-review-paul-mason

McWhinney, J. (2020, January 26). The Nordic model: Pros and cons. Investopedia. https://www.investopedia.com/articles/investing/100714/nordic-model-pros-and-cons.asp

Obama, B. (2011, December 6). Remarks by the president on the economy in Osawatomie, Kansas. https://obamawhitehouse.archives.gov/the-press-office/2011/12/06/remarks-president-economy-osawatomie-kansas

Peterson, M. B., Osmundsen, M., & Bor, A. 2020. Beyond populism: The psychology of status-seeking and extreme political discontent. PsyArXiv. https://doi.org/10.31234/osf.io/puqzs

Qureshi, Z. (2020, November 17). Tackling the inequality pandemic: Is there a cure? Brookings. https://www.brookings.edu/research/tackling-the-inequality-pandemic-is-there-a-cure/

Reagan, R. (1981, January 20). Inaugural address. https://www.reaganfoundation.org/media/128614/inaguration.pdf

Reagan, R. (1989, January 12). Transcript of Reagan's farewell address to American people. *The New York Times.* https://www.nytimes.com/1989/01/12/news/transcript-of-reagan-s-farewell-address-to-american-people.html

Reich, R. (2022, April 12). Inflation is out of control! Urgent memo to Biden and the Democrats! Robert Reich. https://robertreich.substack.com/p/inflation-is-out-of-control-memo?s=r&utm_campaign=post&utm_medium=email

Ridgeway, C. L. (2014). Why status matters for inequality. *American Sociological Review, 79*(1), 1–16.

Roosevelt, F. D. (1937). "One third of a nation": FDR's second inaugural address. History Matters. http://historymatters.gmu.edu/d/5105/

Shrider, E. A., Kollar, M., Chen, F. & Semega J. (2021). Income and poverty in the United States. https://www.census.gov/library/publications/2021/demo/p60-273.html

Stewart, M. (2018, June). The 9.9 percent is the new American aristocracy. *The Atlantic.* https://www.theatlantic.com/magazine/archive/2018/06/the-birth-of-a-new-american-aristocracy/559130/

Szalavitz, M. (2017, December 8). The surprising factors driving murder rates: income inequality and respect. *The Guardian.* https://www.theguardian.com/us-news/2017/dec/08/income-inequality-murder-homicide-rates

Transparency International. (2019). Corruption Perceptions Index (CPI) 2019: Americas. https://www.transparency.org/news/feature/cpi_2019_Americas

Wilkinson, R. G., & Pickett, K. E. (2009). Income inequality and social dysfunction. *Annual Review of Sociology, 35,* 493–511.

Williams, J. C. (2016, November 10). What so many people don't get about the U.S. working class. *Harvard Business Review.* https://hbr.org/2016/11/what-so-many-people-dont-get-about-the-u-s-working-class

World Bank. (2019). GINI index (World Bank estimate)—country ranking. Index Mundi. https://www.indexmundi.com/facts/indicators/SI.POV.GINI/rankings

World Economic Forum. (2017). *The global gender gap report 2017.* https://www.weforum.org/reports/the-global-gender-gap-report-2017

Chapter 11: The Seductive Lure of Authoritarianism

Books

Adorno, T. W. (1950). *The authoritarian personality.* Harper.

Altemeyer, B. (2006). *The authoritarians.* https://theauthoritarians.org/options-for-getting-the-book/

Applebaum, A. (2020). *Twilight of democracy: The seductive lure of authoritarianism.* Doubleday.

Frantz, E. (2018). *Authoritarianism: What everyone needs to know.* Oxford University Press.

Giry, J., & Gürpınar, D. (2020). Functions and uses of conspiracy theories in authoritarian regimes. In M. Butter & P. Knight (Eds.), *Routledge handbook of conspiracy theories.* Taylor and Francis.

Sidanius, J., & Pratto, F. (2001). *Social dominance: An intergroup theory of social hierarchy and oppression.* Cambridge University Press.

Somit, A., & Peterson, S. A. (1997). Darwinism, dominance, and democracy: The biological bases of authoritarianism. Praeger.

Wodak, R. (2015). *The politics of fear: What right-wing populist discourses mean.* Sage.

Other References

Applebaum, A. (2018, October). A warning from Europe: The worst is yet to come. *The Atlantic*. https://www.theatlantic.com/magazine/archive/2018/10/poland-polarization/568324/

Corning, P. A. (2000). The sociobiology of democracy: Is authoritarianism in our genes? *Politics and the Life Sciences, 19*(1), 103–108.

Democracy Digest (2016, November 7). Is "populist international" undermining western democracy? National Endowment for Democracy. https://www.demdigest.org/populism-undermining-western-democracy/

Freedom House. (2022, February 24). New report: Authoritarian rule challenging democracy as dominant global model. https://freedomhouse.org/article/new-report-authoritarian-rule-challenging-democracy-dominant-global-model

Funk, C. L., Smith, K. B., Alford, J. R., Hibbing, M. V., Eaton, N. R., Krueger, R. F., Eaves, L. J., & Hibbing, J. R. (2012). Genetic and environmental transmission of political orientations. *Political Psychology, 34*(6), 805–819.

Kendall-Taylor, A., & Frantz, E. (2016, December 5). How democracies fall apart: Why populism is a pathway to autocracy. *Foreign Affairs*. https://www.foreignaffairs.com/articles/2016-12-05/how-democracies-fall-apart

Kleppestø, T. H., Czajkowski, N. O., Vassend, O., Røysamb, E., Eftedal, N. H., Sheehy-Skeffington, J., Kunst, J. R., & Thomsen, L. (2019). Correlations between social dominance orientation and political attitudes reflect common genetic underpinnings. *Proceedings of the National Academy of Sciences, 116*(36), 17741–17746.

Ludeke, S. G., & Krueger, R. F. (2013). Authoritarianism as a personality trait: Evidence from a longitudinal behavior genetic study. *Personality and Individual Differences, 55*, 480–484.

McLeod, S. (2017). The Milgram shock experiment. *Simply Psychology*. https://www.simplypsychology.org/milgram.html

Milgram, S. (1963). Behavioral study of obedience. *Journal of Abnormal and Social Psychology, 67*(4), 371–378.

Morin, R. (2013, December 9). Study on twins suggests our political beliefs may be hard-wired. Pew Research Center. https://www.pewresearch.org/fact-tank/2013/12/09/study-on-twins-suggests-our-political-beliefs-may-be-hard-wired/

Mounk, Y. (2019, October 9). Democracy in Poland is in mortal danger. *The Atlantic*. https://www.theatlantic.com/ideas/archive/2019/10/poland-could-lose-its-democracy/599590/?gclid=CjwKCAjw1ej5BRBhEiwAfHyh1Mf5Blpx5a5kY8qZgmXnzPfPNUuh5alVlvGhwd5zOWC8sM7CSuuv-RoCriUQAvD_BwE

Simons-Morton, B. and Fahat, T. (2010). Recent findings on peer group influences on adolescent substance use. *J Prim Prev., 31*(4), 191–208.

Venaglia, R., Maxwell, L. (2021, June 28). How we conducted our international study on right-wing authoritarianism. Morning Consult. https://morningconsult.com/2021/06/28/right-wing-authoritarianism-international-study-methodology/

von Hippel, W., & Trivers, R. (2011). The evolution and psychology of self-deception. *Behavioral and Brain Sciences*, *34*(1), 1–16.

Chapter 12: Can Democracy Survive Capitalism?

Books

Kuttner, R. (2018). *Can democracy survive global capitalism?* Norton.

Piketty, T. (2014). *Capital in the twenty-first century*. Harvard University Press.

Reich, R. B. (2016). *Saving capitalism for the many, not the few*. Vintage.

Other References

Autor, D. H., Dorn, D. & Hanson, G. H. (2016). The China shock: Learning from labor-market adjustment to large changes in trade. *Annual Review of Economics*, *8*, 205–40.

Crain, C. (2018, May 7). Is capitalism a threat to democracy? *The New Yorker*. https://www. newyorker.com/magazine/2018/05/14/is-capitalism-a-threat-to-democracy

Inequality.org. (2019). Income inequality in the United States. https://inequality.org/facts/income-inequality/

Levs, J. (2012, December 12). Analysis: Why America's unions are losing power. CNN. https://www. cnn.com/2012/12/11/us/union-power-analysis/index.html

Merkel, W. (2014). Is capitalism compatible with democracy? *Zeitschrift für Vergleichende Politikwissenschaft*, *8*, 109–128.

Ozimek, T. (2019, October 27). Krugman admits he and mainstream economists got globalization wrong. *The Epoch Times*. https://www.theepochtimes.com/krugman-admits-he-and-mainstream-economists-got-globalization-wrong_3128925.html

Chapter 13: Our Fragile Democracy

Books

Applebaum, A. (2020). *Twilight of democracy: The seductive lure of authoritarianism*. Doubleday.

Levitsky, S., & Ziblatt, D. (2019). *How democracies die*. Broadway Books.

Other References

Chowdhury, A., & Sundaram, J. K. (2018). Inequality undermines democracy. Inter Press Service. http://www.ipsnews.net/2018/11/inequality-undermines-democracy/

Cummings, M. (2020, August 11). Study: Americans prize party loyalty over democratic principles. *Yale News*. https://news.yale.edu/2020/08/11/study-americans-prize-party-loyalty-over-democratic-principles

DeParle, J. (2016, September 19). Why do people who need help from the government hate it so much? *The New York Times*. https://www.nytimes.com/2016/09/25/books/review/strangers-in-their-own-land-arlie-russell-hochschild.html

Federal Register. (2020). Executive orders. https://www.federalregister.gov/presidential-documents/executive-orders

Graham, M. H., & Svolik, M. W. (2020). Democracy in America? Partisanship, polarization, and the robustness of support for democracy in the United States. *American Political Science Review, 114*(2), 392–409.

Jefferson, T., et al. (2020). Declaration of independence. National Archives. (Original work published 1776) https://www.archives.gov/founding-docs/declaration

Kapstein, E. B., & Converse, N. (2008). Poverty, inequality, and democracy: Why democracies fail. *Journal of Democracy, 19*(4), 57–68.

Kleinfeld, R. (2021). The rise of political violence in the United States. *Journal of Democracy, 32*(4), 160-76.

Levin-Waldman, O. M. (2016, December 10). How inequality undermines democracy. *E-International Relations*. https://www.e-ir.info/2016/12/10/how-inequality-undermines-democracy/

McCoy, J. and Press, B. (2022, January 18). What happens when democracies be perniciously polarized? Carnegie Endowment for International Peace. https://carnegieendowment.org/2022/01/18/what-happens-when-democracies-become-perniciously-polarized-pub-86190

Mounk, Y. (2022, May 21). The doom spiral of pernicious polarization. The Atlantic. https://www.theatlantic.com/ideas/archive/2022/05/us-democrat-republican-partisan-polarization/629925/

Reed, L. W. (2018, November 9). America's republic: How the great experiment came about (and how we keep it). *FEE Stories*. https://fee.org/articles/america-s-republic-how-the-great-experiment-came-about-and-how-we-keep-it/

Shapiro, A. (Host), & Diamond, L. (2017, August 3). *Decline in democracy spreads across the globe as authoritarian leaders rise* [Interview]. In *All Things Considered*. NPR. https://www.npr.org/2017/08/03/541432445/decline-in-democracy-spreads-across-the-globe-as-authoritarian-leaders-rise

V-Dem Institute. (2021). *Autocratization turns viral: Democracy report 2021*. https://www.v-dem.net/static/website/files/dr/dr_2021.pdf

Chapter 14: America's Drift Toward Authoritarianism

Books

Altemeyer, B. (2006). *The authoritarians*. https://theauthoritarians.org/options-for-getting-the-book/

Levitsky, S., & Ziblatt, D. (2019). *How democracies die*. Broadway Books.

Other References

Amy, D. J. (2020). How proportional representation would finally solve our redistricting and gerrymandering problems. FairVote. https://www.fairvote.org/how_proportional_representation_would_finally

Black, E. (2012, October 16). 10 reasons why the electoral college is a problem. *MinnPost.* https://www.minnpost.com/eric-black-ink/2012/10/10-reasons-why-electoral-college-problem/

Cassidy, J. (2016, May 4). How Donald Trump won the G.O.P. nomination. *The New Yorker.* https://www.newyorker.com/news/john-cassidy/how-donald-trump-won-the-g-o-p-nomination

Corriher, B. (2020, November 18). North Carolina election results show the persistence of partisan gerrymandering. *Facing South.* https://www.facingsouth.org/2020/11/north-carolina-election-results-show-persistence-partisan-gerrymandering

Craig, M. A., Rucker, J. M., & Richeson, J. A. (2018). Racial and political dynamics of an approaching "majority-minority" United States. https://spcl.yale.edu/sites/default/files/files/Craig_Rucker_Richeson_FINAL.pdf

Dews, F. (2017, July 6). A primer on gerrymandering and political polarization. Brookings. https://www.brookings.edu/blog/brookings-now/2017/07/06/a-primer-on-gerrymandering-and-political-polarization/

Edsall, T. B. (2020, December 9). The resentment that never sleeps. *The New York Times.* https://www.nytimes.com/2020/12/09/opinion/trump-social-status-resentment.html

Gellman, B. (2021, December 7). Trump's next coup has already begun. *The Atlantic.* https://www.theatlantic.com/magazine/archive/2022/01/january-6-insurrection-trump-coup-2024-election/620843/

Gross, T. (2021, December 9). *Journalist says Republicans now have more reliable ways to overturn election results* [Radio segment]. In *Fresh Air.* NPR. https://www.npr.org/2021/12/09/1062683521/journalist-says-republicans-now-have-more-reliable-ways-to-overturn-election-res

Havercroft, J., Wiener, A., Kumm, M., & Dunoff, J. L. (2018). Editorial: Donald Trump as global constitutional breaching experiment. *Global Constitutionalism, 7*(1), 1–13.

Husser, J. (2020, April 6). Why Trump is reliant on white evangelicals. Brookings. https://www.brookings.edu/blog/fixgov/2020/04/06/why-trump-is-reliant-on-white-evangelicals/

Ingraham, C. (2020, September 18). The United States is backsliding into autocracy under Trump, scholars warn. *The Washington Post.* https://www.washingtonpost.com/business/2020/09/18/united-states-is-backsliding-into-autocracy-under-trump-scholars-warn/

Jefferson, T., et al. (2020). Declaration of independence. National Archives. (Original work published 1776) https://www.archives.gov/founding-docs/declaration

Ladd, J. M. (2019, April 9). The Senate is a much bigger problem than the Electoral College. *Vox.* https://www.vox.com/mischiefs-of-faction/2019/4/9/18300749/senate-problem-electoral-college

Montanaro, D. (2021). Ranked-choice voting gets a prime-time shot under New York City's bright lights. NPR. https://www.npr.org/2021/06/22/1008807504/ranked-choice-voting-new-york-city-mayors-race

Naím, M. (2017, April 21). How to be a populist. *The Atlantic*. https://www.theatlantic.com/international/archive/2017/04/trump-populism-le-pen/523491/

Nteta, T. (2021, December 28). Toplines and crosstabs December 2021 national poll: Presidential election and Jan 6th insurrection at the U.S. capitol. University of Massachusetts Amherst Department of Political Science. https://polsci.umass.edu/toplines-and-crosstabs-december-2021-national-poll-presidential-election-jan-6th-insurrection-us

Pierson, P. (2017). American hybrid: Donald Trump and the strange merger of populism and plutocracy. *The British Journal of Sociology*, *68*(S1), S106–S119.

Reynolds, M. E. (2020, September 9). What is the Senate filibuster, and what would it take to eliminate it? Brookings. https://www.brookings.edu/policy2020/votervital/what-is-the-senate-filibuster-and-what-would-it-take-to-eliminate-it/

Rohac, D., Kennedy, L., & Singh, V. (2018, May). *Drivers of Authoritarian populism in the United States*. American Enterprise Institute for Public Policy Research. https://cf.americanprogress.org/wp-content/uploads/2018/05/U.S.Populism-report-1.pdf?_ga=2.59619178.631202154.1641853910-143438695.1641853910

Roos, D. (2020, December 14). Why was the Electoral College created? History https://www.history.com/news/electoral-college-founding-fathers-constitutional-convention

Smith, D. (2022, March 26). Republicans' midterms pitch: Never mind the policy, here's the culture war. *The Guardian*. https://www.theguardian.com/us-news/2022/mar/26/republicans-midterms-culture-war-lgbtq-abortion-book-bans

Stafford, T. (2016, October 26). How liars create the "illusion of truth." *BBC Future*. https://www.bbc.com/future/article/20161026-how-liars-create-the-illusion-of-truth

Stanton, Z. (2021, May 20). How the 'culture war' could break democracy. *Politico*. https://www.politico.com/news/magazine/2021/05/20/culture-war-politics-2021-democracy-analysis-489900

Tauberer, J. (2018, October 7). With Kavanaugh vote, the Senate reaches a historic low in democratic metric. GovTrack Insider. https://govtrackinsider.com/with-kavanaugh-vote-the-senate-reaches-a-historic-low-in-democratic-metric-dfb0f5fa7fa

Tausanovitch, A., & Root, D. (2020, July 8). How partisan gerrymandering limits voting rights. *Center for American Progress*. https://www.americanprogress.org/issues/democracy/reports/2020/07/08/487426/partisan-gerrymandering-limits-voting-rights/

Tufekci, Z. (2020, November 6). America's next authoritarian will be much more competent. *The Atlantic*. https://www.theatlantic.com/ideas/archive/2020/11/trump-proved-authoritarians-can-get-elected-america/617023/

Uhrmacher, K., Schaul, K., & Mellnik, T. (2016, March 9). Republicans adjusted rules for their primaries after 2012, and it's helping Trump. *The Washington Post*. https://www.washingtonpost.com/graphics/politics/2016-election/primaries/explaining-the-presidential-primary-process/

von Hippel, W., & Trivers, R. (2011). The evolution and psychology of self-deception. *Behavioral and Brain Sciences, 34*(1), 1–16.

Zakaria, F. (2017, December 1). Why plutocratic populism is working for Republicans. *Charleston Gazette-Mail.* https://www.wvgazettemail.com/opinion/columnists/fareed-zakaria-why-plutocratic-populism-is-working-for-republicans-gazette/article_c9595a09-b1a3-5484-850f-6e2eca660f93.html

Chapter 15: Is Human Nature Compatible with Egalitarian Democracy?

Books

Altemeyer, B. (2006). *The authoritarians.* https://theauthoritarians.org/options-for-getting-the-book/

Chua, A. (2018). *Political tribes: Group instinct and the fate of nations.* Penguin.

Haidt, J. (2012). *The righteous mind: Why good people are divided by politics and religion.* Vintage.

Kahneman, D. (2011). *Thinking, fast and slow.* Farrar, Straus and Giroux.

Kameda, T., and Hastie, R. (2015). Herd Behavior. In R. A. Scott, S. M. Kosslyn, & M. Buchmann (Eds.), *Emerging trends in the social and behavioral sciences: An interdisciplinary, searchable, and linkable resource.* Wiley.

Somit, A., & Peterson, S. A. (1997). *Darwinism, dominance, and democracy: The biological bases of authoritarianism.* Praeger.

Other References

Antonakis, J. (2014, December 17). Does power lead to corruption? *The Guardian.* https://www.theguardian.com/sustainable-business/2014/dec/17/does-power-lead-to-corruption-research-testosterone

Bendahan, S., Zehnder, C., Pralong, F. P., & Antonakis, J. (2014). Leader corruption depends on power and testosterone. *The Leadership Quarterly, 26*(2), 101–122.

Castelloe, M. S. (2020, March 16). Dynamics of emotional contagion. *Psychology Today.* https://www.psychologytoday.com/us/blog/the-me-in-we/202003/dynamics-emotional-contagion

Corning, P. A. (2000). The sociobiology of democracy: Is authoritarianism in our genes? *Politics and the Life Sciences, 19*(1), 103–108.

Fehr, E., Bernhard, H., & Rockenbach, B. (2008). Egalitarianism in young children. *Nature, 454,* 1079–1083.

Fish, M. S., & Brooks, R. S. (2004). Does diversity hurt democracy? *Journal of Democracy, 15*(1), 154–166.

Funk, C. L., Smith, K. B., Alford, J. R., Hibbing, M. V., Eaton, N. R., Krueger, R. F., Eaves, L. J., & Hibbing, J. R. (2012). Genetic and environmental transmission of political orientations. *Political Psychology, 34*(6), 805–819.

Groenewegen, A. (2021). Kahneman fast and slow thinking explained. SUE Behavioural Design. https://suebehaviouraldesign.com/kahneman-fast-slow-thinking/

Ludeke, S. G., & Krueger, R. F. (2013). Authoritarianism as a personality trait: Evidence from a longitudinal behavior genetic study. *Personality and Individual Differences, 55,* 480–484.

Milgram, S. (1963). Behavioral study of obedience. *Journal of Abnormal and Social Psychology, 67*(4), 371–378.

Morin, R. (2013, December 9). Study on twins suggests our political beliefs may be hard-wired. Pew Research Center. https://www.pewresearch.org/fact-tank/2013/12/09/study-on-twins-suggests-our-political-beliefs-may-be-hard-wired/

Nuyen, A. T. (1984). David Hume on reason, passions and morals. *Hume Studies, 10*(1), 26–45.

Pei, M. (2009, January 22). Government by corruption. *Forbes.* https://www.forbes.com/2009/01/22/corruption-government-dictatorship-biz-corruption09-cx_mp_0122pei.html#1e3f0c195979

Pew Research Center. (2021, May 17). Public trust in government: 1958–2021. Pew Research Center. https://www.pewresearch.org/politics/2021/05/17/public-trust-in-government-1958-2021/

Shea, C. (2012, October). Why power corrupts. *Smithsonian Magazine.* https://www.smithsonianmag.com/science-nature/why-power-corrupts-37165345/

Sullivan, A. (2017, September 18). America wasn't built for humans. https://nymag.com/intelligencer/2017/09/can-democracy-survive-tribalism.html

Surve, S. (2008, November 4). Hitler's guide to propaganda—the psychology of coercion. *BrainBlogger.* http://www.brainblogger.com/2008/11/04/hitlers-guide-to-propaganda-the-psychology-of-coercion/

Transparency International. (2020, January 23). Corruption Perceptions Index (CPI) 2019: Americas. https://www.transparency.org/news/feature/cpi_2019_Americas

Van Berkel, L., Crandall, C. S., Eidelman, S., & Blanchar, J. C. (2015). Hierarchy, dominance, and deliberation: Egalitarian values require mental effort. *Personality and Social Psychology Bulletin, 41*(9), 1207–1222.

Venaglia, R., Maxwell, L. (2021, June 28). How we conducted our international study on right-wing authoritarianism. Morning Consult. https://morningconsult.com/2021/06/28/right-wing-authoritarianism-international-study-methodology/

Wicker, B., Keysers, C., Plailly, J., Royet, J.-P., Gallese, V., & Rizzolatti, G. (2003). Both of us disgusted in my insula: The common neural basis of seeing and feeling disgust. *Neuron, 40*(3), 655–664.

Chapter 16: Culture Shapes Human Behavior

Books

Acemoglu, D., & Robinson, J. A. (2013). *Why nations fail: The origins of power, prosperity and poverty.* Crown.

Dawkins, R. (1976). *The selfish gene.* Oxford University Press.

Hobbes, T. (2011). *Leviathan.* Pacific. (Original work published 1651)

Pinker, S. (2011). *The better angels of our nature: Why violence has declined.* Penguin.

Richerson, P., & Boyd, R. (2005). *Not by genes alone: How culture transformed human evolution.* University of Chicago Press.

Vaidhyanathan, S. (2018). *Antisocial media: How Facebook disconnects us and undermines democracy.* Oxford University Press.

Other References

Barrett, P., Hendrix, J., & Sims, G. (2021, September 13). How social media fuels U.S. political polarization—what to do about it. *The Hill.* https://thehill.com/opinion/campaign/572002-how-social-media-fuels-us-political-polarization-what-to-do-about-it

Bouie, J. (2020, September 18). Facebook has been a disaster for the world. *The New York Times.* https://www.nytimes.com/2020/09/18/opinion/facebook-democracy.html

Boyd, R., & Richerson, P. J. (2009). Culture and the evolution of human cooperation. *Philosophical Transactions of the Royal Society B, 364*(1533), 3281–3288.

Caprioli, M. (2000). Gendered conflict. *Journal of Peace Research, 37*(1), 51–68.

Carr, N. (2018, June 29). Is Facebook the problem with Facebook, or is it us? *The Washington Post.* https://www.washingtonpost.com/outlook/is-facebook-the-problem-with-facebook-or-is-it-us/2018/06/28/5949992e-5939-11e8-8836-a4a123c359ab_story.html

Crespo-Sancho, C. (2018, March 28). Can gender equality prevent violent conflict? *Development for Peace.* https://blogs.worldbank.org/dev4peace/can-gender-equality-prevent-violent-conflict

Fish, M. S., & Brooks, R. S. (2004). Does diversity hurt democracy? *Journal of Democracy, 15*(1), 154–166.

Haidt, J., & Rose-Stockwell, T. (2019, December 15). The dark psychology of social networks. *The Atlantic.* https://www.theatlantic.com/magazine/archive/2019/12/social-media-democracy/600763/

Hawks, J., Wang, E. T., Cochran, G. M., Harpending, H. C., & Moyzis, R. K. (2007). Recent acceleration of human adaptive evolution. *Proceedings of the National Academy of Sciences, 104*(52), 20753–20758.

Perreault, C. (2012). The pace of cultural evolution. *PLOS ONE, 7*(9), e45150.

Porter, T. (2021, October 4). A Facebook whistleblower said it knows that its algorithms are pushing QAnon and white nationalist content to Trump fans but denies it. Insider. https://www.businessinsider.com/facebook-pushes-qanon-racism-to-trump-fans-whistleblower-says-2021-10

Romo, V. (2021, October 5). Whistleblower's testimony has resurfaced Facebook's Instagram problem. NPR. https://www.npr.org/2021/10/05/1043194385/whistleblowers-testimony-facebook-instagram

Shakya, H. B., & Christakis, N. A. (2017). Association of Facebook use with compromised well-being: A longitudinal study. *American Journal of Epidemiology, 185*(3), 203–211.

Singer, P. (2011, October 6). Is violence history? *The New York Times.* https://www.nytimes.com/2011/10/09/books/review/the-better-angels-of-our-nature-by-steven-pinker-book-review.html

Chapter 17: Where Are We Going?

Books

Acemoglu, D., & Robinson, J. A. (2013). *Why nations fail: The origins of power, prosperity and poverty.* Crown.

Darwin, C. (1871). *The descent of man, and selection in relation to sex.* John Murray. http://darwin-online.org.uk/content/frameset?itemID=F937.1&viewtype=text&pageseq=1

Dawkins, R. (1976). *The selfish gene.* Oxford University Press.

de Waal, F., & Lanting, F. (1997). *Bonobo: The forgotten ape.* University of California Press.

Kristof, N., & WuDunn, S. (2020). *Tightrope: Americans reaching for hope.* Knopf.

Reich, R. B. (2016). *Saving capitalism for the many, not the few.* Vintage.

Richerson, P., & Boyd, R. (2005). *Not by genes alone: How culture transformed human evolution.* University of Chicago Press.

Sandel, M. J. (2020). *The tyranny of merit: Can we find the common good?* Farrar, Straus and Giroux.

Wilson, E. O. (2012). *The social conquest of earth.* Norton.

Other References

Angier, N. (1997, April 22). Bonobo society: Amicable, amorous and run by females. *The New York Times.* https://www.nytimes.com/1997/04/22/science/bonobo-society-amicable-amorous-and-run-by-females.html

Baboolall, D., Cook, K., Noel, N., Stewart, S., & Yancy, N. (2020, October 29). Building supportive ecosystems for black-owned U.S. businesses. McKinsey & Company. https://www.mckinsey.com/industries/public-and-social-sector/our-insights/building-supportive-ecosystems-for-black-owned-us-businesses

Bennett, M. (2018). McMullin, former congressmen discuss solutions to political polarization, gridlock. *The Daily Universe*. https://universe.byu.edu/2018/10/26/mcmullin-former-congressmen-discuss-solutions-to-political-polarization-gridlock/

Caprioli, M. (2000). Gendered conflict. *Journal of Peace Research, 37*(1), 51–68.

Crespo-Sancho, C. (2018, March 28). Can gender equality prevent violent conflict? *Development for Peace*. https://blogs.worldbank.org/dev4peace/can-gender-equality-prevent-violent-conflict

Institute for InterGroup Understanding. (2021). Tribal behaviors could destroy us as a nation or they can give us a path to peace. https://www.intergroupinstitute.org/peace-thoughts/thought/tribal-behaviors-could-destroy-us-as-a-nation-or-they-can-give-us-a-path-to-peace

Lee I.-C., Pratto, F., & Johnson, B. T. (2011). Intergroup consensus/disagreement in support of group-based hierarchy: An examination of socio-structural and psycho-cultural factors. *Psychological Bulletin, 137*, 1029–1064.

Moore, R., & Brooks, R. (2021, February 8). To end systemic racism, ensure systemic equality. https://www.aclu.org/news/racial-justice/ending-systemic-racism-requires-ensuring-systemic-equality/

Shapiro, D. L., (2017, March 7). Can we overcome our tribalistic nature? *Psychology Today*. https://www.psychologytoday.com/us/blog/transforming-conflict/201703/can-we-overcome-our-tribalistic-nature

V-Dem Institute. (2021). *Autocratization turns viral: Democracy report 2021*. https://www.v-dem.net/static/website/files/dr/dr_2021.pdf

Walker, D. (2020, June 25). Are you willing to give up your privilege? *The New York Times*, https://www.nytimes.com/2020/06/25/opinion/sunday/black-lives-matter-corporations.html

Wright, J. (2019, August 6). 12 things you can do today to improve race relations across America. LinkedIn. https://www.linkedin.com/pulse/12-things-you-can-do-today-improve-race-relations-across-james-wright

Young, M. (2001, June 28). Down with meritocracy. *The Guardian*. https://www.theguardian.com/politics/2001/jun/29/comment

INDEX

ACKNOWLEDGMENTS

I'd like to thank Brooke Dulka, PhD, psychologist, and science writer at Cardinal Health, who has provided editorial support and critical evaluation of content. She gave valuable feedback, chapter by chapter, throughout the entire writing process. I'd like to thank Scott Sugarman, who did a fantastic job copy editing my manuscript. In addition to providing detailed structural edits, he provided valuable insights and suggestions on content. I'd also like to thank Andy Meaden who put it all together with a creative and inviting internal design.

My good friend and colleague Dr. Jim Adelman provided helpful suggestions and feedback regarding development and content throughout the three years I've worked on the book. My Coffee Group, which meets weekly to discuss issues of the day, has given me valuable insights, perspectives, and feedback on many of the issues addressed in the book.

Finally, I'd like to thank my wife Dr. Dora Brodie. She, like me, is a retired physician, forging a new life in retirement. She has provided support and been a constant companion as we worked together—I writing this book and she perfecting her Russian. She grew up in Czechoslovakia where she learned Russian in school during the Soviet occupation. She is now perfecting her Russian with the help of a Russian immigrant.

IMAGE CREDITS

Chapter 1: Human Nature: The Nature-Nurture Debate

Image 1.1 Brown Boobies Building a Nest. Purchased from Shutterstock, October 18, 2019 (ID: 791576575).

Image 1.2 Charles Darwin. Charles Darwin retrieved from Pixabay free images. COO Public domain. Retrieved from https://pixabay.com/en/charles-robert-darwin-scientists-62911/

Image 1.3 Identical Twins. Image/figure created by author.

Chapter 2: Empathy: Evolution's Precious Gift

Image 2.1 Chimpanzee and Infant. COO Public domain. Retrieved December 2019 from https://pxhere.com/en/photo/835255

Image 2.2 Empathy in Rats. Two cute and curious Brown Rats by Gallinago media. Purchased from Shutterstock, December 2019 (ID 295110965).

Image 2.3 Empathy. Hands of elderly man by Alexxnd. Purchased from Shutterstock, December 2019 (ID 576882187).

Image 2.4 Mirror Neurons. Human Brain by DJ. CC BY-SA 2.0. Retrieved and modified from https://www.flickr.com/photos/flamephoenix1991/8376271918

Chapter 3: Emotions: The Essence of Humanity

Image 3.1 Limbic System. Purchased from Shutterstock, December 2019 (ID 295094522).

Image 3.2 Fear. Portrait of a scared young girl. Purchased from Shutterstock, December 2019 (ID 1060527566).

Image 3.3 Disgust. Disgusted and frowning young woman. Purchased from Shutterstock, December 2019 (ID 249074803).

Image 3.4 Shame. Human face expressing emotion. Purchased from Shutterstock, December 2019 (ID 296799968).

Chapter 4: Cooperation: The Driving Force of Evolution

Image 4.1 He Ain't Heavy, He's My Brother. Buddy Carry by Captain Paul Peterson U.S. Marine Corps/Released. United States Government Work. Retrieved April 2020 from https://www.flickr.com/photos/marine_corps/8948219391

Chapter 5: Hierarchical and Egalitarian Instincts

Image 5.1 Bonobos. Purchased from Shutterstock April 2020 (ID 1051536416).

Image 5.2 Brain Anatomy and Psychological Traits. Human Brain Limbic System. Purchased from Shutterstock December 2019 (ID 295094522).

Chapter 6: Tribal Instincts

Image 6.1 Genocide. Genocides by papi8888. Purchased from Shutterstock December 2019 (ID 697260235).

Chapter 8: Social Darwinism

Image 8.1 Herbert Spencer. Smithsonian Institute. Public domain. No copyright restrictions. Retrieved April 2020 from https://www.flickr.com/photos/smithsonian/2552868551

Chapter 9: The Toxicity of Structural Racism

Image 9.1 Segregated Water Fountain in the Jim Crow South. Retrieved from Pixabay free for commercial use. Retrieved March 2021 from https://pixabay.com/photos/discrimination-racism-60512/

Image 9.2 Four Black Youths in a Southern Chain Gang. Four African American Youths by Everett Collection. Purchased from Shutterstock, March 2021 (ID 242820760).

Image 9.3 Signing of the Civil Rights Act, 1964. Retrieved from Pixabay free for commercial use. Retrieved March 2021 from https://pixabay.com/photos/president-lyndon-b-johnson-63219/

Chapter 10: The Growing Crisis of Socioeconomic Inequity

Image 10.1 Income Inequality. Congressional Budget Office. 2020. "The Distribution of Household Income, 2017." Government document in the public domain. Retrieved November 2020 from https://www.cbo.gov/publication/56575

Image 10.2 The Great Gatsby Curve. The Great Gatsby Curve by BoogaLouie. CC By-SA 3.0. Retrieved January 2021 from https://en.wikipedia.org/wiki/Great_Gatsby_curve#/media/File:The_Great_Gatsby_Curve.png

Image 10.3 The Declining Middle Class. Krueger, A. B. 2012. "The Rise and Consequences of Inequality in the United States." Government document in the public domain. Retrieved January 2021 from https://obamawhitehouse.archives.gov/sites/default/files/krueger_cap_speech_final_remarks.pdf

Image 10.4 American Poverty. Beggar in Hood by Andrey Popov. Purchased from Shutterstock, July 2020 (ID 694710103).

Image 10.5 Nordic Nations. Purchased from Shutterstock, April 2020 (ID 1668654172).

Chapter 11: The Seductive Lure of Authoritarianism

Image 11.1 Jarosław Kaczyński. Purchased from Shutterstock, September 18, 2020 (ID 1222751227).

Image 11.2 Recep Tayyip Erdoğan. Purchased from Shutterstock, September 18, 2020 (ID 425646577).

Chapter 13: Our Fragile Democracy

Image 13.1 The Constitution of the United States. Purchased from Shutterstock, December 2020 (ID 1764169292).

Chapter 14: America's Drift Toward Authoritarianism

Image 14.1 Trump Loyalists Storm the Capitol. Pro-Trump supporters storm U.S. Capitol by Alex Gakos. Purchased from Shutterstock, January 2021 (ID 1888727899).

Chapter 15: Is Human Nature Compatible with Egalitarian Democracy?

Image 15.1 Power Corrupts. Giving a bribe into a pocket by Maryna Pleshkun. Purchased from Shutterstock, May 2022 (ID 141755542).

Chapter 16: Culture Shapes Human Behavior

Image 16.1 Law and Order. Judges gavel on wooden table by create jobs 51. Purchased from Shutterstock, May 2022 (ID 6051193491).

Chapter 17: Where Are We Going?

Image 17.1 Empowerment of Women. Strong woman, winning success by KieferPix. Purchased from Shutterstock, May 2022 (ID 1614362578).